Cambridge *Conferences*

REVISED ANNOUNCEMENT

Mr. CHARLES SANDERS PEIRCE

of MILFORD, *Pennsylvania*

ILL give a course of Eight Class Lectures on REASONING AND THE LOGIC OF THINGS, at the rooms of the CAMBRIDGE CONFERENCES, Studio House, 168 *Brattle* Street, on Monday and Thursday Evenings in February and March, 1898, at eight o'clock.

THE SPECIAL TOPICS AND DATES WILL BE AS FOLLOWS

1898

February 10. Philosophy and the Conduct of Life.

February 14. Types of Reasoning.

February 17. The Logic of Relatives.

February 21. The First Rule of Logic.

February 24. Training in Reasoning.

February 28. Causation and Force.

March 3. Habit.

March 7. The Logic of Continuity.

HE COURSE herein outlined will be of UNUSUAL INTEREST AND VALUE to students and teachers of Philosophy. It is hoped that many will avail themselves of the privilege of attending.

In order to render the Lectures available to all who may desire to hear them, the price of admission has been placed at less than the usual class rates :

COURSE TICKETS . . One Dollar Fifty

SINGLE ADMISSION . Twenty-five Cents

Application for admission to the Class Lectures should be made to the Director of the *Conferences*, Dr. LEWIS G. JANES, Studio House, 168 *Brattle* Street, Cambridge, Mass.

Pages i and ii: Advertisement for Peirce's lectures at the Cambridge Conferences. By permission of the Philosophy Department and the Houghton Library, Harvard University.

Reasoning and the Logic of Things

The Cambridge Conferences
Lectures of 1898

Charles Sanders Peirce

Edited by
Kenneth Laine Ketner

With an Introduction by
Kenneth Laine Ketner and Hilary Putnam

Harvard University Press
Cambridge, Massachusetts
London, England
1992

Library of Congress Cataloging in Publication Data

Peirce, Charles S. (Charles Sanders), 1839–1914.
Reasoning and the logic of things: the Cambridge conferences
lectures of 1898/Charles Sanders Peirce; edited by Kenneth Laine
Ketner; with an introduction by Kenneth Laine Ketner and Hilary
Putnam.
p. cm.
Includes bibliographical references and index.
ISBN 0-674-74966-9 (alk. paper).—ISBN 0-674-74967-7 (pbk.:
alk. paper)
1. Logic. 2. Reasoning. I. Ketner, Kenneth Laine. II.Title.
B945.P43R43 1992
160—dc20
92-1038
CIP

Walker Percy
Doctor Humanitatis

Acknowledgments

We are grateful to the Philosophy Department of Harvard University for permission to publish from the Peirce Papers held at the Houghton Library. Many of Peirce's letters cited here are from the William James papers also in the Houghton Library, and we extend our thanks to Mr. Alexander R. James for permission to use them.

Berti Ketner has given invaluable assistance in proofreading, and Arthur Stewart aided in manuscript preparation. We are grateful for the kind assistance of Ms. Margaret Wittenborg of Cambridge, Massachusetts. Both Carolyn Eisele and Max Fisch have been very generous with their advice, guidance, and encouragement, without which the project would not have progressed.

Our gratitude also goes to the staff of the reading room at Houghton Library for assistance with manuscripts, to David McGaughey for computer expertise, and to Elaine Atkinson, Robert Burch, Curtis Collins, Edward George, Nathan Houser, Christian Kloesel, Wendell McClendon, Thomas McLaughlin, and Randall Peters for assistance with textual matters.

Our collaboration in this project was materially encouraged through our joint preparation of the Charles Sanders Peirce Sesquicentennial International Congress held at Harvard during 5–10 September 1989, under the sponsorship of the Peirce Society, Harvard, and Texas Tech University. Financial support from those institutions—and from the National Endowment for the Humanities, Mr. W. B. Rushing of Lubbock, the Mary Baker Rumsey Foundation of Lubbock, the Charles S. Peirce Foundation, and the Society for the Advancement of American

Philosophy—provided the fiscal basis for this large and stimulating conference. This volume is in part a result of that congress.

Finally, we gratefully acknowledge the continuing support of the Institute for Studies in Pragmaticism by the Claude Ventry Bridges Memorial Fund.

K.L.K.
H.P.

Contents

Editorial Procedures

The texts here are from the Charles S. Peirce Papers and the William James Papers at Houghton Library, Harvard University. Editorial work was based upon the archival copies of the Peirce papers housed at the Institute for Studies in Pragmaticism at Texas Tech University. From these resources the lectures as presented were reconstructed. The principal secondary guide has been the Peirce/James correspondence, relevant parts of which are quoted.

A number of references internal to the lecture manuscripts themselves strengthen the hypothesis that these particular texts constitute the actual lectures more or less as delivered. Also, there are timing marks on many of the manuscripts which suggest that Peirce read them aloud against a clock to ascertain whether each piece could be delivered in one hour. Those marks have not been reproduced here.

The aim was to produce a study edition, not a critical text. Therefore, the editorial apparatus has been minimized. The following conventions have been observed. Any material in square brackets, "[ ]," is an editorial insertion, included when it seemed obvious that Peirce had made a simple oversight. Because this was a lecture series, Peirce gave no footnotes. Editorial comments appear as numbered notes and are gathered at the end of the book. No attempt has been made to show all of Peirce's deletions—only those that seem significant have been included; they appear in the endnotes and are indicated with angle brackets, "⟨ ⟩." We include in particular some of his longer deletions, which often provide useful supplemental material. Alternative drafts are available for some lectures, and extracts from those we regard as helpful are presented in the endnotes. Dubious or garbled words are surrounded by pairs of question marks, thus: ??word??. Ampersands are transcribed as "and," but Arabic numbers are not spelled out as words. Peirce's spelling and punctuation style are followed, not modernized, but some obvious misspellings have been silently corrected.

Abbreviations

The following commonly accepted abbreviations are used to refer to the standard editions of Peirce's works.

CP   *Collected Papers of Charles Sanders Peirce,* edited by C. Hartshorne, P. Weiss (volumes 1–6), and A. Burks (volumes 7–8) (Cambridge: Harvard University Press, 1931–1958), followed by volume and paragraph numbers

HP   *Historical Perspectives on Peirce's Logic of Science: A History of Science,* edited by Carolyn Eisele, 2 volumes (Berlin: Mouton-DeGruyter, 1985), followed by volume and page numbers

MS   Peirce manuscripts in Houghton Library at Harvard University, followed by a number identified in Richard R. Robin, *Annotated Catalogue of the Papers of Charles S. Peirce* (Amherst: University of Massachusetts Press, 1967), or in Richard R. Robin, "The Peirce Papers: A Supplementary Catalogue," *Transactions of the Charles S. Peirce Society,* 7(1971):37–57

N   *Charles Sanders Peirce: Contributions to* The Nation, edited by Kenneth Laine Ketner and James Edward Cook, 4 volumes (Lubbock: Texas Tech University Press, 1975–1987), followed by volume and page numbers

NEM   *The New Elements of Mathematics by Charles S. Peirce,* edited by Carolyn Eisele, 4 volumes in 5 books (The Hague: Mouton, 1976), followed by volume and page numbers

PW   *Semiotic and Significs: The Correspondence between Charles S. Peirce and Victoria Lady Welby,* edited by Charles S. Hardwick (Bloomington: Indiana University Press, 1977), followed by page numbers

W   *Writings of Charles S. Peirce: A Chronological Edition,* edited by Max H. Fisch et al. (Bloomington: Indiana University Press, 1982–), followed by volume and page numbers

In addition, items published by Peirce during his lifetime are referenced according to a numbering system in *A Comprehensive Bibliography of the Published Works of Charles Sanders Peirce,* by Kenneth Laine Ketner, second revised edition (Bowling Green: Philosophy Documentation Center, 1986). For instance, "On the Algebra of Logic" of 1880 is *P* 167.

Introduction: The
Consequences of Mathematics

Kenneth Laine Ketner and Hilary Putnam

The general title of Charles Sanders Peirce's 1898 Cambridge Conferences lectures was *Reasoning and the Logic of Things*. If it were within our
power to alter the title, we would, for several good reasons, have it read
The Consequences of Mathematics.

The first of those reasons is that initially, when first asked to prepare a set of Cambridge Conferences lectures, Peirce wanted to use
material about which he had been writing—a study of the "logic of
events." For this project, a somewhat different one from the lectures as
finally presented, the proposed title would be ideal.

In advance of the invitation from Cambridge, Peirce had prepared
a number of provisional lectures for that other project, plus other drafts
on somewhat related topics. These ultimately were not presented in
1898. A few extracts from the abandoned "logic of events" project were
placed in several separate parts of *Collected Papers of Charles Sanders
Peirce*. Also, parts of Lecture One ("Philosophy and the Conduct of
Life"), along with some of the earlier drafts, were published in 1931 as
a chapter in *CP* under the inaccurate title "Vitally Important Topics"
(at 1.616–677). The editors of *CP* also inferred that Peirce gave some
lectures called "Vitally Important Topics," but (as we shall see) he did
not. In the somewhat disorganized way these items were presented in
CP, they have had considerable influence—some of which has been
negative, for students of the *CP* often find the material in that chapter
puzzling. Their questions are understandable, because the editors omitted significant parts. Extracts from either drafts or delivered lectures in
his 1898 Cambridge Conferences series appeared at *CP* 6.1–5, 185–213,

214–221, 222–237; 7.468–517. It would be useful also to publish the unused drafts from the tangled developmental period of the actual lectures in a separate volume in an accurate form, along with materials showing how they are generally related to his Cambridge Conferences project. The availability of these pieces would resolve some questions inadvertently created by the expurgated versions of the unused drafts that appeared in *CP*.

Peirce's abandonment of those drafts is related to the second reason we would, if we had our way, call the series *The Consequences of Mathematics*. When William James first proposed these lectures, Peirce wanted to present a rather technical set of topics—the "logic of events"—for which he planned to draw heavily upon mathematics and mathematical logic. That would have been second nature for him, because his most original intellectual contribution, his "special business," was "to bring mathematical exactitude, [meaning] modern mathematical exactitude into philosophy, and to apply the ideas of mathematics in philosophy."[1] But James urged that mathematics and complicated logic be sacrificed so that a larger audience could be addressed. Yet, the Cambridge Conferences lectures constitute, despite or (more likely) because of William's advice, an admirable popular introduction to Peirce's "special business"—an application of mathematics to philosophy. Nevertheless, Peirce's friend encouraged him to explain himself in a nontechnical way, insofar as possible. So the second reason for the dream title is that Peirce's philosophy is a consequence of his mathematics, and these lectures provide one with a means to enter into his way of thinking on that topic.

But, in the third place, the phrase "consequences of mathematics" has a deeper meaning. Peirce argued that, epistemologically at any rate, mathematics was an observational, experimental, hypothesis-confirming, inductive science that worked only with pure hypotheses without regard for their application in "real" life. Because it explored the consequences of pure hypotheses by experimenting upon representative diagrams, mathematics was the inspirational source of the pragmatic maxim, the jewel of the methodological part of semeiotic, and the distinctive feature of Peirce's thought. As he often stated, the pragmatic maxim is little more than a summarizing statement of the procedure of experimental design in a laboratory—deduce the observable consequences of the hypothesis.[2] And for Peirce the simplest and most basic laboratory was the kind of experimenting upon diagrams one finds in mathematics. (He understood the word *diagram* broadly, encompassing visual, tactile, or audio entities used to model a set of relations under

study.) Mathematics as a study of pure hypotheses is a study of consequences, the method of which study was used by Peirce to develop a
number of wider consequences in other sciences, most notably philosophy. Thus the third sense of our ideal title could be transmitted as
"the ways—which mathematicians use—of studying consequences," especially as they are exemplars of the simplest and purest instance of laboratory method.[3]

This edition, for the first time anywhere, makes available the entire
set of lectures. And it is fortunate that we have them at last, for they
offer a fine, somewhat popular introduction (in the sense used by James)
to Peirce's overall later philosophy. We know of no other single work in
the Peirce corpus of which that statement is true.

It is strange that Peirce, who is internationally regarded as among
the best American intellects, is not known by the general public and
only in a limited way by most academics. We agree with Walker Percy's
terse prophecy: "Most people have never heard of him, but they will."[4]
This set of lectures offers to both expert and layperson the most convenient and complete means for gaining access to those ideas and insights
in Peirce's philosophy which are especially relevant to a number of contemporary issues.

Our goal has been to prepare a study edition of the lectures arranged so that specialists and nonspecialists alike may find them useful
and accessible.

A Portrait in Miniature

The Peirce family was one of the brightest and wealthiest in Puritan
Salem at the peak of its splendid commercial seafaring era. Later generations of Peirces, like many prominent families of the time, such as the
Cabots and the Lowells, migrated from the "provinces" of the Commonwealth toward the orbit of the capital. Charles's grandfather, Benjamin
Peirce (1778–1831), had been a member of the Massachusetts legisla-
ture and, more important for this part of the family's history, Librarian
of Harvard from 1826 until his death. He also wrote a history of Harvard which was published posthumously. With his move from Salem to
Cambridge and Harvard, there began a long association between the
university and the Peirce family, which, as the saying goes, came to have
"blood the color of Harvard Crimson."

Benjamin Peirce, Jr. (1809–1880), was a towering figure for most
of his forty-nine-year career on the Harvard campus. As Perkins Pro-

fessor of Astronomy and Mathematics, he had influence throughout scientific and political circles in this country and the world. If the position of Scientific Adviser to the President had existed in the midnineteenth century, Benjamin Peirce, Jr., would have been the incumbent. His wife, Sarah Hunt Mills Peirce, was the daughter of United States Senator Elijah Hunt Mills, founder of a noted law school of which Franklin Pierce, the fourteenth president of the United States, was an alumnus.

Charles Sanders was the second of the Peirces' five children. His older brother, James Mills, was professor of mathematics and Dean of the Graduate School at Harvard over a long career. One younger brother, Benjamin Mills, died at age twenty-six. The surviving younger brother, Herbert Henry Davis, achieved a distinguished career as a United States diplomat after marrying into a wealthy New England family. Helen Huntington Peirce Ellis was the darling daughter within this family of overachieving men.

Charley, as he came to be known, was born 10 September 1839 in a house on Mason Street that is still standing. The Peirce home was but minutes away from Harvard Yard, closer still to what became Radcliffe Yard. But about 1844 Harvard built on University property a special house for Professor Peirce on Quincy Street, at a site where Sever Hall now stands. Here Charley's father hosted an exciting salon, the informal members of which would constitute a *Who's Who* of the leading political, intellectual, and literary figures of the time. In reflecting late in life upon growing up in this atmosphere, Peirce recalled how little he had seen in his youth of "the ordinary sort of person."

Charley's genius was recognized early by his family and their circle. Benjamin took a special personal interest in his son's education, emphasizing independent, self-directed study and sometimes keeping him up all night in exercises to develop his concentration. In spite of this training (or perhaps better, given the rote pedagogical style of the day, because of it), Peirce had a mixed academic record as he made his way through various private schools, the Cambridge High School, and Harvard, where he was graduated at the age of twenty in the class of 1859.

As an aide to his father's project within the federal Coast Survey, Charley avoided the Civil War. It was a war which the Peirce family generally opposed, contrary to the sentiment of their neighbors in Cambridge. In 1867, when Benjamin became Superintendent of the Survey, Charley acquired the low-sounding but high-placed position of Assistant in charge of gravimetric survey. Peirce had married Melusina Fay (a fellow Cambridge brat, whose family had played a role in the founding of Radcliffe). His life throughout the later 1860s and the 1870s was a mixture of part-time lectures in the University, gravimetric research for the Survey both within the United States and in Europe, participation in the highest levels of international physics, and later a part-time position as lecturer in logic at the new Johns Hopkins University in Baltimore. In the early 1870s, Peirce developed an especially important association with the members of an informal discussion club made up of fellow Harvard students: William James, O. W. Holmes, Jr., John Fiske, Frank Abbot, Nicholas St. John Green, Joseph Bangs Warner, plus their "Dancing Master" and resident elder, Chauncey Wright. James credited Peirce with working out the philosophy of pragmatism during the sessions of this "Metaphysical Club" (a half-jesting title). Others have noted a similar influence of these discussions on the legal philosophy of the future Justice Holmes.

Particularly in the late seventies, Peirce was like Walker Percy's "man on the train." A Victorian, upwardly mobile man of science, he burnt the candle at both ends commuting between what would have been two full-time occupations: he continued his work at the Coast Survey Office in Washington and elsewhere, and he was a central figure in the development of symbolic logic in his work with colleagues and a small group of talented students at Hopkins.

Probably because of this overwork, both Peirce's marriage (which had been a rather practical and conventional union) and his health began to suffer. Ultimately Melusina left him. Then a disaster struck with a bite befitting a Greek tragedy. An enemy informed one of the trustees of Hopkins that Peirce had taken up residence with Juliette Froissy while separated but not yet divorced from Melusina. Also, it did not help matters that Juliette was Peirce's junior by about twenty-five years. Though he had been on the edge of acquiring a permanent professorship in logic, he was abruptly fired by President Gilman in January 1884. This episode became widely known among university administrators in the United States; along with the ecclesiastical fundament of most universities in that period, it is probably the principal reason Peirce never acquired another permanent academic appointment. Another factor was his "ill-adapted" nature as a social being (he was known to be blunt, irascible, and individualistic). Thus it came to pass that one of America's greatest masterminds, who had an impeccable academic endowment and tradition, was banned from the American academy. Even Harvard, despite efforts by James and others, could not take him in, a

Peirce and his wife, Juliette Froissy, at the back door of Arisbe
—post 1900. By permission of the Department of Philosophy
and the Houghton Library, Harvard University.

result no doubt also influenced by the unfriendly attitude that President
Charles Eliot bore toward Peirce's father.

Charley withdrew from Baltimore and refocused his energies on
his work on gravity in Washington and remote experimental sites elsewhere. Although he ultimately married Juliette, his further career in
any circle had suffered a blow that led to its slow death. His father had
died in 1880, depriving him of parent, champion, and protector. After
bringing his gravimetric work to completion, he resigned from the Survey in 1891. He spent the nineties attempting through various schemes
to generate an independent income to finance the royal lifestyle for
which he yearned. But he possessed almost no business ability, and all of
these attempts failed. With a family inheritance, he and Juliette bought a

home in Milford, Pike County, Pennsylvania—a resort community on the Delaware River. He was still "on the train" between New York, Cambridge, Milford, and other places, but now he was downwardly mobile. In these years his commuting took him to odd jobs, or unrewarding big-business appointments, or meetings of the National Academy of Sciences, or occasional lectures at distinguished locations such as the Lowell Institute; he kept trying "just one more time" for an academic appointment, in the meanwhile seeking loans or other forms of help from friends just to stay alive. Had he lived 100 years later, at this stage in his life he could have relied on a pension from his thirty-year career of service as a world-class federal scientist.

This pattern continued roughly until the death of William James in 1910, his close friend and provider (with the help of a number of admirers) of the nearest thing to a pension—a fund for Peirce's minimum sustenance. (In gratitude for James's efforts, Peirce informally added "Santiago"—Saint James—to his name in the later years of his life.)

The most important thing for us, however, is that through it all, the good years and the bad, he continued his lifelong habit of writing constantly. His most beloved topics were philosophy, logic, mathematics, and science: as Lewis Mumford observed, his masterful mind quietly and privately fulfilled itself in his study in the lovely countryside near Milford

There are many great themes in the work of Charles Sanders Peirce, but perhaps the central one is his search for a unified theory of scientific method. Peirce understood science in a very broad sense, a pursuit which he equated with logic (again a broad conception). It was because of this search for unity that he devoted himself to active research in several branches of science: he wanted to be in a position to think deeply about the nature of science from the standpoint of one who knew its practices intimately. In this quality, among the great philosophers he is one of a very select few. He was a founder of contemporary formal logic, and he was proud of the fact that his accomplishments in that field were the basis for his membership in the National Academy of Sciences. Willard Quine, still working today, is the only other person to have been similarly honored.

After Peirce's death from cancer in 1914, one of his few living disciples, Josiah Royce, was instrumental in arranging for his voluminous papers to be transported to Harvard, where they eventually came to rest in Houghton Library under the care of the Library and the

Department of Philosophy. Peirce published in the neighborhood of 10,000 pages, and his manuscripts run to about 80,000 sheets. At times he must have written without stop; perhaps this explains at least in part his difficult nature.

But he was passionately devoted to the unselfish pursuit of truth, so we can admire his accomplishments while trying to forgive his frailties.

Peirce's reputation as an important thinker has grown continually since his death, and we believe it will grow even more. Our favorite piece of evidence for this belief is the international congress held at Harvard during 5–10 September 1989 in honor of the one-hundred-fiftieth anniversary of his birth. On that occasion leading thinkers from many fields and from all regions of the planet, with little financial support from the project, gathered in Sanders Theater (named, as was the honoree himself, after a kinsman of the Peirce family) to continue the process of exploring the resources within his works and to pursue aspects of his research relevant to questions of contemporary interest.

Development of the Lectures

In 1897 Longmans, Green and Company published *The Will to Believe,* by William James. Its printed dedication read:

To
My Old Friend,
CHARLES SANDERS PEIRCE
To whose philosophic comradeship in old times
and to whose writings in more recent years
I owe more incitement and help than
I can express or repay.

At Arisbe, his homestead near Milford, Pike County, Pennsylvania,[5] Peirce received a copy of the volume the evening of 12 March 1897. The next day he conveyed his thanks to James in a long letter, which began, "Your letter and the dedication and the book gave me more delight than you would be apt to believe." After a few other complimentary remarks,[6] Charles used this opportunity to take William into his confidence.

I have learned a great deal about philosophy in the last few years, because they have been very miserable and unsuccessful years, — terrible beyond anything that the man of ordinary experience can possibly understand or conceive. Thus, I have had a great deal of idleness and time that could not be employed in the duties of ordinary life, deprived of books, of laboratory, everything; and so there was nothing to prevent my elaborating my thoughts, and I have done a great deal of work which has cleared up and arranged my thoughts. Besides this, a new world of which I knew nothing, and of which I cannot find that anybody who has written has really known much, has been disclosed to me, the world of misery. It is absurd to say that Hugo, who has written the least foolishly about it, really knew anything of it. I would like to write a physiology of it. How many days did Hugo ever go at a time without a morsel of food or any idea where food was coming from, my case at this moment for very near three days, and yet that is the most insignificant of the experiences which go to make up misery? Much have I learned of life and of the world, throwing strong lights upon philosophy in these years. Undoubtedly its tendency is to make one value the spiritual more, but not an abstract spirituality. It makes one dizzy and seasick to think of those worthy people who try to do something for "the Poor," or still more blindly "the deserving poor." On the other hand, it increases the sense of awe with which one regards Gautama Booda. This is not so aside from the subject of your book as it might seem at first blush, because it implies that much has led me to rate higher than ever the individual deed as the only real meaning there is [in] the Concept, and yet at the same time to see more sharply than ever that it is not the mere arbitrary force in the deed but the life it gives to the idea that is valuable. As to "belief" and "making up one's mind," if they mean any more than this, that we have a plan of procedure, and that according to that plan we will try a given description of behavior, I am inclined to think they do more harm than good. "Faith," in the sense that one will adhere consistently to a given line of conduct, is highly necessary in affairs. But if it means you are not going to be alert for indications that the moment has come to change your tactics, I think it ruinous in practice. If an opportunity occurs to do business with a man, and the success of it depends upon his integrity, then if I decide to go into the transaction, I must go on the hypothesis he is an honest man, and there is no sense at all in halting between two lines of conduct. But that won't prevent my collecting further evidence with haste and energy, because it may show me it is time to change my plan. That is the sort of "faith" that seems useful.

The hypothesis to be taken up is not necessarily a probable one. The cuneiform inscriptions could never have been deciphered if very unlikely hypotheses had not been tried. You must have a consistent plan of procedure, and the hypothesis you try is the one which comes next in turn to be tried according to that plan. This justifies giving nominalism a fair trial before you go on to realism; because it is a simple theory which if it don't work will have afforded indications of what kind of realism ought to be tried first. I do not say probability ought not to be considered. It will be a prominent factor in a well considered plan of research. Probability is simply absurd and nonsensical in reference to a matter of "supreme interest," and any decision of such a question on probable grounds is illogical. But where in does the illogicality lie? Simply in considering any interest as supreme. No man can be logical who reckons his personal well-being as a matter of overwhelming moment.

I do not think suicide springs from a pessimistic philosophy. Pessimism is a disease of the well-to-do. The poor are ready enough to concede that the world in general is getting better, which is the best conceivable world, far better than a "best possible world." But men commit suicide because they are personally discouraged, and there seems to be no good to anybody in their living. There was Mrs. Lunt who drowned herself in a well. I often talked to her when she was coming to that resolution. It wasn't the universe she thought intolerable, but her own special condition.

As for any form of belief in a future state being cheering to anybody, I can't conceive of it. At any rate I am quite sure that it is generally a source of dread. "Phantasms of the Living"[7] to those who believe it must add greatly to its horrors. The old fashioned heaven wasn't half so degraded an existence, — bad as it was.

Religion *per se* seems to me a barbaric superstition. But when you come to Christianity, or as we ought to call it Buddhism,[8] for surely the Indian Prince was an incomparably more perfect embodiment of it than the miracle monger of the Synoptic gospels,[9] if that is to be called religion, — and the distinguishing feature of it is that it teaches the degradation of all arts of propitiating the higher powers, which I take to be the definition of religion, that seems to me essentially the deepest philosophy, having the virtue of *living*. The clergymen who do any good don't pay much attention to religion. They teach people the conduct of life, and on the whole in a high and noble way.

As for morality, it is not a bad thing, taking it in the true evolutionary sense. But it is not everything that evolution results in that is good. Evolution has two results. One is the realization of the dormant idea. That is good. The other is the variation of types. That is indifferent. There really is no evolution in the proper sense of the word if individuals can have any arbitrary influence on the former. If they could, it would fully justify Napoleon's remark to Josephine "Madam, the rules of morality were not meant for such men as I." Even as it is, there is some truth in it. The philosopher is considerably emancipated from morality. I, for example, often say to myself "Your disgust at sports of killing, is really contrary to the traditional morality. You can't be wiser than the experience of the race on a complicated question you have not studied?" But I should think Gautama quite absolved from such a moral law.

I am much encouraged at your thinking well of "tychism." But tychism is only a part and corollary of the general principles of Synechism. That is what I have been studying these last fifteen years, and I become more and more encouraged and delighted with the way it seems to fit all the wards of your lock. It was a truly sweet thing, my dear William, to dedicate your book to me.
C. S. Peirce

Five days later, on the eighteenth, Peirce wrote again with some additional philosophical chit-chat about the new book (see *CP* 8.306–312). The second letter ended with a suggestive post scriptum (omitted in *CP*):

If I write more of these long and empty letters you will wish you had not paid me the compliment of the dedication.

By the way, I wonder if I ever told you that Eliot wrote to me at the time that project of getting me in Cambridge for a year was up and in a tone as if it were only the manner in which the question was sprung and put to him at a distance (perhaps he said by cable) which caused him to decide as he did.

It seems to me a pity, knowing as I do how much my sound logic is needed, that no university should have the benefit of it. I should think psychical researchers would want me to have a chance to teach.

A response from James was penned on the twenty-seventh.

Dear Chas.—Your two inspiring letters have been received duly "and contents noted," though you will excuse me if the laziness of my epistolary nature and the general dislocation of my wits in the multiplicity of different interests that I am supposed to attend to make me disinclined just now to making animadversions in detail on their contents. The matter with me is a "contracted field" of consciousness—a perfectly definite infirmity which forces me to drop one thing entirely if I want to attend to another. To write a decent letter to you would oblige me to throw my lectures for that day to the devil, a thing which *geht nicht!* So I shut down on you, doubtless much to your relief. I am glad you take my book so seriously. Have you looked at Schiller's Riddles of the Sphinx (Swan Sonnenschein 1891)? Loose and somewhat reckless but full of bold constructivism on a pluralistic basis. One of the most *refreshing* things I have read for a long time.

I am sorry indeed that the deplorable state of your affairs should be unrelieved. You write as one who knows misery from within. It seems incredible. You shall have a course of lectures here next year, long or short. I know it can be done, and I will see to it. We all want to hear you, and our graduates *ought* to. But why has the 1st volume of your book so vanished into the kingdom of mere possibles? I tho't that the subscriptions had panned out adequately. Your intensely mathematical mind keeps my non-mathematical one at a distance. But so many of our categories are the same that your existence and philosophizing give me the greatest comfort.
Ever faithfully yours,
Wm. James
P.S. 29th.—I have been trying to get a copy of Renouvier's Logic to present to you, but it is out of print. I have sent my own copy (paid) by express, and must beg you to return it before the summer is out, as I value it a good deal in spite of its grave defects of matter and manner. I think he is at his strongest in his shorter articles.

The mention of "your book" was a reference to Peirce's projected multivolume work, *Principles of Philosophy,* which in 1894 he planned to publish through a subscription plan. Advertisements were printed and distributed, but the project as a whole fell through.[10]

In April, Peirce wrote James that "the Renouvier is at hand" and continued with a long, technical, and interesting critique of the book.[11] James didn't reply, possibly because of the laziness of his epistolary nature, or perhaps because Peirce's long letter made considerable use of mathematical techniques. Nothing more passed between them until Peirce received a letter (dated 12 May) from Paul Carus, the editor of

The Principles of Philosophy:

OR,

LOGIC, PHYSICS AND PSYCHICS,

CONSIDERED AS A UNITY,

In the Light of the Nineteenth Century.

BY C. S. PEIRCE,

Member of the National Academy of Sciences.

Vol. I. (Nearly ready.) *Review of the Leading Ideas of the Nineteenth Century.* Defines the essential ideas involved in and sentiments fostered by political economy, machinery and modern inventions, labor unions, socialism, scientific associations, centennials, nationalism, emigration, various forms of idealism, Hegel's objective logic, the historical method, modern mathematics and its imaginaries, the theory of heat and conservation of energy, statistical methods of research, the kinetical theory of gases, Darwinism, etc. It is believed that these analyses will be found valuable, apart from the conclusions drawn from them. Next, a definite affinity is traced between all these ideas, and is shown to lie in the principle of *continuity.* The idea of continuity traced through the history of the Human Mind, and shown to be the great idea which has been working itself out. (The author's papers in the *North American Review* are here used.) Modern science due to it exclusively. A great part, if not all, of evolution in all departments, and at all times, probably to be ascribed to the action of this principle. The urgent needs of our time may, we have strong reason to hope, be met by the further application of it. Sketch of a thoroughgoing philosophy of continuity. The great opponent of this philosophy has been in history, and is in logic, infallibilism, whether in its milder ecclesiastical form, or in its more dire scientistic and materialistic apparitions.

Vol. II. (Substantially ready.) *Theory of Demonstrative Reasoning.* The first part of this volume contains a plain, elementary account of formal logic, ordinary and relative. It has been very carefully adapted to the use of young persons of mediocre capacities, and has been subjected to experimental tests with success. This is followed by more intricate developments for persons having a turn for such matters, and others may skip this part. (The author's papers in the *Memoirs of the American Academy* and in the *Journal of Mathematics* are here made use of.) Deductive reasoning having thus been accurately described, and the working of it taught, the third part of the volume makes a careful analysis of it, and shows what the natures of its different ingredients are. The principle of continuity is shown to be the crown of the logic of relatives.

Vol. III. *The Philosophy of Probability.* After an analysis of the nature of probability, the principles of the calculus are set forth. The doctrine of inverse probabilities refuted. The theory of inductive and hypothetic inference set forth nearly as in the Johns Hopkins "Studies in Logic," but the position there taken is reinforced with powerful new arguments. Mr. Peirce's rules for inductive reasoning are the strictest that have been advocated. New illustrations are given to show the absurdly bad reasoning into which those fall who follow looser rules. A few inferences admitted by Mr. Peirce as valid are disallowed by some writers. Their inconsistency in this shown, and that those writers simply maintain an unreasonable skepticism concerning some questions which they do not extend to others quite analogous.

Vol. IV. *Plato's World: An Elucidation of the Ideas of Modern Mathematics.* A lucid analysis of the logic and conceptions of the calculus, imaginaries, the theory of functions, and the non-Euclidean geometry. The conceptions of infinity and continuity are now accurately analyzed. The notion that we cannot reason mathematically about infinity refuted. The doctrine of limits as stated by some authors inadequate to its purpose; as stated by others, really involves reasoning about infinity. It is impossible to assign any reason for the dogma that we cannot reason mathematically about infinity; one might as well say we cannot reason mathematically about imaginaries.

Vol. V. *Scientific Metaphysics.* Begins with the theory of cognition. The nature of reality discussed as in the author's papers in the *Popular Science Monthly ;* but the position taken is now set forth more clearly, fully, and in psychological detail. The reality of the external world. Primary and secondary qualities. The evidence of the real existence of continuity. The question of nominalism and realism from the point of view of continuity. Continuity and evolution. Necessitarianism refuted. Further corollaries from the principle of continuity.

Vol. VI. *Soul and Body.* Begins with an analysis of the law of association, which is somewhat generalized. The question of fatigue and its law. Review of psychological phenomena. The apparent discontinuity of sense-qualities considered. Definition of the soul, following out ideas put forth by the author in the *Journal of Speculative Philosophy.* The "unity of consciousness " admits of degrees, and is probably in many cases very low. Phenomena of anæsthesia considered. The author's theory of universal evolution, which supposes matter and its laws to be the result of evolution, is now set forth more systematically and argumentatively. Still, it is to be regarded for the present as no more than a working hypothesis. Explanation of the method of reasoning by which a multitude of unmistakable consequences can be rigidly deduced from the hypothesis. A considerable number of these are shown to be true, while none are known to be false. One prediction of a fact hitherto unknown is shown to be supported by observation. Others remain to be tested by future experience, and the theory will have to stand or fall by the result.

Vol. VII. *Evolutionary Chemistry.* The working out of the consequences of the theory of universal evolution into chemistry. Mendeléeff's law.

Vol. VIII. *Continuity in the Psychological and Moral Sciences.* Mathematical economics. Precisely similar considerations supposed by utilitarians to determine individual action. But, this being granted, Marshall and Walras's theorem leads to a mathematical demonstration of free will. Refutation of the theory of motives. The true psychology of action expounded.

Vol. IX. *Studies in Comparative Biography.* The application of mathematical principles in a new way to this study.

Vol. X. *The Regeneration of the Church.* The philosophy of continuity is peculiar in leading unequivocally to Christian sentiments. But there it stops. This metaphysics is only an appendix to physics; it has nothing positive to say in regard to religion. It does, however, lead to this, that religion can rest only on positive observed facts, and that such facts may prove a sufficient support for it. As it must rest upon positive facts, so it must itself have a positive content. A series of plays upon words will not answer for a religion. This philosophy shows that there is no philosophical objection to the positive dogmas of Christianity; but the question as to their truth lies out of its province.

Vol. XI. *A Philosophical Encyclopædia.* The philosophy of continuity leads to an objective logic, similar to that of Hegel, and to triadic categories. But the movement seems not to accord with Hegel's dialectic, and consequently the form of the scheme of categories is essentially different. Systematic perfection seems to be for the present neither requisite nor attainable; but something like Hegel's Encyclopædia is proposed.

Vol. XII. *Index raisonné* of ideas and words.

Mr. Peirce does not hold himself pledged to follow precisely the above syllabus, which, on the contrary, he expects to modify as the work progresses. He will only promise that he will not depart from this programme except to improve upon it. The work is to be published by subscription at $2.50 per volume. Address:

MR. C. S. PEIRCE,
" Arisbe,"
Milford, Pa.

The Monist, the journal that had published a number of important essays by Peirce.[12] Carus concluded by saying

When I passed through Cambridge, I met, among others, Prof. James, and I was very glad to hear that he appreciates your genius highly and he spoke of an appointment which he expected to procure for you in Cambridge. I suppose you know about his efforts in your behalf and I trust that he will succeed. It would be a great advantage to you in many respects, not only giving you a definite income, but also bringing your name before the University public in a dignified manner. Hoping that your wife will recover from the effects of the operation, and that her health will be perfectly restored, I remain, with kind regards,
Yours very truly,
Paul Carus

Peirce was occupied throughout much of April and May with the question of his wife's operation, which was performed at the hospital in

Holyoke, Massachusetts, on 22 April by Dr. Gill Wylie. A very large noncancerous abdominal tumor was successfully removed. After Juliette's slow recovery seemed secure, on the thirtieth of May—perhaps hoping for a possible end to the financial aspect of his misery—Peirce wrote exuberantly to James.

> I heard some month ago through Dr. Carus that you were endeavoring to get me some opportunity to teach logic in Cambridge.
>
> Since then I have been diligently working upon the Syllabus of a course, and have completed the most elementary parts.
>
> No responsibility could be much more grave in my opinion than that of being charged to imbue a considerable number of young men with ideas of logic. For as I understand logic, the practical issues of it are momentous. Nevertheless, there is no sacrifice which I could make, consistently with duty, that I would not gladly make to have that opportunity of usefulness. I would even give up the possibility of recording my discoveries in logic (the major part of which are unrecorded), although I think they are of measurable importance to mankind. But the letters I get from my former pupils in Baltimore tell me how much I could do for young men; and I could now do far more than I then was able to accomplish.
>
> In the main, — that is, in holding that belief is fundamentally a practical matter, — you and I seem to be in full accord; and if we were together there, we would make an impression upon the philosophical world, and thus upon scientific men, upon teachers, and ultimately upon the current of the world's thought. All that is important. But it would be to my mind secondary to the good to be done for the individual students, and for the dull ones especially. Not that I should expect to make dull young men bright; but I have a particular liking for and understanding of and respect for dull young men, and I understand just what logic can do for them.
>
> If I were to have such a charge, I ought to spend every moment from now till October in preparing the first part of my course. Therefore, I beg you to let me know what the prospects are . . .

The laziness of James's epistolary nature was overcome, for he responded quickly on 5 June that

> Carus gave you a false impression, and I hope that what I say will not be a disappointment. It has long been apparent that a

permanent place for you here is an absolute impossibility. What I said to Carus was that we must get you a short course of lectures here next year, for which I should hope the remuneration would be $1000. I said that I was going to put it through if possible, and I imagine that it could be done, but I have not taken any steps yet, and shall not do so until the fall. The lectures could be on logic, or on the philosophy of nature; I myself should much prefer the later theme, as drawing a larger audience and also being an opportunity for you to get your ideas into finally publishable shape.

On 25 November, perhaps thinking that James had forgotten his pledge to work on a set of lectures for him in the fall, Peirce wrote briefly, commenting on Renouvier in passing, and wondering "could not a small place, say at $50 a month or so, be got for me in the Library . . . ?" Again, response from James was prompt, iterating that there was no chance whatsoever for *any* University appointment. But in regard to a course of lectures in Cambridge, James reported he was making progress. He suggested "not too much logical or mathematical technics" and that he personally wished "for a development of your cosmogony etc. — 'synechism' and 'tychism'." He closed by suggesting that the lectures "would probably best take place not before February."

Shortly thereafter James contacted some mutual friends. For instance, to James McKeen Cattell he wrote (on 5 December):

am trying to raise $1000 to get a course of lectures here by Charles Peirce, whose destitute and ill-"adapted" condition you probably know of. I don't propose to beg you of anything, but it occurs to me that you might possibly *help*, through your circle of acquaintance being other than mine. It would be a shame for P. to pass away without getting himself put down on paper more fully than hitherto; and such lectures help a man to work out his thoughts. Were pensions given to anybody but army bummers, his would be a first rate case.

A few days later, James felt confident enough of his results to write to Peirce that

The road seems now clear to my plan so far as this:
Lectures, once or twice a week at your convenience, afternoon or evening as shall seem most feasible, probably evening; audience, mainly students of philosophy; subject, what you please, but I suggest your Cosmogony; number, from 8 to 12 at your choice; fee,

between 700 and 1000 dollars, as the stars shall decide; Month, February, unless January is much better for you . . .

The place is Mrs. Ole Bull's Cambridge Conferences, of which I enclose a program of the Sunday afternoon performances. Yours would come on weekdays and be advertised in a distinct circular. You may make them more popular, if you please, but I tho't that the student audience would most likely suit you best.

The Cambridge Conferences were founded in 1896 by Sara Bull, the wife of the recently deceased distinguished Norwegian violinist.[13] A woman of some financial means, Mrs. Bull instituted the Conferences at her home as a memorial to her mother, Amelia Chapman Thorp. The house at 168 Brattle Street, Cambridge, in Colonial Revival style, was designed by Arthur Little according to Mrs. Bull's special requirements, which included interior parlors in Norwegian style, in memory of her husband, who had died in 1880. The house was completed about 1890. Its importance in the intellectual life of Cambridge is well captured by Mortimer Smith, Ole Bull's biographer.[14]

After Ole's death Sara became a well-known figure in Cambridge, and her spacious house on Brattle Street, where she lived until her death in 1911, was a famous gathering place for "intellectual" society and for leaders of causes. She presided over her salon with a gentle, unobtrusive and somewhat melancholy grace. Here she could be found introducing Swami Vivekananda and his Vedanta philosophy to her cautious and faintly suspicious Cambridge friends, or discussing religion with William James . . . For two years she conducted in her house what she called "the Cambridge Conferences"; here in a large living room paneled in Indian teakwood and dominated by a bust and innumerable portraits of Ole Bull, one was privileged to listen to the controversial social questions of the day discussed by such figures as Professor James, Thomas Wentworth Higginson, Josiah Royce and Jane Addams. In the audience one could rub shoulders with such varied persons as the patrician Miss Alice Longfellow, Irving Babbitt, Professor Munsterberg, the still active Julia Ward Howe, and even a young woman named Gertrude Stein, then a student at Radcliffe.

The composition of the audience at Peirce's lectures when they were finally delivered is not known, beyond the obvious presence of Royce and James (as we shall see). Santayana scholars think it quite likely that he attended. It will remain for future study to solve this question in a more detailed manner. By 1898, when Peirce's lectures were delivered, the Conferences had moved from the main house to a spacious secondary building, the Studio House.[15] But the speakers and audiences in the new location were no less distinguished. At the time she founded the Conferences, Mrs. Bull had attracted as their permanent director Dr. Lewis George Janes.

On Monday, 13 December 1897, Peirce wrote from Arisbe to express his gratitude for William's efforts in his behalf. He gave a brief outline of a course of lectures he proposed to call "On the Logic of Events." He concluded with:

> I am all alone in the house here and have spent some of the quiet hours over Substance and Shadow and in recalling your father. My experiences of the last few years have been calculated to bring Swedenborg home to me very often.
>
> I am sorry I cannot attempt to thank you as I would wish to do.

Peirce gave a more detailed account of this plan in writing James on the eighteenth from Arisbe.

Eight Lectures on the Logic of Events
1. *Logical Graphs.* A novel method of treating formal logic including the logic of relatives. It splits into two systems; Entitative Graphs and Existential Graphs. The former more philosophical, the latter simpler in the result. There are some hints about it in a Monist paper.[16]
2. *Lessons of the Logic of Relatives.* Showing the erroneousness of current logical notions, due to the particular nature of nonrelative logic. Also, exhibiting the generalizations of logical conceptions obtained by the logic of relatives. Here I might have space to say something on Duns Scotus and how I interpret him differently from Royce.
3. *Induction and Hypothesis.* Though not very fresh indispensable to comprehending my kind of objective logic.
4. *The Categories.* Quality, Reaction, Mediation or Representation.

Pages 20–23: Cambridge Conferences Program for 1897–1898. By permission of the Philosophy Department and the Houghton Library, Harvard University.

Cambridge *Conferences*

168 BRATTLE ST.
CAMBRIDGE, MASS.

November 7th, 1897, to May 8th, 1898

LEWIS G. JANES
DIRECTOR

THE work auspiciously begun last year in the comparative study of *Ethics, Philosophy, Sociology* and *Religion,* at 168 Brattle Street, Cambridge, will be continued during the present season, by the courtesy of Mrs. OLE BULL and Mr. J. H. HATFIELD, in the Studio House at the same address, which is also the residence of the Director.

The following revised program can now be announced, subject to unavoidable changes. Other Classes and Conferences may be introduced, from time to time, of which due notice will be given.

1897. *Sundays,* 4 *P.M.*

November 7. *Opening Meeting.*	Prince Kropotkin, of Cambridge, England. The Moral Influence of Prisons upon Prisoners, based on Personal Observations in French Prisons and Siberia.*

In the unavoidable absence of the Director, Col. Thomas Wentworth Higginson has kindly consented to preside at the opening meeting.

November 14.	Prof. Edward Cummings, of Harvard University. The Dilemma of Philanthropy and Progress.
November 21.	Mrs. Angie M. Mosher, of Cambridge. Brittany and some Bretons : — Abelard, Des Cartes, Lammenais, Chateaubriand, Renan.
November 22. *Monday, 8 P.M.*	Rev. Ida C. Hultin, of Moline, Illinois. Woman's Place in Social Evolution.
November 28.	Mr. George Willis Cooke, of Lexington, Mass. Ethics of Family Life.
December 5.	Mr. Mangasar M. Mangasarian, of the New York Society for Ethical Culture. Ethics of Punishment.

* An admission fee to the lecture of Prince Kropotkin will be required of all who are not members of the Conferences.

December 8. Wednesday.	Rev. Theophilus Parsons Sawin, D. D., of Troy, New York. Ethics of Altruism.
December 12.	Mr. William Potts, of New York, Vice-President of the National Civil Service Reform Association. Social Conditions in Town and Country.
December 15. Wednesday.	Mr. Frank B. Sanborn, of Concord, Mass. Walks With Emerson and Thoreau.
December 19.	Edward Atkinson, LL. D., Ph.D., of Boston. The Ethics of Trade or Commerce.
December 22. Wednesday.	Mr. Leo Wiener, Instructor in Russian, Harvard University. The Popular Poetry of the Russian Jews. With Recitations by Mr. Morris Rosenfeld from his own Dialect Poems.
December 26.	Colonel Thomas Wentworth Higginson, of Cambridge. England Twenty Years After.
December 29.	(*HOLIDAY INTERMISSION.*)

1898. January 2.	Miss Mary White Ovington, Head Worker of the Pratt Institute Neighborship Settlement, Brooklyn, New York. Neighborhood Ethics.
January 5. Wednesday.	Mr. Virchand R. Gandhi, B.A., M.R.A.S., of Bombay, India. The Education of Women in India.
January 9.	Hon. Carroll D. Wright, United States Commissioner of Labor. A Study of the Divorce Question.
January 12. Wednesday.	Mrs. Ellen M. Mitchell, President of "The Round Table," Syracuse, New York. The Social Philosophy of Dante.
January 16.	Mr. Edwin D. Mead, President of the Twentieth Century Club, Boston. Ethics of Citizenship.
January 19. Wednesaay.	Mrs. N. D. Macdaniel, of New York. Brook Farm.
January 23.	Mrs. B. J. Harnett, of New York. Social and Religious Life of Hindu Women.
January 26. Wednesday.	Hon. Albion A. Perry, Mayor of Somerville, Mass. Theodore Parker.
January 30.	Rev. Thomas R. Slicer, of New York. Ethical Problems in Education.

February 6.	Prof. Josiah Royce, Ph.D., of Harvard University. First Lecture of Course on Aspects of Social Psychology.
February 13.	Mrs. Frederick Nathan, President of the New York Consumers' League. Ethics of Domestic Service.
February 20.	Prof. Josiah Royce, Ph.D., of Harvard University. Second Lecture on Aspects of Social Psychology.
February 27.	Prof. Franklin H. Giddings, Ph.D., of Columbia University. Poverty as a Social Problem.
March 6.	Prof. Josiah Royce, Ph.D., of Harvard University. Third Lecture on Aspects of Social Psychology.
March 13.	Mr. Henry Hoyt Moore, President of the Brooklyn Ethical Association. Ethical Aspects of the Saloon Problem.
March 20.	Mr. Joseph G. Thorp, President of the Cambridge Social Union. The Norwegian System of Regulating the Sale of Intoxicants.
March 27.	Mr. John S. Clark, Treasurer of the American Statistical Association. Ethics of Business Life.
April 3.	Prof. Josiah Royce, Ph.D., of Harvard University. Fourth Lecture on Aspects of Social Psychology.
April 10.	Mr. Edward King, of New York. The Rights and Duties of Labor.
April 17.	Prof. Josiah Royce, Ph.D., of Harvard University. Fifth Lecture on Aspects of Social Psychology.
April 24.	Mr. Walter S. Logan, of New York. The Rights and Duties of Capital.
May 1.	Prof. Josiah Royce, Ph.D., of Harvard University. Concluding Lecture on Aspects of Social Psychology.
May 8.	Dr. Lewis G. Janes, M.A., Director of the Conferences. Industrial Conciliation.

Discussion

FOLLOWING each Sunday Lecture, a short time will be devoted to informal discussion and conversation on the topic of the day. When practicable, one or two members will be selected in advance to participate in the discussion.

TO meet the desires of those to whom other dates are impracticable, the lectures of Prof. Josiah Royce on "Aspects of Social Psychology" have been placed in the regular Sunday afternoon series.

The Swâmi Sâradânanda, who may soon return to India, and whose work in the Conferences met with such hearty appreciation last season, will give a series of class lectures on "The Vedanta Philosophy" on Mondays and Thursdays, at 4 P.M., in the second and third weeks in November.

Mr. George Willis Cooke of Lexington, Mass., will give a course of six class lectures on "Woman's Place in the History of Humanity," on Friday afternoons in December and January. Admission to course three dollars. Single admission fifty cents.

Mr. Virchand R. Gandhi, B.A., M.R.A.S., of Bombay, India, will give a course of class lectures on "The History and Philosophy of the Jain Religion and Social Conditions in India," during January, 1898.

The Director, Dr. Lewis G. Janes, will give a series of six class lectures on "Epochs in Early Religious History," on successive Friday afternoons in February and March.

THOUGH the Conferences were primarily intended for students and professional workers in the lines above indicated, the director desires to make them available, as far as possible, to interested non-professional members. A limited number of associate members will accordingly be received, as heretofore, on payment of the annual associate-membership fee of ten dollars. The capacity of the audience-room will probably necessitate the restriction of invitations to members more strictly than was customary last year. Professional, student, and associate members will be continued upon the list unless they otherwise request. Application for membership, and the dues of associate members may be sent to the Director.

Director's *Hours*

THE Director may be consulted at his study in the Studio House on Mondays, Tuesdays and Thursdays, from 4 to 6 P.M. When not otherwise engaged, he will welcome members and their friends at other hours convenient to themselves.

LEWIS G. JANES,
Resident Director.

Studio House,
168 BRATTLE STREET, CAMBRIDGE,
November 1, 1897.

5. *The Attraction of Ideas.* Generalized law of association of ideas to which the cerebral anatomy is adapted. Perhaps 4 and 5 in one lecture.

6. *Objective Deduction.*

7. *Objective Induction and Hypothesis.*

8. *Creation* or the earliest steps in the evolution of the world. Perhaps 2 lectures.

I can't get well started till my return to N.Y. I can't start my steam heater in the house and though the weather is mild the thermometer on my table is below 50° most of the time, so that I have to sit over the fire and can't write.

A partial draft of this letter (given below), probably not sent, shows two features of Peirce's career: (1) that early drafts of his writings often explain some points better than the final one; (2) that his situation was sometimes more desperate than what he expressed, for instance in the relatively cheerful version of this letter (above) that James had actually received.

4. *The Categories:* Quality, Reaction, Representation or Mediation. This is the main thing I have been harping on from the beginning and shows wherein my objective logic differs from that of Hegel.

5. *The Attraction of Ideas.* Generalized law of association of ideas, showing that it is not a mere result of nervous anatomy, but on the contrary that character of the nerves is simply adaptive.

6. *Objective Deduction.* Shows how deduction works in the world, both its simplest and more intricate forms.

7. *Objective Induction and Hypothesis.* Same for these modes of inference.

8. *Creation.* Shows how I would conceive the earliest steps of evolution, beginning with the Germinal Nothing and continuing to the point where the special sciences attack the problem, took place.

I am writing this last Lecture first. I may find I cannot make a *résumé* in a single lecture. If not, I shall have to compress the fourth and fifth lectures into one.

As to my getting myself expressed in a systematic way, of course it is the great object of my life. It certainly cannot be done unless I can devote pretty much all the remainder of my time to it. It may possibly be that things will turn so that I can; I shall endeavor to do what in me lies.

I have been so harassed and persecuted and falsely accused of everything most remote from my habits and nature that I do not much care what becomes of me. Still, I shall stick to what I think I was put into the world for, and try to execute it with as much good sense as I can command.

The lawyers keep me in such a continual stew that I hardly have a quiet moment. That is why I was in the country where I caught a bad cold; and there I must return to an ice-cold house and depending on the baker's daily twist for my subsistence. I can't afford fire. But if I can manage to keep alive till February, I shall certainly have my lectures ready. I had the first and last all written out, but the MSS are both gone after an incredible amount of time had been spent upon them. I have also had most of the others nearly as I should like to give them but cannot get them now.

James responded three days before Christmas. He tried politely to persuade Charles away from formal logic: "I am sorry you are sticking so to formal logic. I know our graduate school here, and so does Royce, and we both agree that there are only 3 men who could possibly follow your graphs and relatives." He added: "Now be a good boy and think a more popular plan out. I don't want the audience to dwindle to 3 or 4 . . . " He concluded his advice about the lecture content with a phrase, marked here with added emphasis, that was to find its place in American intellectual history because of Peirce's later ironical use of it in these lectures and associated works: "You are teeming with ideas—and the lectures need not by any means form a continuous whole. *Separate topics of a vitally important character* would do perfectly well." Then came some details about the financial aspect of the project. The subscribers *"cannot be known."* Juliette was to receive about half the lecture honorarium at a rate of ten dollars per week, and Charles was to receive the other half in weekly installments. In regard to these arrangements, apparently insisted upon by the subscribers, William's advice was to "acquiesce and thank God it isn't worse." After offering some advice about which schedule might draw a larger audience, he concluded, saying: "Write, now, that you accept all these conditions, and pray keep the lectures as un-mathematical as in you lies."

The day after Christmas, heading his letter with "I write from N.Y., but I am going straight back to Pike Co.," Peirce accepted the conditions his friend had stipulated. It must have been difficult, especially since for him philosophy without mathematics was like a wheel without an axle. His letter reflects a tone of restrained displeasure:

My dear William:

I accept all your conditions.

I have no doubt you gauge the capacity of your students rightly. It agrees with all I hear and the little I have seen of Cambridge, though the method of graphs has proved quite easy to New Yorkers, whose minds are stimulated by New York life, — people as remote from the mathematical world as anybody in New York.

My philosophy, however, is not an "idea" with which I "brim over"; it is a serious research to which there is no royal road; and the part of it which is most closely connected with formal logic is by far the easiest and least intricate. People who cannot reason exactly (which alone *is* reasoning), simply cannot understand my philosophy, — neither the process, methods, nor results. The neglect of logic in Cambridge is plainly absolute. My philosophy, and all philosophy worth attention, reposes entirely upon the theory of logic. It will, therefore, be impossible for me to give any idea of the nature either of my philosophy or of any other of any account.

In consequence of your saying you wanted to hear something about *synechism* and the tychism which is a corollary of it, I have already written my Lecture VIII, the most difficult, supposing that all the rest had been given as I planned them. But as long as you think that lectures to 15 or 16 of your students will be more valuable, I will begin again, and will endeavor to write out some of the "ideas" with which I am supposed to be "teeming" on "separate topics of vital importance." I feel I shall not do it well, because in spite of myself I shall betray my sentiments about such "ideas"; but being paid to do it I will do it as well as I possibly can. After all, I have no reason to distress myself that my philosophy does not get expounded. Your Harvard students of philosophy find it too arduous a matter to reason exactly. Soon your engineers will find it better to leave great works unbuilt rather than go through the necessary calculations. And Harvard is only a little in advance of the rest of the country on this road, and this country a little in advance of Europe. The Japanese will come and kick us out, and in the fullness of time *he* will come to the questions which my philosophy answers, and with patience will find the key, as I have done.[17] Some years ago, when J. M. P. had a lawyer trying to do I don't know what with our Pike Co. property, this lawyer induced us to enter into a contract with lawyers up there holding a small mortgage ($1000) that we would keep the house tenanted. It turns out that paper was so drawn that if the house were in any way to remain vacant for one night, they could sell it at public auction for cash at 6 AM next morning, without giving any notice or advertisement whatever. This they now say they will do as a client wants to buy the place. [And] I am therefore kept up there till I find some person to purchase that $1000 mortgage. If I don't do that before Feb. 12, I can't give the lectures. My expenses up there are great and the exposure very severe and it is hard to "teem" with Ideas in a study where the thermometer is 30°–40° F. Never over 50°.

I am perfectly indifferent about times and hours. I shall be clay in the hands of the potter. I wish I had to sing comic songs and dance, though I should do *it* badly. But I am not puritan enough to understand the pleasure of these chins on "topics of vitally important character." The audience had better go home and say their prayers I am thinking.

There seems to be a gap in the surviving correspondence at this point; there may be a missing letter from William, judging from Peirce's letter to James of 4 January 1898. For there he began by saying, "Neither of your interpretations of my letter were correct." He reported that he had commenced all over again by rewriting one lecture, and was halfway through a second one. Peirce also commented that he had "his eye on the Corporation," by which he probably meant that in these lecture drafts he was addressing educational policy at Harvard. This surmise seems borne out by the vigor of his attack on Harvard in the lecture drafts not used. He continued: "But as you know that my style of 'brilliancy' consists in a mixture of irony and seriousness, — the same things said ironically and also seriously, I mean, — I doubt if said Corporation will see the point." Peirce then renewed his complaint that he was forced off the topics he felt qualified to discuss.

I cannot "get down on paper" in this course because my line of thought is too inextricably involved in the most troublesome details of mathematical minutiae. That is my method. But I shall try to think of you and put as much of my philosophy in as I can. But to be popular, it must be without argumentation for the most part, a mere sketch of what I should argue if I could go further into detail.

I propose to entitle the course "Detached ideas on vitally important topics." The first lecture is about Vitally important topics, showing that where they are Vital there is little chance for philosophy in them and that in the sense in which generalization whether cognitive or sentimental is a high thing, vitally important topics are as I say "the outline of huge mountains above which we descry a silvery peak far higher yet."

The second lecture is about detached thoughts and is intended to show that however little time people may have for connected thought outside their business, yet it is better to make it as connected as possible, not shunning detached ideas but seeking to assimilate them. This enables me to say something about Nominalism and Realism and a propos of that of my own philosophical labors.

My third lecture is to be upon the highest maxim of logic, — which is that the only strictly indispensable requisite is that the inquirer shall want to learn the truth.

In another lecture I have determined to say something about Time and Causation and to show that it is not so impossible or even difficult to conceive the universe as it transcends time as has been supposed.

What I shall say in the other lectures I have as yet no idea whatever. I dare say something may occur to me.

To Juliette at approximately the same time Charles wrote that he was still able to maintain only minimal heating in his study, it being so cold there that he could not write. But his closing comment was: "I am getting on well with my lectures," by which one supposes he meant "intellectually." In a second letter from approximately the same time, Charles told Juliette that it was still too cold to write, but meanwhile he was arranging for a caretaker for the house at Arisbe for the period of delivery of his lectures, and he mentioned that "You want to make an important man of me." In a third letter to Juliette of this time Peirce complained of a headache, but that "my lectures come on well in spite of the headache." He concluded with: "I looked in the glass today. I look like an old hermit. White and wild."

By the fifteenth of January, Peirce was ready for another report to James about his progress, and to ask for some special assistance to force misery to retreat long enough for the lectures to emerge.

My Dear William:

I thought as I was writing my last letter to you, "This will sound cold and ungrateful," but it was because I was physically almost frozen to death. I said to myself "I will write again tomorrow"; but the next day I was deep in writing the lectures and have been so ever since. I have completed four which I mail to you, so that if you like to cast your eye over them and see whether they are too technical, you can do so. I would not *ask* such a thing after all the time and trouble you have given. I think No. 1 bad and ought to be rewritten, if possible. No. 2 and No. 3 probably as well as I can average. No. 3 is far the most technical of the whole course. No. 4 I trust about fills the bill. It is thin and commonplace, but those defects are balanced by clearness and earnestness. I *shall want the MS returned* for alterations.

But that which impels me to write to you now and to touch upon the delicate question of money is a letter from my wife asking me to do so for strong reasons which she gives. I am thus led to say (and my wife knows nothing of these feelings on my part) that $50 per lecture seems a reasonable price for such lectures, and therefore since you say you have $350 to be paid over to me, we will make the number of lectures 7. I enclose their titles. [This list has not been found.] As to the $10 a week for 45 weeks to be presented to my wife, I cannot regard [it] in any other light than as alms from totally unknown persons. Clearly it is not payment for my lectures. I shall not tell my wife how I look upon it, for we are in truth very poor, and she is ill, and if she sees her way to accepting it, I shall simply take care it is spent on her personal comfort. So much for that.

But now she wishes me to ask you to send me an advance of $100, and if you choose to do so, it can be regarded as half payment for the four lectures I enclose. If on the other hand you like to send it to Mrs. C. S. Peirce 108 W. 89th St. New York, we can see hereafter which part it comes from. I don't want her to be compromised by the acceptance of this $100, so that she cannot decline the $450 should she wish to do so. I simply wish to avoid interfering myself about that.

I will now mention the reasons she gives for my asking for the advance.

1st, that I am ill (a mere trifle) and that we ought not to be forced to have two households, as I am obliged to do unless I make a deposit to pay a caretaker. In fact I could not leave here for a single day without that because owing to peculiarities of Pennsylvania law *etc.* were I to do so a party who wants to buy the place at winter cash sale could have it sold *without notice* the minute my back was turned, and certainly would do so. I am alone here. I get a Vienna loaf once in 3 days and live on that.

2nd, It is important I should be in New York where negotiations to get me as Professor in the Cosmopolitan University which was almost decided upon, are broken off and in danger of adverse decision by my staying here. Besides, I cannot earn a cent here and my wife is in personal distress, while there I could earn a little.

3rd. There is a leak in the roof here and I don't think it will practically be mended until I am prepared to pay for it. Of course this is ruinous to the house, and all the worse that two men are coming up to inspect the house, one with a view to purchase and the other with a view to consolidating the 3 small mortgages (total $2500) very greatly to our advantage and safety. Now a neglected leak would probably negative both propositions, — not to speak of the effects of damp.

4th. She wants me to have decent clothes for the lectures, to which supposing the money was mine I should agree. Also that as things stand now, I should neither be able to leave here, nor have the money to go to Cambridge, or if I did go there [I] might perhaps be too ill to give the lectures.

I have thus delivered my message. With warmest thanks for all your sacrifice of time and energy, to which thanks I fancy Royce is also entitled to a share.

Peirce continued to make good progress upon the plan of lectures announced in the foregoing. This is confirmed by a letter of mid-January to his wife. Everything seemed to be developing according to the plan Peirce had announced. James responded that he had sent the list of lectures Peirce had provided to Dr. Janes (manager of the Conferences) at 168 Brattle Street, under the title "Detached Ideas on Vitally Important Topics," saying that an eighth lecture would probably be added. James was disappointed that the plan seemed to leave no place for tychism or synechism. He reported that he had sent a check for one hundred dollars. And, most important, he remarked that "the lectures have arrived, but I haven't had a chance to look at them, and busy as I now am (and fagged also) I shall have to make my glance very cursory and send them back in a few days."

Peirce wrote on the twentieth of January acknowledging the check, and suggesting 3 or 7 February as a date for the first lecture. He also asked James to try to find temporary lodging for him. A second letter to James was penned on the twenty-first, in which Peirce commented on William's request for lectures on Tychism:

> About my lecturing on Tychism and Synechism, I wish to avoid any further treatment of the former by itself, because I want it clearly understood that I am a Synechist at bottom and a Tychist only because Tychism is a corollary of Synechism.
>
> On Synechism I should only be too glad to give any number of lectures that will be listened to. But in the first place, it is against my deep principles to represent that or any philosophy as a matter of "vital importance," and therefore I will call a lecture which I should be glad to put in the plural, an *appended* lecture or lectures. In the second place, continuity is a most difficult conception, — *the* most difficult of all conceptions. The easiest way to treat it, by far, is by means of geometry. A lecture or lectures about continuity itself, and the way to reason about it, and the way to apply that mode of reasoning to metaphysics, which is absolutely novel and well worth the consideration of every philosopher, I shall be able to make instructive to the merest babe. Only he must not rebel at its being mathematical.

Peirce told his wife in a separate letter on the twenty-first that he would finish his fifth lecture that evening. He also seemed to exhibit a celebratory mood, for he asked:

> When you get the $100 will you kindly send me *tobacco* and *tea*? I am getting on so well with my work I think it best not to bother with correcting my habits at present. For the discomfort would spoil my work. Having suddenly come into the great fortune you sent $2 + $5. I yesterday indulged in a Happ's mince pie and a piece of American cheese. I even thought of getting a little whiskey which I have had only one swig of since I have been here this last time. That was last Sunday when the men that came about buying the place gave me a drink. But I decided that I would not go into that luxury.

Peirce's jovial euphoria continued through the next day, when he sent another letter to Juliette: "What do you think happened yesterday? I washed my face. I wash my hands often and I brush my hair very frequently, sometimes twice in the same week."

But his financial exuberance and tonsorial splendor were sharply interrupted by a sudden turn of events expressed in a letter from William dated the twenty-third, only parts of which survive.

> I mailed you your 1st lecture yesterday, but have been too "driven" to add a word until now. I will send the other three by express tomorrow, Monday.
>
> The lectures can just as well as not begin on Feb. 7, or for the matter of that the following Thursday or Friday.
>
> Reading the lectures rapidly prompts me to make some remarks—with fear and trembling, as in the presence of a most peppery personage.
>
> 1. The fourth lecture seems to me a model of what a popular lecture ought to be. It is anything but "thin" (as you call it). It establishes your "atmosphere" of thought in an earnest and sympathetic way, it makes connection with things already in the air, and it would tempt any and every hearer [irresistibly] to listen to what is to follow, if it were given first.
>
> Therefore I remark that I implore you on bended knees to *give it first,* instead of the one you have written, which being full of "sass" to the audience and paradoxical irradiations in all sorts of directions, would have, I fear somewhat of an opposite effect.
>
> I don't see then why you shouldn't re-establish your former title "The logic of events." You could work in the more important parts of the original first lecture, in other places. I think the way you work the distinction between topics of Sentiment and those of thought is highly interesting—even tho' it have a somewhat paradoxical sound.

Some parts of the letter are missing at this point, but the conclusion has survived:

> I must say that your *sweep* is as glorious as it is vertiginous! So good luck to the enterprise!

Peirce responded on the twenty-sixth in a surprisingly good humor, although he declined (in a joking way) to return to his original title.

> Dear William: Yours of the 23rd was missent by the P.O. I received it this morning.
>
> All the changes you desire shall be made as far as practicable. There will be hardly anything about the Logic of Events. The course might be called "Hints toward a logic of Events," on the

ground that a good deal is instilled in a casual way in the course of the lectures. I suppose Lecture IV to make it Lecture I will have to be rewritten. Miracles will have to be struck out. Old Lecture I can be rewritten and put in somewhere toward the end. I will try to temper its paradox, — though it ought not to be found paradoxical. The two lectures to be added can be given to the Law of Continuity and to the Logic of Events.

The course might be entitled

The Logic of Events and Allied Topics
Prolegomena to the Logic of Events
On the Fringes of the Logic of Events.

Be it understood then 8 lectures and we shall appear at any lodgings that may be found for us Feb. 9.

The lecture you like I called "thin" because there is nothing in it not substantially in Plato. As to "things already in the air" perhaps you allude to Morison's oration for which I gave hints.

The "Training in Reasoning" of course does not approach the logic of events but the "Time and Causation" does. It is the most solid of the lot. Too much so, no doubt. I will try to make the four I still have to write (including old No. IV) perfect ballet-girls.

I must have all the time possible so I write to Dr. Janes to name Feb. 10 as the date of the first, citing you as saying it can be so.

His mention of Morison's oration refers to the 1896 Phi Beta Kappa oration delivered at Harvard by George Shattuck Morison (1842–1903, Harvard class of 1863), friend and business associate of Peirce. After graduation, Morison first entered the practice of law, but he soon moved into civil engineering. By this time he was perhaps the world's leading bridge designer. In a letter to Peirce dated 2 June 1896 (*MS* L 300:41), Morison mentioned: "I am going to give the Phi Beta Kappa oration at Cambridge this year, perhaps rather a curious thing for an engineer to do, and I hope you will pardon me if I steal a few of your ideas in regard to a university." Peirce wrote the *Century Dictionary* definition for "university," and prominently there we find it described as "an association of men for the purpose of study." This and other Peircean ideas on the topic can indeed clearly be seen in the oration.[18]

Approximately two days after writing James, in a letter to his wife, Peirce gave vent to attitudes that he had kept from his friend.

My sweetest wife: I sent you that telegram in consequence of a letter received yesterday to say lectures must begin Feb. 3. But this morning the same stage which carried away the telegram brought another letter to say the lectures need not begin till the 10th. So, as I need all the time I can have I postpone them one week. I have had a terrible struggle with my sixth lecture which will, however, be finished tonight. The letter of today changes the subject of my courses completely and compels me to write 3 new lectures, one of which is the first, and to change all of them! Did you ever hear the like? There was quite a heavy fall of snow last night and that and the necessity of striking while the iron was hot on the terrible 6th lecture prevented my going out. Nor have I had time to read your last two letters. You see these lectures are life and death, and I have been at work night and day on them; but when this is finished tonight I shall attend to matters before writing my first lecture. It is harder work than you think.

Peirce sent two separate short notes to James on the twenty-ninth, mentioning vexatious worries about his wife (still in New York), asking that William send fifty dollars against the lecture earnings, and still showing anxieties about successfully finding a caretaker for the house in Milford. Then he gave a progress report on his lecture preparations.

I found I could not do precisely as you desired. But I am just halfway through a new lecture I which is particularly free from paradox, is on the contrary perfectly clear, does not satirize any person or body, and in short is according to your views.

Do not fail to send the money [to Juliette]. For I have the course 3/4 written. Five lectures complete, 1 half done and two upon which a good deal of work has been spent quite equal to another half lecture.

Peirce seems to have begun to see the light at the end of the tunnel on the thirtieth, for the following happy report went to James on that date.

My dear William:

I have now finished my first lecture and I have no doubt that when you hear it you will admit that it is far superior to the one on the First Rule of Logic. Every trace of personal vexation as well as of condemnation for the present state of the university has been completely erased. One sentence of 5 words "There is a lesson there" is all I utter in recommendation of the cultivation of mathematics.

As for the paradoxes, since the doctrine remains the same, they are really untouched; but I have treated them as the well-known doctrines of famous philosophers, and put their paradoxical character almost entirely into the background, so that I do not think the general effect is paradoxical.

I have developed the subject in an entirely different way which I think will be found decidedly interesting, and which is also original and fresh, and which brings the thought constantly down to concrete history.

I wanted particularly to please you; but you would not have been pleased to have the logic of the course deranged; and that logic quite imperatively called for this lecture at the outset, while the other one could only have been brought to the beginning by treating the subject in a totally different way in which my success would have been highly problematical.

I now have six lectures complete, of which the second and third are the worst.

The whole course has been greatly improved by giving the unity to it which is given by the last modification of the subject; and though it is not so systematic as I had originally intended to make it, I have no doubt the lectures are much better adapted to the audience than they would have been if the unity had been as complete as I wished originally to make it . . .

I introduce a paragraph into the first lecture saying that the subject of the course had been changed and that that causes me sometimes to wander from the present subject.

Progress continued, for on the thirty-first Charles wrote his wife that he had finished the first lecture and about a quarter of the seventh. By this time the formal announcement for the lectures had been issued.

Peirce decamped Milford in early February, presumably having solved the caretaker problem. After arrival in Cambridge he received an invitation to dine at the James house:

Arrived home last night. I learn that you are also arrived—solus. Pray come and dine tonight, if you can at 6.30, — I will ask Royce.

From his lodging at 3 Berkeley Street in Cambridge, Peirce informed Juliette on the eleventh that his first lecture "went off brilliantly last night." The series apparently continued well, with a happy conclusion, for Charles reported to Juliette on the sixth of March that

> My lectures are now all but one finished. They have been well re-
> ceived. The 7th was the one which seemed to excite most interest.
> A meeting of philosophers has been arranged to meet me; and this
> could not be arranged for an earlier night than next Friday.

These sentiments and evaluations about the lectures were echoed in a
letter the following day from James to Mrs. Peirce.

> The lectures ended tonight felicitously, with a very dignified and
> touching peroration. They have been a great success, from the
> point of view of esteem, everyone speaking of them with the great-
> est admiration; and in some shape or other they ought to get into
> print before it is too late. I have just been walking home with Royce,
> who is extraordinarily full of appreciation.

James was not simply making a social compliment to Mrs. Peirce.
His admiration of Peirce was apparent in a letter he wrote to Paul Carus
on March eighteenth.

> Chas. Peirce has just been giving a course of lectures here, with
> great success—abstruse in parts, but always something popular and
> inspiring, and the whole thing leaving you with a sense that you
> had just been in the place where ideas are manufactured. They
> ought in some shape or other to get into print. I am sure there is
> stuff there for several more Monist articles, and I tip you this hint
> accordingly. I enclose you one of Peirce's programs . . .

On the twenty-sixth of August in 1898 in Berkeley, California,
James delivered the famous lecture[19] on pragmatism that marked the
beginning of the public life of the doctrines Peirce had initiated at the
Metaphysical Club in Cambridge in the early 1870s.[20] Royce's writings
after 1898 began to drift toward Peirce's ideas, in a path that culminated
in *The Problem of Christianity* (1918). One is led to wonder if these events
in the careers of James and Royce, and in the career of pragmatism
itself, were not influenced by Peirce's performance in Cambridge in
1898. It is our hypothesis that Peirce's Cambridge Conferences lectures
did have this effect.

Now the complete lectures are presented in print for the first time.
At last the wish of William James for their accurate publication has
been honored. We hope that through this edition study of our historical
hypothesis can be facilitated. Moreover, the ideas contained in these

lectures will now be available for examination, and thereby their role in intellectual life may steadily grow.

Peirce's Continuum

This section attempts to explain a conception which is important not only for understanding these lectures, but also for understanding virtually all of Peirce's larger metaphysical projects. That is the concept of continuity.

In the present lectures Peirce said that he would like to call his metaphysics Synechism because "it rests on the study of continuity" (Lecture Eight). He also mentioned, in Lecture Seven, "all the hard work I have done for the last fifteen years" in "trying to bring all the action of the universe" under this single principle of continuity. Yet that statement will be totally misread by anyone who understands continuity as it is understood in present-day mathematics, as simply a well-understood and well-defined property of certain functions, curves, and lines. Peirce's own notion of continuity does begin, indeed, with a metaphysico-mathematical analysis of the "continuity" of the line, but it culminates in a grand generalization of that notion of continuity in a direction that will be quite unexpected to most twentieth-century readers. A metaphysics of continuity, in Peirce's sense, is not merely or primarily a metaphysics which insists that there are a lot of important continua in nature, or a lot of important continuous functions in physics; it is a metaphysics which identifies ideal continuity with the notion of inexhaustible and creative possibility. We hope to explain how the analysis of continuity led Peirce to such an identification.

If the following remarks are more mathematical than you might expect, there is at least the excuse that Peirce himself, when he lectured to the Cambridge Conferences, would have liked to be much more technical than he was allowed to be. We hope, at any rate, that the discussion that follows is the sort of thing that would have pleased Peirce himself.

Peirce's "metaphysical speculations," as he called them, are characterized by enormous originality and profundity in conception combined with precision in technical detail, and they cannot be understood without reconstructing the detail. It is fair to assume that most readers are not mathematicians, and since with some of you the mathematics you learned in school may be "rusty," let us begin by very briefly recapitulating what one learns about the continuum—that is, about the line—in elementary mathematics.

The conception of the line which developed during the nineteenth century and which became virtually the exclusive mathematical conception in the twentieth century, or at least the exclusive conception until the recent appearance of something called "nonstandard analysis," is that the line is isomorphic to the real numbers. So let us recall what the real numbers are.

First of all, we must remember what the rational numbers are. A rational number is what in ordinary language we call a fraction, say 2/3 or −31/10. The real numbers are simply the rational numbers together with all the numbers which can be expressed as the limits of sequences of rational numbers. Following the work of the nineteenth-century mathematician Karl Theodor Weierstrass, we can explain what it is for a sequence of rational numbers to be convergent without using the notion of a real number; that is, it is possible to define the notion of convergence in terms of the intrinsic properties of the sequence of rational numbers itself. Instead of saying that the real numbers are the *limits* of convergent sequences of rational numbers, one can identify the real numbers with *equivalence classes* of convergent sequences of rational numbers under an appropriate equivalence relation, and this is what is done in formalized systems of mathematics such as *Principia Mathematica*. The square root of two, for example, is the limit of the sequence 1, 1 + 4/10, 1 + 41/100, 1 + 414/1000, . . . and is thus a real number, as are all the numbers one can express in decimal notation, whether the number of digits after the decimal point be finite or infinite.

Descartes taught us to use letters of the alphabet such as x, y, z to stand for the lengths of line segments, whether those lengths be rational or not. Perhaps as a result of this, the assumption gradually grew up that there is a complete isomorphism between the system of points on the line and the system of real numbers. Indeed, mathematicians often refer to the system of real numbers as "the real line." Peirce, however, decisively rejected the idea that the geometrical line, as it shall be called here, is isomorphic with the system of real numbers. And it is Peirce's conception of the geometrical line that will be discussed, although the discussion will require us to take a look at Peirce's set theory and at his metaphysics of possibility as well.

Although it is doubtful that his view was the same as that of Peirce, it may be useful to point out that a great philosopher-logician of our time, Kurt Gödel, remarked that,[21] at least intuitively, if you divide the geometrical line at a point you would expect that the two halves of the line would be mirror images of each other. Yet, this is not the case if the geometrical line is isomorphic to the real numbers.

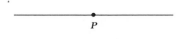

Fig. I.1

A division of the real numbers at point P into two sections, say, a left section L and a right section R, is called a "Dedekind Cut." (The term is also applied to divisions of the rational numbers with the following four properties.) Since it is supposed to correspond to a division of the line, it has the properties that (1) L and R are not empty; (2) if a number belongs to L, then so does every smaller number; (3) if a number belongs to R, then so does every bigger number; (4) every number belongs to exactly one of the two sections. A theorem, called the "Dedekind Cut Theorem," says that no matter how the Dedekind Cut is made, it is always the case that *either* the left section L has a greatest member *or* the right section R has a least member (but of course not both, since then neither section would contain the numbers between the greatest member of L and the least member of R). The two halves of a Dedekind Cut—an arbitrary "division" of the real numbers—are not mirror images of each other. For, if they were mirror images, then if L has no greatest member, then R should have no least member (which is impossible by the Dedekind Cut Theorem), and if L does have a greatest member, then R should also have a least member (which is also impossible, as we just remarked). If the geometrical line is isomorphic to the real number system, then when we divide the line at P, we must either include the point P itself in the right half of the division (but not the left half, since a "division" is an *exclusive* affair) or else include the point P itself in the left half of the division (but not the right half). Then one of the "half lines" created by the division will have an end point and the other will be an "open" half line, a half line with no end point, and the two half lines will not be mirror images.

But how could Gödel have thought that the geometrical line might fail to obey the Dedekind Cut Theorem? We cannot answer with confidence, but there is a very old view, one that surely was known to Gödel, which was very likely in the background of his reasoning. This is the Aristotelian view that points are simply conceptual divisions of the line.

At first blush, it does not seem that Peirce could have had an Aristotelian conception of the line, since he did speak in at least one place of the line as "a collection of points." Later on, it will be argued that, apart from terminology, Peirce's view is broadly Aristotelian, although it has many elements that could not have been present in Aristotle. It will also be argued that what makes it possible for Peirce to incorporate

Aristotelian elements in his view is a certain conception that Peirce had of "collections." But that is getting ahead of the story. Sticking for the moment with Aristotle, if we adopt his view, the line is an irreducible geometrical object and not a collection of more elementary objects. If a line is divided into two parts, that is what is done: the line is divided into two parts. And the two parts are mirror images of each other. But to ask to which half does the point of division belong makes no sense on the Aristotelian view. (Here, of course, a modern question is answered on Aristotle's behalf; Aristotle himself did not consider this question.) For him, points don't *belong* to lines, although they lie on them; that is, points are divisions of lines (and also terminations of them, in the case of line segments and curves with endpoints). To elaborate Aristotle's view in a way which will facilitate comparison with that of Peirce, consider not a line but a line interval (Figure I.2a):

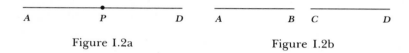

A   P   D   A   B   C   D

Figure I.2a   Figure I.2b

Suppose we divide the line interval at a point *P* and then separate the two broken halves by moving the right half a short distance to the right (Figure I.2b). This moving of a line segment to the right must not be thought of, as it is on the modern conception, as a one-to-one mapping of one collection of points onto another collection of points, of course, but as a primitive and irreducibly geometrical transformation, as it presumably was for Euclid. And in Figure I.2a the endpoints *A* and *D* are not to be regarded as *members* of the line segment *AD*, but simply as loci distinguished by the fact that an object we have constructed *ends there*. What about Figure I.2b? The left half of the original segment *AD* (which has not been moved) still has two endpoints. In the Aristotelian conception, there is no such thing as an "open" line interval; a line interval by the mere fact of existing as a line interval "defines," as it were, its endpoints. They are abstract properties of the line interval itself, and the notion of a line interval with no endpoints is senseless. Now look at the right half of the original segment *AD*, which has become the right-hand segment *CD*. The endpoints of this segment are again abstract properties of the line segment itself, and not "members" of the line. Where did *C* come from? Well, *C* was originally the point of division of the two halves of *AD*, that is to say, *C* was originally *P*. But *B*, the right-hand endpoint of the left half, is the original *P*. Dividing and separating the line segments has had the effect of dividing the point *P* into two points, or, if you like, performing this geometrical transformation has "mapped" the original point *P* onto two points: it is its own image under the transformation, but equally its image may be said to be *C*. To use the language which Peirce used about such a construction in Lecture Three, the point *P* has "become" the two points *B,C*. (Peirce's example differs only in that he considered breaking a closed curve rather than a line segment.)

Although what Peirce said about this sort of case makes sense on the Aristotelian view, there is another case that Peirce considered in Lecture Three that appears to make no sense on that view. (Again, Peirce considered a curved line rather than a straight one, but such "affine" properties as straightness are irrelevant to the present discussion.) Imagine the following: start with a line interval, and instead of dividing the line in the middle, we simply take the right-hand endpoint and move it a short distance to the right, thus:

Figure I.3

This construction, which does make sense for Peirce, would seem not to make sense for an Aristotelian, for it treats the point not as an abstract property of the line but as a real geometrical part of the line. But for Peirce this is also a case of one point "becoming two points." But it is time to let Peirce speak for himself.

In Lecture Three Peirce said a number of things which sound completely bizarre to today's mathematical sensibility. Then he challenged anyone who might think he is crazy to show that he had actually contradicted himself. What is worse, it looks very easy to show that he has indeed contradicted himself.

According to Peirce, if the transformation shown in Figure I.2 is reversed, then the two points *B* and *C* will become "one single point" again. Now this much an Aristotelian will say too. But an Aristotelian would not say that *B* and *C* might *keep their order* after they have "become one single point" again. Peirce said that one point

> might burst into any discrete multitude of points whatever, and they would all have been one point before the explosion. Points might fly off, in multitude and order like all the real irrational

quantities from 0 to 1; and they *might* all have had that order of succession in the line. Men will say this is self-contradictory. It is not so. If it be so prove it. The apparatus of the logic of relatives is a perfect means of demonstrating anything to be self-contradictory that really is so, but that apparatus not only refuses to pronounce this self-contradictory, but it demonstrates, on the contrary, that it is not so.

Well, suppose just two points fly off in the "explosion." Let B and C be the two points that were "one point before the explosion." This explosion might be imagined to happen, for example, by just the transformation depicted in Figure I.2b, the case in which one point has "become two." The order of B and C after the explosion is that B is to the left of C and C is not to the left of B. Suppose B and C had "that order of succession in the line" before they flew apart (when they "have been at one point"). That is to suppose that B and C had that order even in Figure I.2a, when B and C "have been at" the one point P. Then at that time the following was the case (read xLy as "x is to the left of y"):

$$BLC \ \& \ -CLB \ \& \ C = B$$

But this *is* a contradiction in predicate calculus with identity, which is certainly a part of Peirce's Logic of Relatives. Had Peirce then simply lost his marbles in 1898?

Well, first of all, we should be suspicious of the symbolization of the inference that if C and B were "at one point," then at that time it was the case that $C = B$. For consider the following statements: India is larger than Pakistan and Pakistan is not larger than India, and Pakistan and India stood in that relation when they were still one country. If we symbolize (what we might take to be a consequence of) that statement in the following way (read i for India, p for Pakistan, and "xLy" as "x is larger than y"),

$$iLp \ \& \ -pLi \ \& \ i = p$$

then we have a contradiction in the Logic of Relatives. But in 1940 clearly it was true that what we now call India and Pakistan were one country, and yet that India was larger than Pakistan. What "A and B are one country" means in such a sentence is that A and B are both parts of one country. This is an equivalence relation, but it is not the relation of identity. Once we see that "India and Pakistan were one country in 1940" does not (in such a use) mean that India and Pakistan were identical in 1940, then we see that the statements about India and Pakistan are consistent.

Similarly, if we suppose that what we ordinarily call a "point" can in some sense have *parts*—and the argument here will be that this is what Peirce believed—then the "contradiction" between Peirce's statements also disappears. *B* and *C* are separate *point parts* which have become separate points as the result of moving the line segment *CD*. Before that line segment was moved, on the interpretation of Peirce's view proposed here, they were parts of what we ordinarily call one point but they had the order that *B* was to the left of *C* but not vice versa.

Notice, by the way, that in his formulation of the paradox Peirce said that the points have been *at* one point, and that the symbolization "=" is not a natural one for *being at one point*, although it does sound natural for the other locution Peirce used, apparently interchangeably, of having *been one point*. Another problem, of course, is that Peirce spoke as if things could be identical at one time but not at another, yet in the Logic of Relatives, as in present-day predicate Calculus, identity is treated as a tenseless relation. But if "being at one point" is not an identity relation, even for points, then this problem disappears.

What is the justification for putting the notion of a "point part" into Peirce's mouth when he did not explicitly use any such notion?

Although he did not make it explicit in this set of lectures, we know from his other writings[22] that he believed in the existence of infinitesimals. Indeed, he said things in a number of places in these very lectures which directly imply the existence of infinitesimals, including geometric infinitesimals, that is to say, line intervals whose length is not zero but is less than any positive real length whatsoever. For example, in Lecture Five Peirce made it quite clear that he believed in infinitesimals; he had just mentioned that the commonest form that a certain fallacy takes is treating every collection as if it were finite—he then continued:

> Somewhat more subtle forms of this fallacy are Euclid's assumption that every whole is greater than its part, and that reasoning of the doctrine of limits which thinks it proves a quantity to be zero by saying, if not, let E be its value, and goes on to show that the value is less than E. What this does prove is that the value of the quantity is less than that of any quantity chosen as E has been chosen, generally as a finite quantity. This proposition really proved is *less* than

the truth, even though the proposition supposed to be proved is *more* than the truth.

The inference that Peirce here declared to be a fallacy is the inference from a proof that a quantity is less than any finite quantity to the conclusion that the quantity is zero; and the only way the inference can be fallacious is if there are quantities less than every finite quantity but not zero, that is, if there are infinitesimals.

Infinitesimals were indeed standard in mathematics, but their use gradually died out during the nineteenth century. As the result of Abraham Robinson[23] and others, they have been revived, and we now have a well-developed theory, called nonstandard analysis, which can be used to construct models for mathematics in which there really do exist infinitesimals.

We can understand the bearing the existence of infinitesimals has on what we have been discussing by supposing that there is somewhere on the line an infinitesimal segment, that is, a segment with endpoints AB whose length is infinitesimal. Let P be any other point on the line. By the axioms of Euclidean geometry, it is possible to find two points, P' and P'', such that P' is to the left of P and P'' is to the right of P and the intervals $P'P$ and PP'' are congruent to the interval AB. In short, if there is even one infinitesimal segment on the line, then there are infinitesimal segments beginning and ending with any point whatsoever. The line has the same structure in all of its parts. In nonstandard analysis we say that two points P and Q whose distance is infinitesimal are "identical modulo the infinitesimals" and we symbolize this by using a wiggly equals sign: $P \approx Q$. If P is a point, the collection of all points Q such that $P \approx Q$ is called the *monad* of P. It can be shown (ignoring points at infinity,[24] if there are any) that every point has to lie in the monad of a "standard" point, that is, a point whose distance from the origin (assuming that we have arbitrarily picked a point as the origin and a unit of length) is a (standard) real number. To see this, let P be any point on the line which is not a standard point. Divide the *standard* points into two sets: those which are to the left of P (L) and those which are to the right of P (R). By the Dedekind Cut Theorem, either L has a greatest member or R has a least member, and since L,R is a division of the *standard* points, this distinguished point is itself standard; call it $P°$. There is no *standard* point between P and $P°$; for if $P°$ is the greatest member of L, then any standard point to the left of P is in L and hence to the left of or identical with $P°$ (and similarly we get a contradiction if we suppose $P°$ is the least member of R and some standard point is between P and $P°$). But every interval of finite length contains standard points. So the interval $PP°$ must be of less-than-finite length, that is, it is infinitesimal. Thus, if there are any nonstandard points, they all lie in the monads of the standard points.

Now here is the proposed interpretation of the apparently crazy passage from Peirce's third lecture. Suppose that Peirce's view there was that what we ordinarily call "points" are really monads. While this doesn't account for everything that Peirce mentioned in the lecture, it does remove the appearance of "self-contradiction" to which Peirce himself alluded. In accordance with the hypothesis about what Peirce meant here, in the remainder of this section, individual points on a line will be designated as "point parts" and "points" will refer to monads. In this language, Peirce is telling us that within a single point one can find at least c different point parts, where c is the power of the set of real numbers. This is true, because if there is even one infinitesimal interval AB, then for every positive real number r there is an infinitesimal interval whose length is r times the length of AB. (Proof of this requires certain geometric assumptions, of course.) It is easy to show that within one monad one can find a set of points (point parts) which is ordered exactly as the real numbers between 0 and 1 are ordered—and this, according to the interpretation advanced, is exactly what Peirce claimed!

What Peirce was doing, then, was first imagining a transformation as the result of which these point parts fly apart, without changing their relative order, that is, they are mapped onto distinct points (distinct monads) having the order type of the real numbers between 0 and 1; and Peirce was saying that even before the transformation—that is, even when the point parts were parts of a single point (were "at" a single point)—they had that same order. On the proposed reconstruction, he is quite right in claiming that there is no contradiction in this point of view.

If someone wonders how we could know that Peirce really did believe in the existence of *geometric* infinitesimals, the proper reply seems to be that Lecture Three itself clearly implies their existence, although Peirce did not draw the conclusion for his lay audience. For Peirce *did* insist in the lecture that the cardinal number of the points on the line is much greater than c; that is, he claimed that the points on the line are of a higher order of infinity than the real numbers. This implies the existence of nonstandard points on the line, and hence of infinitesimals.

Peirce referred to the infinite cardinals of Georg Cantor. (He remarked that Cantor's work became generally known only after 1890.) Following Cantor, Peirce defined what it is for two collections to have the same cardinality, and he gave Cantor's proof that the set of all subsets of a given set is of a higher cardinality than the set itself. He introduced Cantor's term "denumerable" for an infinite collection which has the same cardinality as the set of all integers. It was also known from Cantor's work that the set of all real numbers is of the same cardinality as the set of all collections of integers, so by Cantor's proof the set of all real numbers is nondenumerable or, as Peirce said, "abnumerable."

The set theory that Peirce informally presented in Lectures Three and Eight has points of resemblance to that of both Ernst Zermelo and John von Neumann. Like both of these it seems[25] to envisage a universe of sets arranged in cumulative types (cumulative because, unlike Bertrand Russell's types, each type—or "rank," to use von Neumann's term—in Zermelo–Frankel–von Neumann set theory includes all the lower ones). For the purposes of understanding Peirce's lectures, we might think of the individuals as the finite cardinal numbers (the "finite multitudes," in Peirce's terminology). Call the collection of all the finite multitudes N, and take N to be rank zero. Then the union of the set of all subsets of N—that is, the collection of all collections of finite multitudes—with N itself would be rank one; and for n greater than zero, the set of all subsets of rank n would be rank $n + 1$. Rank zero is denumerable; rank one has the cardinal which is above called c and which Cantor called $2^{cardinal\ of\ rank\ n}$. Peirce's (informally presented) set theory resembles von Neumann's set theory in that in addition to including what have been here called "sets" ("collections of discrete individuals," in Peirce's terminology), Peirce also allows collections of sets which do not themselves occur in the hierarchy of sets; for example, the union of all the ranks (call it **V**) is a collection, but not a "collection of discrete individuals." For von Neumann there would be many more ranks than there were for Peirce, because von Neumann extended the series rank zero, rank one, rank two, and so on, through the transfinite. But for von Neumann as for Peirce the union of all the ranks recognized by the set theory is a special kind of collection: von Neumann called it a "proper class." The proper classes are all the collections of sets which are not themselves sets, that is, which do not themselves belong to one of the ranks.

The cardinal number of his universe of collections of discrete individuals (which is here called **V**) was recognized by Peirce as a special kind of cardinal (call it Ω): a cardinal which is not itself a set but only an ideal limit of the cardinals in **V**.

In his informally presented set theory Peirce said, in fact, that the multitude of the points on the line is not only greater than c; it is greater than the cardinal number of any set. In fact, it is similar to the multitude of the whole universe of sets ("collections of discrete individuals"). If we call the cardinal of the universe of sets Ω, there are Ω points on the line!

Now if there are more than c points on the line, then almost all the points on the line must be "nonstandard." But, as already pointed out, every nonstandard point has to lie in the "monad" of a standard point. Thus, at least provisionally, we may think of Peirce's continuum as consisting of the standard points together with all of the nonstandard points in their monads. In fact, in the monad of each standard point there must be Ω nonstandard points!

This reconstruction of Peirce's view of the continuum is still far from complete.

To determine what Peirce's view was, we have to see how he could come so close to what earlier was called the "Aristotelian" view. First, a couple of corrections to earlier remarks are needed: although the terminology of contemporary nonstandard analysis has been used in order to explain Peirce's conception of the line, that terminology is in a way extremely misleading. When one does nonstandard analysis, one starts by expanding the real number system by adding nonstandard real numbers which are infinitesimally close to the standard real numbers (as well as infinite nonstandard real numbers) and then one assumes that the nonstandard geometric line is isomorphic to the nonstandard real numbers. But this was not Peirce's view at all. Peirce did not propose to add nonstandard numbers to the real number system. He simply proposed that there are nonstandard points on the geometrical line. This means that it would make no sense on Peirce's view to ask which point in a given monad is *the* standard point. On his view (as reconstructed here), what we mean when we ordinarily talk of points on a line are monads (and sometimes parts of monads, as when a point "becomes two points"), and not points (which have here been called point parts) at all. The real numbers do, at a first pass, give us all the points until we begin to divide those points and thereby to construct nonstandard point parts.

But this advances ahead of the argument. For the moment, it is important to suggest that we should think of the line as consisting of monads which can be put into one-to-one correspondence with the real numbers, each of which contains Ω potential point parts. (What is meant by calling them *potential* point parts will become clear shortly.) Within a given monad, none of the point parts is any more "standard" than any other point part in that monad. This view is a very different one from the idea of a monad in nonstandard analysis as we have it today. The monad corresponding to $x = $ *the square root of 2* can be divided into Ω point parts, but none of those point parts is *the* point $x = $ *the square root of 2*.

Saying this is not to further interpret Peirce, but to *subtract* from the earlier account certain extraneous elements which had been introduced through use of ideas from nonstandard analysis.

Now, back to the Aristotelian examples in Figures I.2a and I.2b. To someone familiar with nonstandard analysis it would seem that introducing infinitesimals will not bring us any closer to the Aristotelian view. For present-day nonstandard analysis is constructed in such a way that the Transfer Principle holds. This principle says that all theorems of usual mathematics (with the usual conception of the continuum) which do not explicitly contain the words "standard" and "nonstandard" continue to hold when we add the nonstandard elements to the line or to the real number system. In other words, it makes no difference whether a mathematician proves a theorem using the methods of standard analysis or of nonstandard analysis; if a theorem can be proved using nonstandard analysis, then the theorem will still be valid even if one doesn't believe that there really are infinitesimals. However, the Transfer Principle was no part of anything to which Peirce had a commitment. The reason for discussing the Transfer Principle is this: if the Transfer Principle is true, then the Dedekind Cut Theorem must hold for the nonstandard line as well as for the standard line; that is, even if we add infinitesimals, it must remain the case that when we make a division in the line, the two halves will not be mirror images of one another. Now, Peirce did not explicitly say that he accepted the Aristotelian intuition, that the two halves are mirror images of one another, but there seems to be no reason to *doubt* that he thought this, since he did think that (in Figure I.2b) AB and CD both have endpoints.

At this point, the following speculation is a reasonable one, given Peirce's views. Suppose that when we divide the line at a point P what we do is actually divide the monad of P into two halves. The points in the left half of the monad of P become the new "endpoint" of the left half of the line (become the point B in Figure I.2b), and the points in the right half of the monad of P (or their images under the translation which moves that half of the line to the right) become the new "endpoint" of the right half of the line (become the point C). Then AB and CD will still have two endpoints, as Peirce asserted that they do; and it is still possible (although incompatible with the Transfer Principle, to be sure) that *AB* and *CD* should be mirror images of one another.

Still, the problem remains: even if some divisions of the line produce halves which are mirror images of each other, how can *every* division of the line have this property? Why can't the line be divided by putting the monad of *P* in the right half of the division, together with every point which lies to the right of *P* by some *finite* amount, and putting all the other points (the points which lie to the left of *P* by some *finite* amount) in the left half of the division? It would seem that this would divide the line cleanly into two pieces in such a way that the left hand of the division would contain no greatest "point," that is, it would contain no greatest monad. This would violate both the Aristotelian intuition and that much of it to which, as we have seen, Peirce himself is definitely committed—namely, that if we divide a line or a line interval and then separate the two segments, then the left half of the division will have a right-hand endpoint. We believe we know the answer to this question, and not surprisingly it takes us deeper into Peirce's metaphysics than anything we have talked about so far, because what we have said so far does not really appeal to much of Peirce's metaphysics. It appeals only to his belief in the very large cardinality of the points on the line. In particular, we have not so far interpreted Peirce's mysterious idea that when a multitude becomes that large, then its individuals *lose their distinct identities*.

Let us go back for the moment to the Aristotelian view. On the Aristotelian view, as well as on Peirce's view, we can understand the transformation shown in Figure I.2 as causing two points to arise from a single point. But let us consider the simpler case shown in Figure I.1. Suppose we ask an Aristotelian whether the point *P* existed before he divided the line. The Aristotelian would, of course, say that there is an ambiguity in the notion of existence; he would say that *P* existed *in potentiality* before we divided the line, but that it existed *in actuality* only when we made this particular construction. And Peirce's language in Lecture Three is close to this:

> But the line is a mere conception. It is nothing but that which it can show; and therefore it follows that if there were no discontinuity there would *be* no distinct point there, — that is, no point absolutely distinct in its being from all others.

This suggests that for Peirce as for the Aristotelian, points are in some way the results of mathematical or conceptual operations, such as dividing a line or noting that a curve has an extremity. It is true that he also speaks of a line as a collection of points, but in the same paragraph he stated, "No point in this line has any distinct identity absolutely discriminated from every other." We provisionally interpreted this as meaning that what we ordinarily call points are really monads, or large aggregates of point parts. But what is a "large aggregate"?

In Lecture Eight, Peirce repeatedly referred to infinite sets as *potential* aggregates. For instance, he stated:

> We have a conception of the entire collection of whole numbers. It is a *potential* collection indeterminate and yet determinable. And we see that the entire collection of whole numbers is more multitudinous than any whole number.

What this language suggests is that Peirce had in fact what Putnam has called elsewhere a *modal logical view of set theory*.[26] Peirce apparently did not think of sets (or "collections") as mathematical "objects." His language suggests that we *could*—not, of course, physically or psychically, but in the sense of logical or "metaphysical" possibility—aggregate the natural numbers, and that when we consider the collection of natural numbers what we are contemplating is this possibility, and not an object. In this respect, Peirce's picture is like that of L. E. J. Brouwer, the founder of intuitionist logic and mathematics, but with one all-important difference. Peirce thought of both points on the line and sets as the results of conceptual construction processes: one lists objects and forms an aggregate, or one divides a line or curve or determines that a line segment or curve has an extremity and thereby determines a point. But the difference is this: for Brouwer, *our finiteness* is an omnipresent consideration. For Brouwer, it does not even make *mathematical* sense to imagine completing an infinite number of operations. Peirce had no such scruples. For Peirce, completed infinite processes are perfectly conceivable as long as the cardinal number of steps in the process is less than Peirce's ideal limiting cardinal, here called Ω.

This is not as speculative, as an interpretation of Peirce, as it may seem. For Peirce said, following the sentence just quoted above, that

> In like manner the potential aggregate of all the abnumerable multitudes [Peirce was not referring to the set of all nondenumerable cardinals here, but to the idea of "a collection of distinct individuals which is an aggregate of one collection of each of these multitudes"—that is, to a union consisting of sets of all the different nondenumerable cardinalities] is more multitudinous than any mul-

titude. This potential aggregate cannot be a multitude of distinct individuals anymore than the aggregate of all the whole numbers can be completely counted. But it is a distinct general conception for all that, — a conception of a potentiality.

This language is very consistent with the idea that the collection of points on a line (which is of the same cardinality as the potential aggregate of the abnumerable multitudes) is, like the collection of the abnumerable multitudes, "the conception of a potentiality."

There is, then, a sense in which a line is a collection of points and a sense in which it is not. A line, taken in intension, is a perfectly definite relation: in fact, the ordering relation of the line is the line, taken in intension. For Peirce tells us in Lecture Eight that when one has a collection of the kind we have been discussing, a collection of cardinal Ω, then the members of that collection are never distinguished by each having its own individual *quality*. Peirce made it clear that the difference of the points on the line is entirely a relational difference; and characteristically he thought that the underlying relation is triadic. The relation, however, is not a relation which obtains between individuals which exist in any one possible world. The indeterminate relation between points on a line can be made partially determinate in a possible world by actually constructing *aleph-null* or c or 2^c or . . . points on the line; but one can never construct *all possible* points on the line, because there is no possible world in which there are actually Ω "distinct individuals." The reason that the line is a collection of points which "lack distinct individuality" is that it is a collection of *possibilia,* and possibilia are not fully determinate objects, for Peirce. To say that the line is a collection of possibilia is to say that one can construct things which stand in a certain triadic relation, the relation "Proceeding to the right from A you reach B before you reach C." *What answers to our conception of a continuum is a possibility of repeated division which can never be exhausted in any possible world, not even in a possible world in which one can complete abnumerably infinite processes.* That is what we take Peirce's daring metaphysical hypothesis to be.

To complete this reconstruction of Peirce's view one thing remains, and that is to say what constructing an infinitesimal distance could be. But we don't have far to seek. The examples considered thus far are almost all that is needed. If we first perform the transformation represented by Figures I.2a and I.2b and then reverse the transformation, we have conceptually divided what was originally an indeterminate point P into two parts B and C, which have to be an infinitesimal distance apart. This can be regarded as the construction of one infinitesimal interval. Are there point parts between B and C? As we have seen, there are *in potentiality*, which is the only way points exist until they are actually constructed. The midpoint of the infinitesimal segment BC (here referring to C after the right-hand segment has been "moved back," of course) is itself between B and C. Once we have an infinitesimal interval, we can also subdivide that interval into n equal subintervals, for any natural number n. One should also regard *division* of the already constructed points as also a construction, one which always creates *both* a right-hand endpoint of the left half of the division and a left-hand endpoint of the right half of the division. And if we lived in a possible world in which we could complete infinite processes, all of these constructions could be performed abnumerably many times. For example, in c steps we could actually construct monads corresponding to all the real numbers. The terminology here of "possible worlds" could be regarded as a *façon de parler;* that is, "there is a possible world in which X is the case" could be regarded as merely a way of saying that "there *could* be a world in which X is the case." However, the *façon de parler* is not wholly inappropriate, since at times Peirce does seem close to the David Lewis view in which other possible worlds really exist. At least Peirce explicitly held that possibility open, and he also said that the whole collection of possible worlds (which he called "a Platonic world," and—metaphorically—"the mind of God") is itself only one of a number of really existing systems; there is not only our logical space, but other whole logical spaces.

There are still a few loose ends to tie up. In the beginning of this section we listed two difficulties with attributing an "Aristotelian" view to Peirce. One was that associated with a quotation in which Peirce said of a certain curve, "This line is a collection of points." But the sentence which follows glosses that remark, namely: "For if a particle occupying at any one instant a single point, moves until it returns to its first position, it describes such a line, which consists only of the points that particle occupied during that time." But with that gloss, no Aristotelian would disagree; and, as already indicated, Peirce added, "But no point in that line has any distinct identity absolutely discriminated from every other." The other difficulty was that Peirce accepted a construction which would not make sense to an Aristotelian, a construction in which we remove a point from the end of a line and move it. But if we accept the hypothesis that by a point Peirce meant a monad, then the point of this difficulty becomes somewhat different. The difficulty now is this: if we move a whole monad from the end of a line, then how can what is left of the line still have an endpoint? This endpoint must, after all, belong to the very monad that we moved, since after all if we reverse the transformation, and return the point to the end of the line, the new endpoint of the line and the point "returned" will "keep their order" even though they will now "be at one point." The answer is this (and again, the spirit will be somewhat Brouwerian): when we move a monad, we must think of that as moving *the monad as so far constructed.* But by moving it (in effect, making a Dedekind Cut in the already constructed points) I extend the construction. The monad that is moved is not a "collection of distinct individuals" but a "notion of a possibility." When we move it, we act on it in a way that further determines that structure, and we determine it by specifying that some of the points in that monad (the ones previously constructed) are to be (mapped onto points) infinitesimally close to a point at the new location, while other points in that monad (one of which, namely the new endpoint of the line segment, we have constructed by the transformation itself) all become point parts of the new endpoint of the line segment.

Now suppose that someone tries to block this move by specifying that the monad to be moved is *the whole proper class* of points which *could ever be constructed* in the monad of the original point. Peirce's answer would probably have been that this is simply not a possible *construction.*

Peirce's view, if we have it right, is that moving a point away from the end of a line segment or curve always produces new points (point parts) distinct from the points that were moved, just as dividing a line or curve does. The metaphysical intuition which is behind all of this is that we live in a world—since Peirce did think that there actually are continua in the real world—in which there are an enormous number of possibilities, *compatible* possibilities. Moreover, the reason that they cannot all be actualized is not that the realization of some of them logically precludes the realization of particular others, although that kind of case exists too. That is not what is involved in Peirce's statement that there cannot exist Ω distinct individuals. The Peircean picture is that the multitude of possibilities is so great that as soon as we have a possible world in which some of these possibilities are realized—say, a possible world in which some abnumerable multitude of the divisions are made—then we immediately see that there is a possible world in which still *more* divisions can be made, and hence there is no possible world in which all of these *nonexclusive* possibilities are *all* actualized. We might summarize this by saying that the metaphysical picture is that possibility intrinsically outruns actuality, and not just because of the finiteness of human powers or the limitations imposed by physical laws.

THE AIM OF THIS section was not, of course, to expound upon the entire Cambridge Conferences lectures, but to reconstruct one key element, which, if it could not be shown to be consistent, would represent a fatal flaw in the whole edifice. And that, we believe, has been done.

Comments on the Lectures

Hilary Putnam

While we don't propose to summarize Peirce's lectures, we offer as a guide to readers particular background materials that might not be conveniently available. We also want to mention some of the quite real connections between Peirce's efforts and contemporary discussions. Readers will no doubt notice many others.

Lecture One

Peirce's opening lecture speaks to a question with which all of the great pragmatists were concerned, but takes a position which may surprise some readers. Pragmatism is (not incorrectly) associated with a strong form of "cognitivism" in ethics, that is, with the ideas that ethical statements are true or false and that ethical truths can, in principle, be established by methods of inquiry continuous with those employed in the sciences. Indeed, the appeal to use "the scientific method" in ethics is the heart and soul of the philosophy of one great pragmatist, John Dewey. But if this means that we should rely on "the scientific method in ethics" to solve our practical problems, we find Peirce beginning his Cambridge Conferences lectures with a powerfully voiced dissent. Indeed, Peirce, while affirming that *in principle* there exists a science of ethics, was utterly pessimistic about the value of what is nowadays called "applied philosophy," pessimistic, in fact, about the whole idea of applying reason to "vital questions."[1] "In everyday business, reasoning is tolerably successful," our author tells us; "but I am inclined to think that it is done as well without the aid of a theory as with it." And more than that, "Men many times fancy that they act from reason when, in point of fact, the reasons they attribute to themselves are nothing but excuses which unconscious instinct invents to satisfy the teasing 'whys' of the *ego*. The extent of this self delusion is such as to render philosophical rationalism a farce."

Incidentally, Peirce anticipates the distinction (to come in Lecture Two) between induction (the establishment of frequencies by sampling, as when we estimate the frequency with which voters will vote for a given candidate by taking the frequency in a random sample), "probable inference" (the inference from the frequency in a population, when that is known, to the probable frequency in a randomly drawn sample), and "abduction" or "retroduction" (the decision to accept an explanatory theory in science on the basis of the successes of the theory). The first two methods are typified by the practices of, say, insurance companies, which estimate frequencies of all sorts of things and base practical deci- sions on them; Peirce granted that this kind of reasoning is of use in mundane practical affairs. But abduction is not useful in connection with "vital questions," Peirce thought, for two reasons: only a few (those who can master the new symbolic logic, called by Peirce "the logic of relatives," and the theory of the three kinds of inference Peirce will describe in Lecture Two) are really good enough to use this method when great questions in metaphysics or in ethics are at stake—Peirce himself would make a stab at using it in metaphysics in Lecture Eight— and even those few will be corrupted if they allow their desire for moral improvement of either the individual or the species to enter their minds. "But in philosophy, touching as it does on matters which are, and ought to be, sacred to us, the investigator who does not stand aloof from all intent to make practical applications, will not only obstruct the advance of the pure science, but what is infinitely worse, he will endanger his own moral integrity and that of his readers."

Although William James would certainly have disagreed with this, James himself did accept some of Peirce's premises. James also believed that many great questions of religion and ethics could not be presently settled by reason.[2] But on what to *do*, given that this is the case, Peirce disagreed with James. Yet even the disagreement is not a diametrical opposition.

James's view, announced two years earlier in "The Will to Believe" (the opening gun in the war for James's own "Pragmatism," with which Peirce ultimately utterly disassociated himself), was that when a question of vital importance to us cannot be settled by reason, "our passional nature not only may, but must, decide." On the surface, this does not look so different from Peirce's declaration that "Reason, for all the frills [it] customarily wears, in vital crises, comes down upon its marrow-bones to beg the succour of instinct . . . Reason, then, appeals to sentiment in the last resort. Sentiment on its side feels itself to be the man. That is my simple apology for philosophical sentimentalism." But there are important differences between what followed from this declaration for Peirce and what was intended by the similar-sounding statement by James.

One difference is, quite simply, political. Peirce was deeply conservative by temperament, and in his view "Sentimentalism implies Conservatism; and it is of the essence of conservatism to refuse to push any practical principle to its extreme limits, — including the principle of conservatism itself. We do not say that sentiment is *never* to be influenced by reason, nor that under no circumstances would we advocate radical reforms." James was a progressive in politics who advocated many reforms that were regarded as radical in his day. For James, if any principle was of the essence it was to listen to "the cries of the wounded."[3] But there is more at stake than a difference between two political visions (not that we wish to minimize the importance of such a difference).

The fact is that Peirce argued for a position[4] very like that advocated by Karl Popper, according to which science consists not of established truths but of unrefuted conjectures.

> Pure science has nothing at all to do with *action* . . . Nothing is *vital* for science; nothing can be. Its accepted propositions, therefore, are but opinions at most; and the whole list is provisional. The scientific man is not in the least wedded to his conclusions. He risks nothing upon them. Some of them, I grant, he is in the habit of calling *established truths;* but that merely means propositions to which no competent man today demurs.

James, on the other hand (and even more John Dewey), believed that this Peircean idea of a distance between pure science and applied science is fundamentally unsound; that science is and ought to be a guide to practice, and that, indeed, science would not progress if it were not used as a guide to practice. As the reference to Popper indicates, this philosophical split is still with us today. But even this is not all. For James social ethics, in particular, *requires* social experimentation. James would concede to Peirce that the results of such experimentation do not have the status of "scientific" truths. But James denied that (as Peirce thought) they are merely rationalizations of sentiment. As James put it in "The Moral Philosopher and the Moral Life,"

> In all this the philosopher is just like the rest of us non-philosophers, so far as we are just and sympathetic instinctively, and so far as we are open to the voice of complaint . . . His books upon ethics, therefore, so far as they truly touch the moral life, must more and more ally themselves with a literature which is confessedly tentative and suggestive rather than dogmatic, — I mean with novels and dramas of the deeper sort, with books on statecraft and philanthropy and social and economic reform. Treated in this way ethical treatises may be voluminous and luminous as well; but they can never be *final* except in their abstractest and vaguest features; and they must more and more abandon the old-fashioned, clear-cut, and would-be "scientific" form.

In point of fact, the dispute we see here, the dispute between philosophers who think that serious philosophy must be based on symbolic logic and exact science, and philosophers who are not afraid to suggest that a work of serious philosophy might be "allied" with "novels and dramas of the deeper sort" is still very much with us today![5]

Peirce closed this lecture with something which was quite common, and of great interest, in his time, but which has essentially disappeared from the intellectual scene today, and that is a classification of the sciences. Alisdair MacIntyre has well described the intellectual milieu in which this kind of classification was produced in "Adam Gifford's Project in Context"[6]:

> Baynes [the editor of the ninth edition of the *Encyclopedia Brittanica* (1875–1889)] made it clear that he intended his contributors not merely to provide detailed information on every major topic but to do so within the framework of a distinctive architectonic of the sciences as that had emerged in the late nineteenth century . . . Sciences were generally taken to be individuated by their subject matter, not by their methods . . . In all sciences there seem to be four constitutive elements: first there are the data, the facts, and here the sciences of the nineteenth century were held to have provided the degree of comprehensiveness necessary to reason adequately from the facts. Secondly there are unifying synthetic conceptions supplied by reflection upon the facts, if such reflection begins from a true and adequate comprehension of the facts and

if it is informed by adequate inventiveness, it will supply unifying conceptions which order the facts by making them intelligible as exemplifying laws. And thirdly there are the methods so employed, the methods by which we move from facts to unifying conceptions in theoretical discovery and from such conceptions back to the facts in the work both of explanation and of confirmation of our theories. Fourthly . . . it was taken to be the outcome of the successful application of methods to facts that there is continuous progress in supplying ever more adequate unifying conceptions which specify ever more fundamental laws. So it is characteristic of genuine science, as contrasted with the thought of the prescientific and the nonscientific, that it has a particular kind of history, one of relatively continuous progress.

We do not wish to suggest that Peirce's classification can be reductively explained by appeal to the general conceptions that MacIntyre describes; Peirce's classification of the sciences was based upon much deeper principles than the classifications MacIntyre describes (and unlike the contributors to the ninth edition of the *Encyclopedia Brittanica*, Peirce classified sciences by their method). Peirce burst the frame of the culture that produced him, but this much knowledge of that frame is helpful in reading him.

Lecture Two

In this lecture Peirce gave a very concise account of his highly original views on the nature and justification of different types of reasoning, and especially of the probabilistic inferences and the nondeductive reasoning on which all empirical inquiry depends. The lecture begins with a discussion of logic, and although Peirce postponed any description of his own symbolic logic[7] until Lecture Three, what he said here is informed by that logic, although partly couched in the vocabulary Peirce inherited from Kant and partly in the still older vocabulary of traditional Aristotelian logic. At the outset, Peirce rightly protested against the usage (which he however employed) of "hypothetical proposition" to mean any compound proposition (so that even a conjunction is called a "hypothetical proposition"). Peirce briefly discussed the question of the existential import of categorical statements and the paradoxes of material implication and supported the "Philonian" view (which is now standard, as the result of the acceptance of symbolic logic) according to which "All

A are B" is true if the class of As is empty, and according to which "If p, then q" is equivalent to "either not-p or q."[8]

In addition to defending this "Philonian view," Peirce laid down a series of interesting but unargued obiter dicta on the philosophy of logic and language. Examples: The fundamental unit of meaning is the *verb* not the noun. Part of what Peirce meant is that it is *predicates* and not individual constants that are essential to a language, and this view would be shared by many logicians today. But Peirce went further, to argue that proper names and demonstratives (*this, that*) are not really constituents of propositions but *stimulants to looking*. The idea seems to be that in the proposition "This is red" it is not the demonstrative *this*, but the thing the interpreter's attention is called to with the aid of the word *this*, that is a *constituent* of the proposition. (If this is the correct interpretation of Peirce's thought, Peirce held a view Russell developed at about the same time.) Several pages are devoted to arguing something that at first blush seems rather forced, namely that all hypothetical propositions can be (and *should* be) regarded as "categoricals." An example may illustrate what Peirce meant. "If John is a banker, then he is timid" says, on Peirce's philosophically motivated reinterpretation, that every "case" in a certain "range of possibilities" in "this here world" is a case in which if "it bankers" then "it timids." This last statement is a categorical proposition.[9] The fact that in Peirce's own system of quantification theory, the system of existential graphs (which he will introduce in Lecture Three), there are no individual constants is undoubtedly what Peirce had in mind when he claimed that this analysis is the only one which "corresponds to [an adequate] theory of inference."

The construction of the remainder of this lecture is curious: after a lengthy preliminary discussion of the syllogism, Peirce distinguished (following his essay of 1867) three types of scientific inference (probability inference from a population to a sample, the acceptance of a scientific theory on the basis of "retroduction"[10] from cases it explains, and inductive inference from a sample to a population), and showed that the first three figures of the syllogism can be regarded as extreme cases of *these* inferences. The purpose is not, as one might suppose, to show that classical deductive inferences (syllogisms in figures one, two, and three) are really probabilistic or nondeductive inferences in disguise; for the limiting cases are necessary (a notion he discussed in Lecture Eight) while Peirce recognized that at least one of the nonextreme cases (hypothetico-deductive reasoning or "retroduction") is nondeductive. However, the idea that deductive and nondeductive reasoning are in many ways analogous was important for Peirce, and he returned to it in Lecture Four.

The problems with which Peirce wrestled here have been at the center of philosophy of science for over a hundred years. A central tool employed by Peirce was the notion of probability, and Peirce saw the need to say something about the notion of randomness. In the present century such a notion was introduced into mathematical probability theory by von Mises, whose definition of randomness was, however, quickly shown to be inconsistent.[11] A successful definition could not, in fact, be arrived at until the development of modern recursion theory by Church, Turing, and Gödel. In addition, although there were already controversies over the question whether probability can be identified with frequency (the "frequentist" view) or is a primitive logical (or, some would say, psychological) notion in the nineteenth century, the fact that there are at least *two* notions of probability was not understood until Carnap made this clear in the 1950s. Needless to say, Peirce had none of these tools available in 1898.

The depth with which he understood the problems, in spite of the lack of the proper mathematical and conceptual tools, is well illustrated in this lecture, although at certain points the answers he gave are, inevitably, unsatisfactory, precisely because the concepts he had available will not suffice without a proper theory of randomness and a distinction between probability as frequency and probability as degree of confirmation.

Since many readers today will not know what "the figures of the syllogism" are (in Peirce's time, this would have been part of the knowledge of every educated person), it will be useful quickly to review them. Consider the following four schemes:

__ M are P	__ P are M	__ M are P	__ P are M
__ S are M	__ S are M	__ M are S	__ M are S
$\therefore$ __ S are P	$\therefore$ __ S are P	$\therefore$ __ S are P	$\therefore$ __ S are P
(I)	(II)	(III)	(IV)

Each of the schemes becomes a syllogism (though not necessarily a valid one) if the blanks are filled in (in any way at all) with the logical constants "all," "some," "not all," and "no." ("Not all A are B" traditionally would be written "Some A are not B.") A syllogism is said to belong to the "first figure" if it comes from the first scheme, the "second figure" if it comes from the second scheme, etc. Here is an example of one valid syllogism from each figure:

All M are P	All P are M	Not all M are P	No P are M
All S are M	Not all S are M	All M are S	Some M are S
∴ All S are P	∴ Not all S are P	∴ Not all S are P	∴ Not all S are P
(I)	(II)	(III)	(IV)

The way in which Peirce regarded the first three of these inferences as limiting cases of probabilistic inference from a population to a sample, induction, and "retroduction" may be illustrated with the valid syllogism in the first figure above (its traditional name, from medieval terminology, which Peirce used, is *Barbara*). Consider the following *probability inference:*

> The proportion r of the Ms possesses the haphazard property π.
>
> These Ss are drawn at random from the Ms.
>
> ∴ Probably and approximately, the proportion r of the Ss possesses π.

If we let r, the proportion in question, have the value one, then (if the population is finite,[12] Peirce should have said) the first premise in the probability inference just says that all Ms are πs, the second premise says that all of "these Ss" are Ms (as Peirce noted, the fact that they are drawn at random is irrelevant when $r = 1$, as is the fact that π is "haphazard"), and the conclusion is that—deleting "probably and approximately"—all of "these Ss" are πs. And this is just the syllogism *Barbara*. As we remarked, however, Peirce did not regard this as a justification of *Barbara*, nor, of course, did he regard it as a justification of the probability inference. His aim was to provide a natural classification of the three types of arguments.

To understand the problems with which Peirce was wrestling, let us first look at his explanations of the key terms "random" and "haphazard."

Peirce considered a method of selection random if it has two characteristics (he limited the discussion to finite and countably infinite populations): (1) if the method of selection were applied indefinitely, every member of the population M would sooner or later be selected; (2) "the Ss that are π and the Ss that are not π should be drawn with equal frequency." It will be noted that Peirce was a "frequentist," that is, he always identified probability with a proportion or a frequency (or a limit of a relative frequency, in the case of infinite populations). The function of clause (1) in the definition of "random" seems to be to impose an order upon the population, that is, to let us think of the population as a series in which there are limit relative frequencies. (In the case of a finite population, these become ordinary frequencies.) The real work is done by the sloppily worded clause "the Ss that are π and the Ss that are not π should be drawn with equal frequency"—but what in the world does this mean?

It does not, of course, mean that the frequency of Ss that are π must equal the frequency of Ss that are not π, for this would be to define "random" so that in a "random" sample π must be expected to occur with a probability of exactly 0.5. Peirce was, perhaps, trying to find a frequentist equivalent to the idea that the *single case* probability[13] of any S being selected at any point is *independent* of whether it is π or not. All that one can say for sure is that Peirce saw the need to define "random," but he did not succeed in doing so in a satisfactory way, nor could he have, lacking the requisite distinction between *recursive* and *nonrecursive* subsequences of an ordinary infinite series.[14]

At any rate, it is clear what situation Peirce envisaged in the inference under discussion. We have a population M from which we are sampling. The sampling is to be such that the attribute π occurs *randomly* in the sequence of Ms generated by the method of sampling ("the Ss").

In addition, Peirce saw that there are apparent counterexamples to the probabilistic inference if we allow π to be just any attribute. Suppose we know, or take it that we know, that the immense majority of the members of M "will never be seen by mortal eye." (M is the set of all the "small objects which fall to the bottom of the sea.") Let π be the attribute of being *seen by mortal eye*. Then π occurs with very low frequency in the population M. Yet, if one draws up a sample to examine, one will not say "probably and approximately, the percentage of these Ss with π will be very small," for one will know in advance that all of them are going to be π. What has gone wrong?

It will be easiest to explain what has gone wrong if we begin by stating Peirce's probability inference in contemporary language:

The proportion r of the Ms possesses the property π.

These Ss are drawn at random from the Ms.

[The foregoing is all the relevant information we possess bearing on the proportion of these Ss that are π.]

∴ Probably (that is, with a high degree of confirmation) the proportion of the Ss that possess π is approximately r.

With this statement of the inference before us, we can easily see what is going on in Peirce's little example. In this case the population is finite ("small objects which fall to the bottom of the sea"). If we take a "sample" to be just *any finite subset of the population* (whether looked at "by mortal eye" or not), then it is true (provided the sample is reasonably large) that the frequency of samples in which the proportion of the property π is close to the proportion of π in the whole population (that is, the statistical probability that a sample is "representative" of the whole population with respect to π) is relatively high—just how high can be determined from the sample size and what we specify "close to" to mean. Thus there is a *frequency sense* in which the probability that an arbitrary sample S will be *representative* in the sense of having a proportion of π not far from the proportion of π in the population M is very high.

If M in this example were not finite but infinite, then we could not speak of the *frequency* of π in M, but (since we imagine that the members of M form a countably infinite sequence) it makes sense to speak of the *limit* of the relative frequency of π in M in longer and longer initial sections of the sequence, and this is how Peirce understood the probability (or "proportion") of π in the case of a (countably) infinite population. And if we take a "sample" to be, say, any collection of N consecutive members of the infinite sequence, then (given the assumption of the random distribution of π) the Law of Large Numbers (Bernoulli's Theorem) will enable us to calculate the limit frequency of samples in which the proportion of π is close to r. And again it is true (provided the sample size is reasonably large) that the (limit) *frequency* of samples which are *representative* in the sense that the proportion of the property π is close to the proportion of π in the whole population is relatively high— just how high can be determined from the sample size and what we specify "close to" to mean. However, whether M is finite or infinite, if one wants to know the probability that in *this* sample the probability of π is very high, what one is asking for is not a frequency but a degree of confirmation. And the probability inference yields degrees of confirmation only when the added clause, that the Peircean premises represent *all* our relevant knowledge bearing on the conclusion, is satisfied. If we know that all the members of S are going to be examined by mortal eye, then, in the present example, this *total relevant evidence requirement* is violated. It is to ensure that this requirement is not violated that Peirce required that π be a "haphazard" characteristic, which he explained by writing, "π must be composed of elements which the course of thought naturally throws together. It must not be a recondite or artificially composed character. It must not be suggested by the manner in which the instances are presented, nor by the character of those instances. The safest way will be to insist that π shall be settled upon before the Ss are examined."

In a way which is slightly more complicated[15] than the way in which he showed that *Barbara* can be regarded as the limiting case of the probability inference in which $r = 1$, Peirce showed that the valid syllogism in the third figure exhibited above is the limiting case of *induction*, that is, the following inference from the composition of a sample to the composition of the population:

These Ss are drawn at random from the Ms.

The proportion r of these Ss possesses the haphazard property π.

[Peirce should have added: The foregoing is all the relevant information we possess bearing on the proportion of the Ms that are π.]

∴ Probably and approximately, the proportion r of the Ms possesses π.

In a similar way (by a "tedious and formalistic discussion" which Peirce omitted, and which we certainly cannot supply!) Peirce claimed that a valid syllogism in the second figure (but which?) is a limiting case (in what sense?) of the following strange "kind of reasoning":

All things of the nature of M have the ("haphazard") property π.

S has property π.

∴ Provisionally we may suppose S to be of the nature of M.

What Peirce had in mind is that we are forming a hypothesis to the effect that S is of a certain nature. If the hypothesis were true, certain consequences π_1, π_2, π_3, . . . would follow. That the thing S is such that these consequences obtain is "π," and the requirement that π be "haphazard" was Peirce's way of saying that we do not already know whether they obtain or not (Peirce's standard substitute for the needed total relevant evidence requirement). Thus Peirce immediately transformed the above "kind of reasoning" into the more standard form of hypothetico-deductive reasoning which consists in observing that if a hypothesis were true certain consequences π_1, π_2, π_3, . . . would follow, looking and finding out that π_1, π_2, π_3, . . . are all in fact borne out by observation, and *provisionally supposing* that the hypothesis is true. The novelty is that Peirce spoke of *provisionally supposing* and not of "inferring" or "concluding"; for Peirce retroduction is not an "inference" but a strategy of making refutable conjectures.[16] "Here [in Retroduction], not only is there no definite probability to the conclusion, but no definite probability attaches even to the mode of inference. We can only say that the Economy of Research[17] prescribes that we should at a given stage of inquiry try a given hypothesis, and we are to hold to it provisionally as long as the facts will permit. There is no probability about it. It is a mere suggestion which we tentatively adopt."

Peirce had interesting and important things to say about the sense in which the inference from a population to a sample and the inference he called "induction" are justified. (It is to be regretted that owing to the nature of this lecture series he said them so briefly; undoubtedly the fact that he could not assume a knowledge of Bernoulli's Theorem—the so-called Law of Large Numbers—on the part of his audience accounts for his decision to state facts without justification.) As a matter of fact, given the premise that the sampling is random, it follows (if we know the sample size and the degree of approximation ϵ involved) that we can determine the probability (in the frequency sense) with which a "sample" of, say, N consecutive members of the sequence of Ms will have the same proportion of π as the entire population to an accuracy of plus or minus ϵ. In this sense, the *probability* that the conclusion of a probability inference from a population to a sample is true (given the premises) is a matter of pure mathematical deduction, and this was Peirce's reason for regarding the probability inference as a form of Deduction in a wide sense.

However, things are not quite so simple. As we saw, Peirce needed to go from a statistical frequency—the frequency of samples in which the proportion of π is within plus or minus ϵ of the proportion r with which π is found in the whole population—to a degree of confirmation for a statement about a single case ("These Ss"). It is plausible that this step represents a valid principle of inductive reasoning (a principle which could be taken as constitutive of our notion of confirmation), but it goes beyond the Law of Large Numbers.

Similarly, given the premise that the sampling is random, we can say with what frequency the inductive inference will succeed when applied to a given population. Knowing this is not knowing the *probability* that the conclusion "the proportion r of the Ms possesses π" is true, for if M is fixed there is no such thing as a probability in the *frequency* sense here: either the proportion of π in M is r or it isn't. Rather, it is knowing the frequency with which inferences of this *structure* will succeed in the case of M. Again, Peirce did not note that the step from a knowledge of frequency to a degree of confirmation requires the principle of confirmation theory just mentioned. Nevertheless, what Peirce noticed about "induction" is extremely important. The idea that a mode of statistical inference can be justified, even in the absence of a numerical figure for the (statistical) probability of the conclusion *by a knowledge of the frequency with which inferences of the same structure will succeed* is at the heart of modern Neymann-Pearson statistical sampling theory with its notion of "likelihood."[18] Moreover, Peirce's conception of "induction" is unusual and worth pondering: by requiring that "induction" include a premise to the effect that the sampling method is *random*, Peirce was telling us that all induction requires prior knowledge of *lawlike* statements. For the statement that a method of sampling is random (even in Peirce's unsatisfactory explication of that notion) requires knowledge of *the equality of certain future frequencies,* and is thus a species of lawlike knowledge, knowledge of generals. Thus Peirce was not pretending to answer Hume by justifying a form of nondeductive inference from just statements about particulars to a general law; rather, Peirce was saying that inductive reasoning always requires the presence of assumptions about the general course of the world (that certain ways of sampling are random). Those assumptions, in Peirce's view, themselves come from Retroduction, and are thus not knowledge but hypotheses which are "provisionally adopted." It is the making of hypotheses and not the empiricist's beloved "induction" that makes empirical knowledge possible.

Lecture Three

In this lecture, Peirce discussed three huge topics (how his audience must have felt about being asked to absorb so much in a single lecture we can only conjecture!). First he briefly introduced his three famous metaphysical categories of Firstness, Secondness, and Thirdness. Since there has been more written on this aspect of Peirce's thought than almost any other, we shall not attempt to further interpret these categories here! Next he briefly sketched a discovery that few people had heard of at that time, but that has revolutionized the practice of philosophy today, and has also led to remarkable discoveries in areas such as mathematics, computer science, and linguistics—the new subject (devised independently by Frege and by Peirce and his student O. H. Mitchell) of quantification theory or (to use Peirce's term) the "Logic of Relatives."

Peirce used two notations for his "Logic of Relatives" or first-order logic (a term we owe to him, by the way; he attributed these notations to Mitchell). One, using Π for the universal quantifier and Σ for the existential quantifier, is the ancestor of the now-standard notation.[19] The other is the graphical notation which he explains here; on the basis of this notation, Peirce constructed an elegant diagrammatic method for doing deductions in propositional calculus and quantification theory which has been shown to be correct and complete.[20] In the present lecture, Peirce only introduced the notation; he evidently felt that it would have been inappropriate to go into the deductive method itself. We should like to say a word about both Peirce's diagrammatic way of doing logic and the philosophical significance which he attached to it.

Formulas are represented by graphs and subgraphs. The empty graph represents truth (think of this as a tautologically true graph); enclosing a graph or subgraph once negates it. Thus Figure C.1 represents contradiction (the negation of the tautologically true).

Drawing two subgraphs next to each other to form a single graph represents conjunction. A propositional letter is a graph, as is a predicate letter with the appropriate number of "lines of identity" (think of these as existentially quantified variables). The quantifiers and the basic truth functions can thus be represented as in Figure C.2.

Note that it is existential quantification that Peirce took as primitive (a line of identity represents an *existentially quantified* variable), and that the scope of the quantifier is determined by how many enclosures the line of identity crosses. Thus if the second figure had been drawn as in

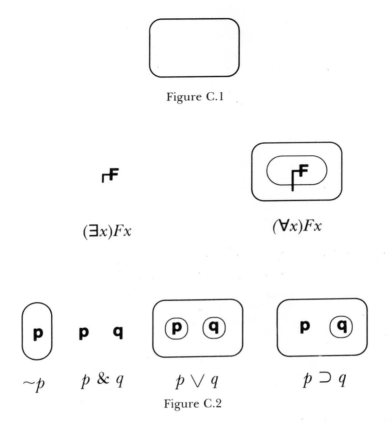

Figure C.1

$(\exists x)Fx$ $(\forall x)Fx$

$\sim p$ $p \,\&\, q$ $p \lor q$ $p \supset q$

Figure C.2

Figure C.3, it would have corresponded to the formula, $\sim\sim(\exists x)Fx$, and not to the formula $\sim(\exists x)\sim Fx$ (that is, $(\forall x)Fx$). We shall mention just three of Peirce's rules for manipulating graphs.[21] One is, in effect, a *rule of double negation:* it allows one to enclose any graph or subgraph with a double enclosure or to erase a double enclosure, where by a "double enclosure" is meant a pair of enclosures with nothing inscribed in the space between them. For example, the two graphs in Figure C.4 are intertransformable by this rule.

But the two enclosures in the graph corresponding to $p \supset q$ cannot be erased, because p is inscribed between them, and the two enclosures in the graph representing $(\forall x)Fx$ (see Figure C.2) cannot be erased because a portion of a "line of identity" lies between them.

In working with Peirce's "existential graphs" one classifies every part of the diagram as "evenly enclosed" (enclosed by an even number of enclosures, regardless of whether there is anything between them, or

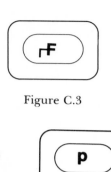

Figure C.3

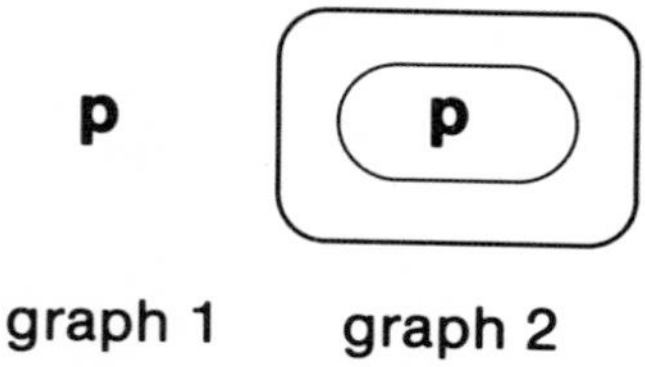

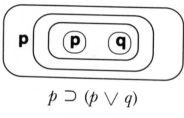

graph 1   graph 2

Figure C.4

$p \supset (p \vee q)$

Figure C.5

by zero enclosures) or as "oddly enclosed." A second rule allows one to inscribe an arbitrary formula (subgraph) in any oddly enclosed region of a graph, and a third rule allows one to copy (Peirce would say "iterate") any formula that occurs unenclosed in a graph or subgraph over again in any other part of that same graph or subgraph (even inside enclosures). Here is an example to show how all this works.

Suppose we want to prove the tautology $p \supset (p \vee q)$. Since we want to prove this absolutely, that is, from no premises, we must start with a blank graph and transform it into the graph corresponding to this formula (Figure C.5). Inspecting this graph, we see that it is intertransformable (by the double negation rule) into the simpler graph shown in Figure C.6. And this suggests our strategy. We begin with the blank graph and transform it into a graph with two enclosures (step 1 in Figure C.7). Then we inscribe p and the graph corresponding to $\sim q$ in the oddly enclosed region between the two enclosures (step 2). Finally (step 3), we copy p over into the innermost enclosure (which is a proper

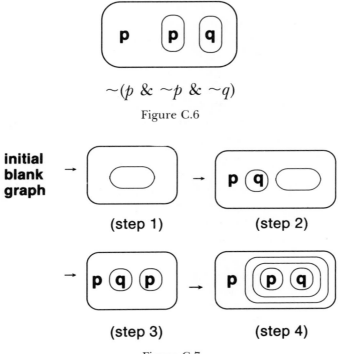

$$\sim(p \ \& \ \sim p \ \& \ \sim q)$$

Figure C.6

Figure C.7

part of a *subgraph* in which *p* is unenclosed, even though *p* is, to be sure, enclosed in the whole graph).

With a little practice, it is remarkably easy to find such "graphical" proofs. For quantification theory, Peirce added a few simple rules allowing one to iterate, join, and break "lines of identity" under certain conditions; proofs are, again, remarkably easy to find.

The philosophical significance of a fully developed calculus of propositional functions and quantifiers capable of representing and analyzing proofs which involve relations and multiple generality is a huge topic and has been widely discussed (although the recent fashion has been to give too much of the credit to Frege and to slight Peirce, whose work was actually far more influential for a long time). We shall not add to this discussion here. However, the significance Peirce attached to the possibility of seeing logic as manipulation of *diagrams* is extremely interesting, and worthy of more discussion. That significance can perhaps best be brought out by contrasting Peirce's attitude to logic with Frege's. For Frege, the possibility of a completely formal symbolic logic ("completely formal" in the sense that no appeals to "intuition" have to be made in the course of a proof) was a refutation of the philosophies of arithmetic of both Kant and Mill. For both Kant and Mill the model of a mathematical proof was a geometrical construction. Arithmetic was to be understood on the model of geometry. For Kant such a construction required the "intuition" of points and lines, and since pure extensionless points and lines cannot be *literally* visualized, the requisite kind of "pure intuition" is something distinct from sensibility. For Mill (whose account is much more subtle than those who have only read Frege's polemics against him are likely to know), geometrical intuition is not something over and above sensibility but a special use of the imagination. Frege accepted the need for something like Kant's pure intuition in *geometry,* but he thought that, by reducing arithmetic to logic and showing that logic can be reduced to mechanical application of formal rules, he had shown that there is no analogy at all between arithmetic and geometry.[22]

Present-day readers of Frege's famous texts often suppose that the view that something like geometrical intuition has a role in arithmetic (let alone in logic itself!) was, in fact, overthrown by Frege once and for all. (Present-day readers are likely to think that we don't even need "intuition" in *geometry* itself, since we can arithmetize geometry.) But Peirce's view highlights the fact that this is, to put it mildly, not obviously right. Peirce argued that *the recognition that a structure is a deduction* is itself akin to geometrical intuition (which Peirce conceived more on the lines of Mill than of Kant, we believe). Doing logic diagrammatically highlights the way in which such a proposal might be right; however the view can also be held if one uses "proof trees" or linear proofs or some other system. We believe that this issue is far from sufficiently explored at the present time. But it is fascinating that the two inventors of predicate calculus (which we today regard as the heart of symbolic logic) disagreed on so fundamental a metaphysical issue, Frege seeing logic as totally nonempirical and Peirce seeing logic itself as involving something like mental experimentation with diagrams.[23]

The last, and longest, part of this lecture develops Peirce's notion of the continuum. We have discussed this topic at length in the Introduction.

Lecture Four

This lecture is perhaps the clearest of the whole series, and very little elucidation is necessary. In it one sees very clearly the respects in which

Peirce was and was not a "pragmatist," as that term has subsequently come to be understood. His emphatic stress on the revisability of all knowledge claims is characteristic of all the pragmatists, and James and Dewey were happy to accept Peirce's great maxim "Do not block the way of inquiry," as well as the "first rule of logic" of which Peirce said it is the corollary ("In order to learn you must desire to learn, and in so desiring not be satisfied with what you already incline to think"). Likewise, they were happy to accept Peirce's "great rule of predesignation," which says that any valid induction (indeed, any valid inquiry) must start with a definite doubt or at least a definite question. (Doubting is not as easy as lying, Peirce argued, throughout his career.[24]) Moreover, the idea that knowledge does not need to start with a *foundation* in the traditional epistemological sense has rarely been more beautifully expressed than in the metaphor with which Peirce described the "ground" on which science stands as a "bog": "It still is not standing upon the bedrock of fact. It is walking upon a bog, and can only say, this ground seems to hold for the present. Here I will stay till it begins to give way." (Note the suggestion that science would never "move on" if it weren't "walking upon a bog"!)

In other respects, however, Peirce's views are much more in line with the tradition of metaphysical realism (or as Peirce called it elsewhere,[25] "scholastic realism") than with the pragmatism of James or Dewey. For James and Dewey, there is no such thing as Nature's own language; *we* make languages, guided by our interests, ideals, and by the particular "problematic situations" (as Dewey would say) that we find ourselves in. To be sure, Dewey accepted Peirce's definition of truth as that to which inquiry would converge if continued indefinitely (and James spoke of truth in this sense as a "regulative notion"): but neither of them supposed that *that to which inquiry would converge* is independent of *us,* of what interests and ideals we have, and what questions those interests and ideals lead us to formulate. Those interests and ideals (and the problematic situations we are in) shape our very categories; there is no such thing as discovering Nature's own categories, for James and Dewey. For Peirce, Nature has a set of "joints" which any group of determined inquirers will discover if they pursue their inquiry long enough; in pure science, as opposed to practical life, our language is ultimately controlled by the structure of reality, not by our interests (apart from the interests of pure inquiry itself). This strain of Peircean realism has recently been endorsed and emphasized by two influential British philosophers, Bernard Williams[26] and David Wiggins,[27] who join Peirce in insisting on a sharp separation between what is true "humanly speaking" and the "absolute" truth (their term) to which science is "fated" to converge in the long run. Peirce would thus reject James's and Dewey's claim that scientific practice is ultimately dependent on our practical interests and goals (both in the vulgar and in the philosophical sense of "practical"), and best tested by its success in enabling us to fulfill and achieve them. For Peirce (as he already made clear in Lecture One), it is precisely by prescinding from all practical interests that science succeeds. (Some readers may find it fascinating to compare and contrast the account of inquiry in the present lecture with the account in Dewey's *Logic, the Theory of Inquiry*.)[28]

This lecture is also valuable as giving us a capsule account of Peirce's philosophy of mathematics (and logic, which, as Peirce has already made clear in Lecture One, he regarded as simply a part of mathematics). Peirce saw mathematics as quasi-empirical, and at the beginning of the lecture, immediately after introducing the idea of science as a *self-correcting activity*, he listed a number of analogies between deduction, induction, and retroduction. Thus, he argued, deduction requires the joining together ("colligation") of the right premises just as induction does, it requires "observation" of proofs (for example, the diagrams presented in the previous lecture), and it even requires experimentation. In these respects, Peirce's view resembles Mill's, and Peirce did give Mill a favorable mention.[29] Some of Peirce's analogies are, indeed, forced, as when he compares looking at the same datum twice in the course of an induction to an application of his rule of "iteration" (copying over)[30] in deduction. And Peirce anticipated the objection which will arise in the mind of any reader: the objection that there is the possibility of error in an inductive conclusion, but "theoretically" no possibility of error in a deductive conclusion. His reply is deeply interesting:

> to speak thus "theoretically," is to use language in a Pickwickian sense. In practice and in fact, mathematics is not exempt from the liability to error that affects everything that man does. Strictly speaking, it is not certain that twice two is four. If on an average in every thousand figures obtained by addition by the average man there be one error, and if a thousand million men have each added 2 to 2 ten thousand times, there is still a possibility that they have all committed the same error of addition every time.

Epistemologically speaking, Peirce did not see mathematical necessity as absolute. (Peirce's idea of using the *ubiquitous possibility that we have made a mistake in checking a proof* to argue for the quasi-empirical character of mathematics has recently been revived by Philip Kitcher.)[31] There is, however, an important difference from Mill's view, in spite of the obvious kinship: for Mill, mathematics is simply empirical. But Peirce did not deny that there is a kind of metaphysical necessity that mathematics has, and that ordinary empirical statements lack. What is "necessary" metaphysically speaking holds not only in our actual world but in the whole "Platonic world" of possibilia alluded to in the concluding lecture of this series (Lecture Eight). (That lecture holds open the possibility that there may also be *other Platonic worlds,* however!) What Peirce denied is the *epistemological necessity* of mathematics, not its metaphysical necessity (in this respect, he anticipates Saul Kripke's famous distinction[32] between the two).

What Peirce wrote here will, of course, not satisfy philosophers who (not unreasonably) ask whether we *know what it means to say* that we might all be "making a mistake" when we say that twice two is four. Still, one move against Peirce is already anticipated and blocked: that is the Fregean move of arguing that "twice two is four" is (epistemologically) necessary because the thought that twice two is four is ("in disguise") just a theorem of predicate calculus, viz.:

> {There are exactly two F & There are exactly two G &
> ($H = F \cup G$) & Nothing is both F and G}
> $\supset$ There are exactly four H.

Or, in (present-day) predicate calculus symbolization:

> $\{(\exists x)(\exists y)(Fx \ \& \ Fy \ \& \ x \neq y \ \& \ (z)(Fz \supset z = x \lor z = y))$ &
> $(\exists x)(\exists y)(Gx \ \& \ Gy \ \& \ x \neq y \ \& \ (z)(Gz \supset z = x \lor z = y))$ &
> $(x)(Hx \equiv Fx \lor Gx) \ \& \ (x){\sim}(Fx \ \& \ Gx)\}$
> $\supset \{(\exists x)(\exists y)(\exists z)(\exists w)(Hx \ \& \ Hy \ \& \ Hz \ \& \ Hw \ \& \ x \neq y \ \& \ x \neq z$ &
> $x \neq w \ \& \ y \neq z \ \& \ y \neq w \ \& \ z \neq w) \ \& \ (u)(Hu \equiv u = x \lor u = y \lor$
> $u = z \lor u = w)\}$

We believe that it is obvious what Peirce would say in reply to this argument: (apart from the possibility of error in constructing this "equivalent" to "twice two is four"!) verifying that this *is* a theorem of predicate calculus (or, as Wittgenstein taught us to say, a "tautology") requires checking a moderately complicated proof, and that is exactly the sort of observation that Peirce here argued to be essentially fallible. The issues here are extremely deep; for example, they preoccupied Wittgenstein throughout his philosophical life.

Lecture Five

To be a philosopher, or a scientific man, you must be as a little child, with all the sincerity and simple-mindedness of the child's vision, with all the plasticity of the child's mental habits.

What are the exercises conducive to this? Extensive reading to begin with. A hundred volumes a year, or 3⅔ days per volume does not sound like hard work. Fifty volumes are easily read, if you can find so many good books. Real reading consists in putting yourself into the author's position, and assimilating his ways of thinking. Conversation with all sorts of people whom we do not altogether understand, freshens the mind; but then interesting people are as hard to find as interesting books.

Reading this charming lecture in the right mood is as close as one can come to spending a pleasant evening in conversation with C. S. Peirce. (Think of it as a "Dinner with André"—or rather, a dinner with Charley.) To comment on most of it would be an impertinence; but at one or two moments it suddenly digresses into technicality, and it is on these moments that we shall comment.

The first of these digressions into technicality occurs at the beginning of the discussion of "habituation." Peirce wrote, "A continuous curve, that is one whose differential coefficients are continuous[,] is one which can be described in general terms, that is, has an equation. True the curve may have singularities, which are no doubt discontinuities. In reply to this objection, I shall at present content myself with remarking . . ."—and Peirce is off on a tangent, one whose motivation and content are deeply obscure. (Perhaps that *is* what it was like to have dinner with Charley.)

A knowledge of mathematics is not all that much help here. We do not define a continuous curve as "one whose differential coefficients are continuous"; but it seems likely that what Peirce meant is what we today call an *analytic* curve. Such a curve can have singularities of various kinds; but why is this a problem for Peirce?

Here is a suggestion, in line with the interpretation we give in the general introduction of Peirce's theory of the continuum. As we wrote there, the metaphysical intuition which is behind Peirce's theory is that we live in a world—since Peirce did think that there actually are continua in the real world—in which there are an enormous number of possibilities: compatible possibilities. Moreover, the reason that they cannot all be actualized is not that the realization of some of them logically precludes the realization of particular others, although that kind of case exists too. That is not what is involved when Peirce said that there cannot exist Ω distinct individuals. The Peircean picture is that the multitude of possibilities is so great that as soon as you have a possible world in which some of these possibilities are realized—say, you have a possible world in which some abnumerable multitude of the divisions are made—then you immediately see that there is a possible world in which still *more* divisions can be made, and hence there is no possible world in which all of these *nonexclusive* possibilities are *all* actualized. We might summarize this by saying that the metaphysical picture is that possibility intrinsically outruns actuality, and not just because of the finiteness of human powers, or the limitations imposed by physical laws.

If this is right, then it seems reasonable to suppose that for Peirce "generality" in the sense of Thirdness involves the same elements. That is, a mere All-statement, for example, "All swans are warm-blooded," is not, in itself, even if true, automatically an instance of Thirdness. Indeed, all interpreters of Peirce agree that, at the very least, a "generality" in Peirce's sense must involve Law or "Habit" (recall that it is the topic of "habituation" that provoked this digression), and that Law involves modality—the notions of what *would be* and what *could be* the case. Many interpretations stop here. But, we wish to suggest, the identification of generality with continuity (in Peirce's understanding of continuity) is correct only if Peirce is prepared to say that an ideal Law or Habit, in his sense, must allow for Ω possible realizations,[33] that is, must allow for such a richness of possible exemplifications that in no possible world are all of its possible exemplifications actualized. Moreover, these exemplifications must be, in some sense, *dense*. The slim textual evidence does not permit any further development of these ideas; but they at least make sense of the claim that "from a logical [read: metaphysical] point of view, generality is continuity." The problem then arises that his own paradigm of continuity, the analytic function, sometimes has singularities, and he worried this problem for a few minutes and then promised to return to it in the future.

The remarks about Firstness and Secondness which immediately follow the discussion of continuity are of great importance for the interpretation of those categories. (Note that the identification of Firstness with Immediate Consciousness, which was already made in the previous lecture, shows a streak of Objective Idealism in Peirce— and indeed, Peirce was capable of describing himself as a "Schellingian Idealist.")

The lecture consists of a discussion of three fallacies: in retroduction it is fallacious to claim that we should always "choose the most probable hypothesis," Peirce argued, since in the case of true retroductive inference the notion of "the probability of the hypothesis" does not even make sense. (Here Peirce is a consistent anti-Bayesian, like a great many present-day theorists of probability.) In deduction, the most common fallacy is "not reasoning at all, but only going by rule of thumb." (We are back to Dinner with Charley.) The examples given are recherché ones: thinking it is a logical truth that a whole cannot be the same size as its part—Cantor's counterexample, with which Peirce was familiar, is that the set of all whole numbers is exactly the same cardinality as the set of all even numbers—and thinking it a logical truth that infinitesimals cannot exist (which, were it a logical truth, would exclude Peirce's own theory of the continuum). Finally, the most common fallacy in induction is violation of a requirement Peirce stated in Lecture Two. As he put it there, the requirement was that the characteristic π involved "must not be suggested by the manner in which instances are presented, nor by the character of those instances. The safest way will be to insist that π shall be settled upon before the S's are examined." In Lecture Two Peirce already gave a number of examples of what can go wrong when this requirement is violated; here he used the opportunity to criticize Paul Carus (whose criticism of Peirce, on an unrelated point, was repudiated by Peirce with scorn in material written for Lecture Four, but not included in the lecture as delivered.) It is unfortunate that Peirce got "carried away" by his desire to show how badly Carus erred, since an otherwise elegant lecture ends on a note of unnecessary technicality.

Lecture Six

Thus it is that uniformity, or necessary law, can only spring from another law; while fortuitous distribution can only spring from another fortuitous distribution. Law begets law; and chance begets chance; and these elements in the phenomena of nature must of their very nature be primordial and radically distinct stocks. Or if we are to escape this duality at all, urged to do so by the principle of retroduction, according to which we ought to begin by pressing the hypothesis of unity as far as we can, the only possible way of doing so is to suppose that the first germ of law was an *entity* which itself arose by chance, that is as a First. For it is of the nature of Chance to be First, and that which is First is Chance; and fortuitous distribution, that is, utter irregularity, is the only thing which it is reasonable to explain by the absence of any reason to the contrary.

In the last three lectures of the series, beginning with this one, Peirce laid out a daring metaphysical system. In the next lecture Peirce will explain his motives for undertaking such a construction, telling us that what pushed him to "these metaphysical speculations" was asking himself, "how are we ever going to find out anything more than we do now about atoms and molecules? How shall we lay out a broad plan for any further grand advance?" The metaphysics presented here was thus meant to be an *empirical* metaphysics; it is to lead to predictions that we shall be able to test. In this respect it is, and is intended to be, very different from what is usually thought of as metaphysics, even if the language resembles that of (what we think of as) metaphysics more than the language of (what we think of as) empirical science.

Peirce began with some penetrating remarks on the subject of causation. He pointed out that the conception of a cause has changed repeatedly through time (quoting with approval his "friend Carus"— apparently the anti-Carus mood that characterized the close of the previous lecture has worn off!); and he argued brilliantly that the notion of cause used in classical mechanics (Peirce was thinking of celestial mechanics) has properties quite contrary to those that we typically assume causation to have. For example, if we know the positions and masses of all the bodies in the universe, then (in Newtonian gravitational theory) we know the accelerations of all the bodies (since Newtonian gravitation acts instantaneously at a distance), but we cannot predict the future state of the system unless we are also given the velocities of the bodies. But the velocity of something is simply the ratio of the distance between its positions at two sufficiently near times to the difference between the two times. Thus what Newtonian celestial mechanics allows us to do is predict the condition of the universe at a future time (to an arbitrarily preassigned accuracy) *if we are given the positions and masses of all the bodies at two sufficiently near earlier times*. Instead of saying that Newtonian causation determines the future condition of the universe as a function of its condition at *one* earlier time, we should say that it determines the future condition of the universe as a function of its condition at *two* earlier times![34] Moreover, in Newtonian physics, a cause and its effect can be simultaneous,[35] and the same equations that enable us to predict the future condition of the universe, given the condition at two suitable earlier times, allow us to "postdict" the past condition of the universe, given its condition at two suitable later times. The causality of fundamental physics is completely "time-reversible."[36]

Yet, Peirce pointed out, the causality of our psychic life (and even the causality we observe in everyday events) seems full of *irreversible* phenomena. As far as we can tell, it has, in fact, just the intuitive properties that the causality of celestial mechanics violates.[37] Peirce's problem (and ours[38]) is to explain how two so very different species of "causation" (the species governed by conservative forces, such as gravitation and electromagnetism, and the species which seems to obey our intuitive "principle of causation") can exist in the same world.

Peirce noted that the latter sort of causation (he called it "nonconservative" causation) we see all around us always involves a statistical element. (He illustrated this with the equilibration of temperature in the atmosphere.) Peirce turned, therefore, to a discussion of the nature and the ubiquity of what he called "fortuitous distributions" (or, as we call them today, "normal distributions").[39]

The definition Peirce gave of "fortuitous distribution" is actually a much better definition of *randomness* than the one he gave in Lecture Two. According to Peirce (in the present lecture, he uses an example in which an infinite series of objects are classed as "colored" and "white"), the distribution is fortuitous if an object's being colored or not is *independent of its bearing to other objects in the series any relation definable in terms of the successor relation in the series, color, and whiteness*. For example, the probability that an object is colored given that the three objects immediately preceding it in the series are, respectively, white, white, and colored is exactly the same as the probability that it is colored given that those three objects have any other distribution of the attributes "white" and "colored." (This definition still contains a vague term— "definable"—but if we specify that what is meant is that the probability that an object is colored is independent of its membership in any infinite subseries definable *by recursion* in terms of the successor relation in the series and the attributes of other objects in the series, we get exactly Church's definition of a random sequence.)

Having characterized random ("fortuitous") distributions, Peirce made the important observation that the existence of a fortuitous distribution is always explained (for example, in statistical mechanics) by postulating that some *other* distribution in the past was fortuitous. Explanations of the presence of "chance" (in the sense of fortuitous distribution; chance in the sense of violation of determinism is not yet under discussion, although it will come under discussion in Lecture Seven) always involve the assumption of chance, and explanations of the presence of regularity always involve the assumption of regularity. "Law begets law; and chance begets chance." And at this point Peirce made the great retroductive leap (quoted at the beginning of the present comments) to the hypothesis that "the first germ of law was an *entity* which itself arose by chance, that is as a First."[40] (This cryptic remark will be spelled out in the evolutionary cosmology which is one of the subjects of Lecture Seven.)

Now Peirce wrote, "These things having become clear to us, let us now, remembering that the whole aim of this discussion is to find some clue by which physical and psychical action may be unified, examine, a little, certain other features of the two classes of phenomena governed respectively by conservative forces and by the principle of causality [that is, the requirements that causality be irreversible, that an effect always precede its cause, and that "the state of things at one instant is completely and exactly determined by the state of things at *one* other instant"], and see how bright or how darkling a light is shed upon them by what we have thus far made out."

In an ordinary lecture, such a transitional paragraph would lead one to expect some application of the ideas so far presented, but Peirce was no ordinary lecturer: what follows these words is nothing less than the opening sketch of a whole new metaphysical account of space and time!

Using Kantian language, Peirce suggested that space is "that form of intuition in which is presented the law of mutual reaction of those objects whose mode of existence consists in mutually reacting."[41] He sketched a number of what he called "consequences" and "corollaries" of this view, and while it is unclear exactly how these are supposed to be derived, they do serve to make the view somewhat clearer. The ultimate constituents of the physical world are capable of acting on one another ("reaction"), and reaction is *hic et nunc* (here and now). From this it "necessarily follows" that these ultimate constituents are point particles ("Boschovichian[42] atomicules"). How does it "necessarily follow"? Very likely the argument Peirce had in mind is that any reaction involving an extended body is the sum of a multitude of reactions, one at each of its point parts.[43]

The idea that space is only a form of intuition in which the reactions between these agents are represented carries with it the denial that spatial locations (points) are real things. Thus there cannot be a law that particles are attracted to one or another particular *place*, since such a law would require a place to have physical properties. (In particular, the world-view of general relativity, according to which space and matter are constantly interacting and modifying one another, is completely contrary to the metaphysics sketched here.) Motion can only be relative, but Peirce introduced a reference frame, because he thought physics requires such a frame. The frame, he said, is an improved version of Cayley's "absolute." Here Peirce was referring to a way of subsuming metric geometry under projective geometry discovered by Cayley in 1859. That method defines a metric in *projective* geometry[44] on any line, provided we have chosen two arbitrary points on that line (the "gauge points"). Such a metric can also be defined on the whole space provided we have chosen a surface with the properties that (1) at least two of its points are on every line of the field, and (2) (preserving the duality characteristic of projective geometry) at least two of its lines intersect every point of the field. The simplest figure with these properties is a conic. This conic is now called the *metric-gauge conic* or more simply *the metric gauge.* The term "absolute" has been dropped nowadays because of "the false implication of the word absolute; there is nothing absolute about the metric gauge."[45]

This frame is itself an "object" in Peirce's cosmology, albeit a geometrical one. It should be noted that for Peirce the topology of space is the topology of *projective* geometry (in which every line contains a point at infinity and all the points at infinity lie on a line at infinity). Such a space is infinite, but every line in it returns on itself.

This is getting ahead of our story, however. To begin with we have only the idea of space as a way of representing the existence of a multitude of interacting things, each represented as occupying one point at a given time (time is absolute, in Peirce's metaphysics, and totally different from space). To define a notion of "nearness" on this space (that is, to impose a topology), Peirce considered points "nearer" if objects at those points would tend to interact more strongly.[46] To define the notion of "straight line" (to "impose an affine structure," in present-day parlance), Peirce specified that the successive positions of an elementary particle which is not acted on by any other agent lie on a straight line. To define distance (to "impose a metric"), Peirce specified that the distances covered by such a particle in equal times[47] are equal. That this metric will agree with the metric defined by a suitable gauge conic (one of Cayley's "absolutes") is a fundamental assumption of Peirce.

Space, however, is not just a way of representing the fact that there are particles which "react" to one another; it is a way of representing *law,* the law governing the mutually induced motions of those particles. From this Peirce derived a number of consequences, freely employing his metaphysical categories of Secondness and Thirdness. For example, since Space is a kind of incarnation of Law, or Thirdness, and since ideal Thirdness, or Generality, is also continuity, it "follows" that space is continuous. Moreover, since reaction is Secondness, all reactions must be analyzable into reactions of just *two* things at a time: "Space presents a law whose prescriptions are nothing but conditions of reactions, and since reaction is Duality, it follows that the conditions of prescriptions of space are necessarily Dual."

From this idea, Peirce derived "five corollaries." The third corollary is that

> when the places of an isolated body at two instants are given the law prescribes its places at all other instants. That is, the first differential coefficient, or mere difference between the places at two instants determine[s] its places at all other instants. That is, the velocity remains constant.

Peirce added that

> From these corollaries again, together with the general principle from which they are derived, it follows that when a body is acted upon by another body, that which is directly affected is the uniform velocity in a straight line, and that in such a way that in so far as the action of the active body remains the same, two velocities, or what comes to the same thing, three positions with their dates, determine all the velocities the particle will take. This explains, therefore, why the force should produce acceleration rather than any other differential coefficient of the space relatively to the time.

This is Peirce's metaphysical derivation of Newton's law that force equals mass times acceleration.

Other derivations have more surprising consequences. For example

> when one particle, A, acts on another, B, this latter, B, will likewise act on A; and moreover this action cannot impart to both the same acceleration, because the law is such as to affect their relative places.[48] This follows by the aid of the third principle already enunciated, as we shall see. Hence, it can only impart opposite accelerations to A and B.[49] *Secondly, those two accelerations must be equal, so that the masses of all atomicules are equal.* [Emphasis added.]

All of this is reminiscent of Kant's attempts to derive some of the principles of Newtonian physics from his philosophy.[50] But there is one decisive difference: Kant's arguments were meant to show that some parts of Newtonian physics were a priori; Peirce's arguments were meant to spell out the consequences of a hypothesis that Peirce *wanted* to have implausible consequences so that it shall be subject to empirical disconfirmation.

> [Certain consequences of my theory of space] I am happy to say, are extremely doubtful. I say I am happy because this gives them the character of predictions and renders the hypothesis capable of experiential confirmation or refutation.

Turning from his theory of space to the topic of chance, Peirce explained the irreversibility of stochastic phenomena with the remark that

> it is because of the independence of different instants of time. A change having been made there is no particular reason why it should ever be unmade. If a man has won a Napoleon at a gaming table he is no more likely to lose it, [than] he was to lose a napoleon at the outset.

This argument is strange, in view of an obvious objection: the laws of probability do not distinguish a direction of time any more than the laws of fundamental physics do.

Peirce closed this lecture by suggesting that just as space may be "that form of intuition in which is presented the law of mutual reaction of those objects whose mode of existence consists in mutually reacting," so time may be "the form under which the law of logical dependence presents itself to intuition," and the significance of the "discontinuity at the actual instant" (that is, the present) may be that "here new premises not logically derived from Firsts are introduced." The idea seems to be that the derivation of consequences from laws is represented in intuition as the materialization of those consequences in time. If this is right, then time is intrinsically irreversible (the reverse of a deduction is not, in general, a deduction); and this is clearly what Peirce believed. From time to time (that is, at various points in the derivation) new "premises" arise spontaneously by chance, and this is what we experience as the "present moment."

Lecture Seven

We now seem launched upon a boundless ocean of possibilities. We have speculations put forth by the greatest masters of physical theorizing of which we can only say that the mere testing of any one of them would occupy a large company of able mathematicians for their whole lives; and that no one such theory seems to have an antecedent probability of being true that exceeds say one chance in a million. When we theorized about molar dynamics we were guided by our instincts. Those instincts had some tendency to be true; because they had been formed under the influence of the very laws that we were investigating. But as we penetrate further and further from the surface of nature, instinct ceases to give any decided answers; and if it did there would no longer be any reason to suppose its answers approximated to the truth. We thus seem to be reduced to this alternative. Either we must make some very broad generalizations as to the character of Nature's ways, which may at least tell us that one theory about molecules and ether is better worth trying than another theory, or else we had better abandon altogether a line of inquiry, — I mean into the inmost constitution of matter, — which is likely to prove a mere waste of time.

In this lecture Peirce laid out a large part of his cosmology—both his metaphysical picture of the physical universe and his account of the psychical; some speculations at a still deeper metaphysical level will occupy the next and last lecture of the series. This speculative side of Peirce seems to have embarrassed many of his followers, judging by the comparative lack of attention it has received, but it is vital to understand it, and to understand the motivation for undertaking this project which moved Peirce to "all the hard work I have done for the last fifteen years in trying to reason this matter out" if we are to understand his conception of the place of philosophy among the sciences at all.

These lectures were delivered at the end of the nineteenth century, when certain problems—the possible non-Euclidean nature of space, suggested (as at least a possibility) by the work of Lobatchevsky and Riemann beginning in the 1820s, the problems about the nature of the ether, the controversy about whether atoms were more than useful fictions—were provoking discussion among some scientific thinkers. To be sure, the dominant view was that Newton (with his theories of gravitation and of optics) and Clerk Maxwell (with his equations for electromagnetism) had, between them, solved all the problems, at least in principle. Thus the great mathematician David Hilbert, in his famous list of problems to the World Congress of mathematicians in 1900, listed *putting the foundations of physics on a satisfactory basis* as a problem for *mathematicians!* But this dominant view was clearly not shared by Peirce. Peirce clearly anticipated that it would take fundamental new ideas to penetrate to the nature of "molecules and ether," to get down to the level of "Boschovichian atomicules" (the point particles, which Peirce believed to be the ultimate constituents of matter), and to answer questions about the geometry and topology of space. Not only was he right about this, as relativity theory and quantum mechanics have shown, but he was also right that these new ideas would never be found by merely trying to extend Newtonian dynamics to smaller and smaller regions.

Faced by this situation, Peirce concluded (see the epigraph to this section) that physics itself, let alone our understanding of the psychic or our metaphysics, could not progress further without philosophical guidance. That guidance was to be provided by a metaphysics based on his categories of Firstness, Secondness, Thirdness, as he applied them to such problems as the nature of space, time, and causation. But that metaphysics was to be a testable metaphysics. In sum, Peirce regarded it as not just consistent with his philosophy but as a consequence of that philosophy that metaphysics was still possible. The traditional conception of philosophy as a subject which probes to the deepest and most hidden levels of reality is very much Peirce's; what he rejected about traditional metaphysics is its unempirical character, its failure to produce *falsifiable* hypotheses, and its insufficient grasp of the mathematical method. In this respect, Peirce was also very different from James and Dewey, neither of whom ever claimed that philosophy could offer substantive guidance to the working physicist. On the contrary, Dewey wrote[51]

> [Philosophy's] primary concern is to clarify, liberate, and extend the goods which inhere in the naturally generated functions of experience. It has no call to create a world of "reality" *de novo*, nor to delve into secrets of Being hidden from common sense and science. It has no stock of information or body of knowledge peculiarly its own; if it does not always become ridiculous when it sets up as a rival of science, it is only because a particular philosopher happens to be also, as a human being, a prophetic man of science.

This is certainly a repudiation of the sort of enterprise that Peirce undertook in the present lectures!

If Peirce was prescient in his grasp of the difficulties the sciences of the next century would face, it must be admitted that his attempt to suggest to future scientists "that one theory about molecules and ether is better than another theory" was not a success, at least by present lights. Although some features of later science were anticipated by Peirce—the non-Euclidean character of space and the existence of indeterministic events—many of the features of our most successful scientific theories run directly contrary to other of Peirce's conclusions. Thus Peirce never doubted the absolute difference of space and time, the existence of an absolute "now" (as we saw in the previous lecture), or the existence of absolute motion. And such indeterminism as Peirce postulated consists in the *very rare* occurrence of chance events[52]—even he did not suppose that indeterminism would prove to be ubiquitous at the micro-level. Thus, those who would suppose (with Dewey) that philosophy *cannot* play the role of directing physical investigation that Peirce wanted it to play might argue that it would have been a disaster if twentieth-century physics had indeed accepted Peirce's proffered philosophical guidance. But it is not our aim to take sides on this issue in these comments, but only to call it to the reader's attention.

The structure of the present lecture is as follows: Peirce laid out most of his physical cosmology in the first part. Then there is a section on the ethics of terminology (which we have placed in brackets because of uncertainties as to just where in the lecture it was actually situated), which is followed by Peirce's discussion of "psychical action." Finally, in the last few pages, Peirce drew general conclusions and offered his most far-reaching metaphysical hypothesis yet: *That the laws of nature are the result of an "evolutionary process."* We shall say something about each of these in turn. Peirce stated his aim at the beginning of what we are calling the first part of the lecture thus: "what I wish to show is that causation, as distinct from the action of conservative force, is a real, and fundamental, and vital element both in the outer and in the inner world." To understand what follows, it is necessary to be very clear as to what Peirce meant by this. Although (in Lecture Six) Peirce had already begun to speak of the irreversible causation of everyday life as "nonconservative," that does not mean that he was guilty of simply assuming that irreversibility must be incompatible with the universal validity of time-reversible deterministic laws at the deepest level. Although he did not actually mention the word "entropy" he was aware that irre-

versible phenomena have been (allegedly)[53] explained by the Second
Law of Thermodynamics, and he was further aware that the Second
Law has itself been (allegedly) explained by means of probability theory.
This was what Peirce was referring to in the paragraph which begins,
"As to those explanations which physicists propose for irreversible phe-
nomena by means of the doctrine of chances as applied to trillions of
molecules, I accept them as one of the finest achievements of science."

The following is a very clear and simple summary of "those explanations" by Hans Reichenbach.

> It was the discovery of the Vienna physicist Boltzmann that the
> principle of irreversibility is explainable through statistical consider-
> ations. The amount of heat in a body is given by the motions of its
> molecules; the greater the average speed of the molecule, the
> higher the temperature. It must be realized that this statement re-
> fers only to the average speed of the molecules; the individual mole-
> cules may have very different speeds. If a hot body comes into
> contact with a cold body, their molecules will collide. It may occa-
> sionally happen that a slow molecule hitting a fast one loses its speed
> and makes the fast one even faster. But that is the exception; on
> the average there will be an equalization of the speeds through the
> collisions. The irreversibility of heat processes is thus explained as
> a phenomenon of mixture, comparable to the shuffling of cards, or
> the mixing of gases and liquids.
>
> Though this explanation makes the law of irreversibility appear
> plausible, it also leads to an unexpected and serious consequence.
> It deprives the law of its strictness and makes it a matter of proba-
> bility.[54]

The Boltzmannian explanation of irreversibility to which Reichenbach refers, if accepted, makes irreversibility fully compatible with the
time-reversible causation of Newtonian physics which Peirce referred to
throughout as "conservative force," because the forces involved are all
conservative forces. That Peirce was aware of this compatibility is clear,
since he spoke of "Those nonconservative actions which *seem* to violate
the law of energy, and which physics *explains away* as due to chance-
action . . ." [emphasis added]. Indeed, Peirce rejected all criticisms of
the Boltzmannian explanation, although today it seems undeniable that
some of those criticisms raise deep problems. (What Boltzmann showed
in a famous theorem, stated in technical language, is that *after a minimum*, entropy will tend to increase. But, since the laws of probability and

the laws of Newtonian physics are both indifferent to which direction of time we consider to be the "future" and which direction we consider the "past," it inevitably turns out that the same theorem implies that *before a minimum* entropy will tend to *decrease*. Thus, the "Boltzmann H-Theorem" cannot *by itself* account for the fact that irreversible processes all "go in the same direction" (for example, the direction in which entropy increases on Mars is the same as the direction in which entropy increases on Earth.)[55] But Peirce was not content to conclude that we live in a deterministic world obeying time-reversible laws, in which all the apparent irreversibility is due to the statistical considerations mentioned, valid as they are. Peirce had already given one reason for not resting content with this conclusion in Lecture Six: it would leave chance (the existence of Gaussian distributions, or "fortuitous distributions" as Peirce called them) an *unexplained* feature of reality. Peirce believed that such distributions arise through chance in another sense, *absolute* chance, and (as he will explain) he believed that Law is capable of arising from the same source. (Here he was clearly impressed by the various evolutionary theories—Lamarck, Darwin, Spencer, not to mention Hegel—of the nineteenth century.) Such a hypothesis would, if true, give both fortuitous distributions and regularities the same *ultimate* origin, and should thus be metaphysically preferred. (An additional argument will be offered at the end of the present lecture.)

However, Peirce complicated the reader's life with a string of technical observations (occupying several pages) of no great interest in themselves. These observations, which begin immediately after the reference we have identified as being to Boltzmann, concern different ways in which conservative actions could simulate the properties of irreversibility and tendency to a specified final state which Peirce took to be characteristic of "nonconservative actions." Some of these are clear (the friction example); others involve speculative changes in the laws of physics (considering what would happen if the force were not exactly an inverse-square force, or even what would happen if it were an inverse-cube force.) In reading these pages (which should be skimmed on a first reading), it is important to realize two things:

(1) As we pointed out in the discussion of Peirce's theory of the continuum in our general introduction, Peirce believed in actual infinitesimals. As we explain there, for years this way of doing the calculus was believed to be just a *mistake*, but since it was put on a rigorous basis by the work of Abraham Robinson a few decades ago, it has become again a recognized way of doing the calculus, under the name "nonstan-

dard analysis." As we point out, however, Peirce's own theory of the continuum differs from Robinson's "nonstandard" construction (although we believe it also could be shown to be fully consistent, relative to our present-day set theory). This is relevant because some of Peirce's discussions involved the significance of singularities in certain equations, and Peirce pictured these in terms of what would happen in "an infinitesimal moment of time" as the singularity is approached.

(2) Because of his belief that projective geometry is more fundamental than metric geometry,[56] as well as his belief in actual infinitesimals and actual infinites,[57] Peirce believed in the reality of the "point at infinity" at the end of any line and a "line at infinity" in any plane (and of a point at infinity in *time*). Thus it is that when he discussed the case of a body moving forever in a hyperbolic trajectory, he wrote, "could the motion continue *beyond the infinitely distant moment of time* it would continue through *the infinitely distant line in the plane* and complete the closed hyperbolic orbit" [emphasis added]. (Although he did not think this is "completely satisfactory" as a solution to the paradox—as he took it to be—that here a conservative force produces an irreversible effect.)

These musings are followed by a remark of great interest, which Peirce apparently crossed out in green pencil (here we have reconstructed the end of the uncompleted sentence):

> Now let me call your attention to the facts, first, that there is no reason whatever to believe that the sum of the angles of a triangle is precisely two right angles, and second, if it is not so, there is no motion save [should be *with*] the properties we familiarly associate with *translation*. For example, we conceive of translation as a purely relative motion, so that two particles unacted on by any forces and relatively at rest for a moment will, however fast or slow they may be moving relatively to other bodies, remain forever at rest relatively to one another. But this is not so in non-Euclidean geometry. The two particles moving side by side [is,] unless the sum of the angles of the triangle is precisely 180°, [an impossibility].

Here Peirce took seriously the idea that space may be non-Euclidean, and pointed out, in effect, that in a non-Euclidean space a system consisting of two free particles whose trajectories are parallel is not possible.

Immediately after the green-penciled remark just cited, we find another fascinating passage: a discussion of the famous controversy between Newtonian and Machian views of the nature of motion and inertia. By our present lights, Peirce came down on the wrong side (with

Newton against Mach), but, in our opinion, he is quite right in regarding
Newton's seventeenth-century arguments as much better than those of
his contemporary, Mach. Newton believed in absolute space not on a
priori grounds, but because this was a hypothesis that accounted for
inertial phenomena. Peirce correctly pointed out that it is a consequence
of Mach's theory (that inertial motion is motion relative to the fixed
stars, and not relative to an absolute space) that the centrifugal force
(say, of a sling shot) would be "influenced by the angular motion of stars
very far away, and more influenced by the more remote than by the
nearer stars." Mach has indeed been borne out by general relativity, but
not only did Mach himself not have even the germ of general relativity,
but he rejected even special relativity, to Einstein's sadness. In the context of the Newtonian physics which Mach accepted, his theory made
no dynamical sense, as Peirce was right in pointing out. At this point we
find a passage which is certainly somewhat difficult to interpret. Peirce
wrote,

> It is true that Space, insofar as it is a continuum, is a mere law, —
> a mere Thirdness. But that does not stand in the way of its being
> a *thing* too. If besides its continuity it presents arbitrary *thisness*, we
> must admit that it is something more than a mere law. The question
> of the relativity of motion is a question of the measurement of
> space, not of the nature of space itself; and therefore, although
> motion be not relative, it would not necessarily follow that space
> *itself* is non-relative, however good the inference may be, considered
> as a retroduction. But there are characters belonging to space *per
> se* which seem to involve *thisness,* such as its having three dimen-
> sions . . .
>   Now if you examine the matter more closely than I have time
> to do in this lecture, you will find that it is precisely in those respects
> in which Space shows such indications of Secondness that motions
> act as though governed by the law of causality [that is, "non-
> conservatively"], while in those respects in which Space preserves
> all its Thirdness the motions preserve their dynamical character.

The problem is that, at first blush (and following hard upon the
criticism of Mach's belief in the relativity of motion), one is inclined to
read this as an endorsement of absolute space. But in Lecture Six, Peirce
had already told us that

> since space *has only the being of a law* [emphasis added], its places
> cannot have distinct identities in themselves, for distinct identity

belongs only to existent things. Hence place is only relative. But since, at the same time, different motions must be comparable in quantity, and this comparison cannot be effected by the moving and reacting particles themselves, it follows that another object must be placed in space to which all motion must be referred. [This is Cayley's "absolute," or in present-day terminology, the metric-gauge conic.[58]]

The appearance of contradiction can be avoided (and it is unattractive to have to assume that Peirce changed his mind between Lecture Six and Lecture Seven) if we assume that the respects in which space exhibits "Secondness"—that is, irreducible properties not determined by any law—correspond to the unexplained physical *constants* which Peirce will talk about at the very end of this lecture (the number of spatial dimensions is such a constant), and not to any absoluteness of location ("place"). The reason that the argument against Mach's view does not also count against Peirce's own view in Lecture Six is that the "absolute" is not a dynamical object (like a star, or the whole collection of the fixed stars) but a geometrical object, a locus of points. What Peirce thought is that the laws of physics intrinsically involve a metric which is fixed *relative* to a particular gauge conic. Since the gauge conic in projective geometry is not *unique*—contrary to the misleading connotations of Cayley's term "absolute"—and different gauge conics lead to different metrics,[59] there is still the question as to why these laws should involve one particular gauge conic rather than another (or why they do not involve a gauge conic in motion relative to the gauge conic which yields the right physics for the actual world, on Peirce's view). Presumably the answer is that this is a fact of the same order as the arbitrariness of some of the ultimate physical constants, an arbitrariness which Peirce exploited metaphysically in what follows.

This part of the lecture ends with two examples. The first is an example of a case in which Peirce seemed to think that physics is almost irrelevant ("altogether insignificant") and the metaphysical absoluteness of the flow of time itself (in Peirce's language, the passage out of "the problematical state of [futurity] into the state of a *fait accompli*") is all that is essentially involved. The second, which is really a digression, is an example of two swinging pendulums; Peirce pointed out that the mathematical description does not treat either pendulum as "the agent" or "the patient" while "our natural tendency to prefer the formula of causation" leads us to regard the pendulum which is ahead as the agent and the one which lags behind as the patient. (In this case, which involves conservative forces, Peirce clearly preferred the mathematician's description to the "natural" one.)

The charming section on the ethics of terminology which follows is very clear (and, incidentally, gives Peirce a chance to express his admiration for the terminological exactitude of the scholastic philosophers). An interesting present-day essay in a somewhat similar vein is Quine's essay on terminological and other abuses in mathematics in *Quiddities*.[60]

There follows a short section in which Peirce sketched his version of psychology. That version, like the psychology of the time (compare, for example, James's *Principles of Psychology*) is simultaneously introspectionist, associationist, and respectful of psycho-physical parallelism ("the established cerebral theory"). Peirce distinguished two introspectable parameters of mental events: their intensity (for example, a thunderclap is said to be more intense than the sound of a few people clapping their hands, and also more intense than the light of a star), and their vividness (a mental event in the full center of my attention is more vivid than one in the periphery, and an impression is more vivid than a memory image or an image of the imagination; note that an event which is not very intense may be quite vivid). This section ends with "the law of the action of ideas," which is really a collection of five principles of association.

After describing the "action of ideas" in the style of the psychology of his day, Peirce concluded this lecture by returning to the question which had occupied him since the beginning of Lecture Six: whether the irreversible causation we see in our mental life can be shown to be "conservative causation at bottom" or whether "all conservative action is causational at bottom." Here he confessed the "vague and shadowy hope" of showing one or the other would never have moved him to "all the hard work I have done for the last fifteen years in trying to reason this matter out," and gave the reasons for constructing a retroductive metaphysics which we have cited in the epigraph to this section. Peirce had already given one reason for trying the grand retroduction that Law arises from Chance in Lecture Six: the desire for unity in our explanations, given the impossibility of reducing Chance to Law in an ultimately satisfactory way.[61] He concluded the present lecture with a second reason: the laws of nature involve arbitrary constants. ("These are mere arbitrary Secondnesses. The explanation cannot then be a purely rational one.")

"What kind of an explanation can there be then?," Peirce asked. "I answer, we may hope for an evolutionary explanation." And the lecture ends, for once, not in a technical digression, but on a truly Wagnerian note as Peirce presented his great hypothesis that there is a "generalizing tendency" inherent in reality which reinforces itself (one form of evolution) and which also accounts for the formation of all other laws. In the next and final lecture, the metaphysical drama will be expanded, as Peirce will go on to speak of the evolution of logic itself, and of much more besides.

Lecture Eight

Peirce's lack of experience in addressing a general audience is nowhere more apparent than in this final lecture. Although the lecture concluded fittingly by extending the grand metaphysical vision of an evolutionary cosmology and metaphysics which he had begun to present in the two preceding lectures to almost unimaginable reaches (some readers will want to delete the "almost" in this sentence!), the first half is almost entirely a lecture on projective geometry and topology, with an admixture of Peirce's own conception of the continuum. On a first reading, we recommend that the reader review our description of Peirce's theory of the continuum in the general introduction, and then begin reading the present lecture with the paragraph that begins with the remark (on page 257), "Every attempt to understand anything, — every research, — supposes, or at least *hopes,* that the very objects of study themselves are subject to a logic more or less identical with that which we employ."

We shall not comment in detail on Peirce's explanations of projective geometry and topology, since it is the metaphysical part of the lecture that will most interest present-day readers. Suffice it to say that, like many mathematicians, Peirce regarded the projective properties of space as more fundamental than the metrical properties, and the topological properties as more fundamental still. The reason is that the metric properties are thought of as the properties invariant under rigid motion (like Reichenbach[62] after him, Peirce thought of a metric as being imposed on space by the behavior of bodies and light rays),[63] the projective properties are invariant under a wider class of continuous transformations, and the topological properties are invariant under the widest class of continuous transformations. (Again like Reichenbach after him) Peirce held, contrary to the opinion of his time, that the human mind *can* visualize non-Euclidean spaces and spaces with strange topologies. (To do so, we just have to *imagine the experiences we would have in such a space.*)

What Peirce meant by the remark that "Every attempt to under-stand anything, — every research, — supposes, or at least *hopes,* that the very objects of study themselves are subject to a logic more or less identi-cal with that which we employ" in the present context quickly becomes clear. He added that whatever "may be said for or against [the hypothe-sis that the logic of the universe is "more rudimentary" than our subjec-tive logic], that which we of these times ought to try is rather the hypoth-esis that the logic of the universe is one to which ours aspires rather than attains." The picture, then, is of a universe in which something is realized to which our logic can only "aspire" to do justice, which for Peirce meant a universe which contains (and, indeed, *evolves*) continua.

At this point Peirce made two very important remarks about con-tinua. The first is that "continuity is shown by the logic of relations to be nothing but a higher type of that which we know as generality. It is relational generality." What did Peirce mean by this?

As far as Peirce's conception of the continuum is concerned, the most important thing to hold in mind is, as we expressed it in the general introduction, that the reason that the line is a collection of points which "lack distinct individuality" is that it is a collection of *possibilia,* and pos-sibilia are not fully determinate objects, for Peirce. To say that the line is a collection of possibilia is to say that one can construct things which stand in a certain triadic relation, the relation "Proceeding to the right from *A* you reach *B* before you reach *C.*" *What answers to our conception of a continuum is a possibility of repeated division which can never be exhausted in any possible world, not even in a possible world in which one can complete abnumerably infinite processes.*

We have also proposed an interpretation of Peirce's repeated insis-tence on the intimate connection between continuity and generality in our comments on Lecture Five, where we noted that the identification of generality with continuity (in Peirce's understanding of continuity) is correct only if Peirce is prepared to say that an ideal law or Habit, in his sense, must allow for Ω possible realizations, that is, must allow for such a richness of possible exemplifications that in no possible world are all of its possible exemplifications actualized. Moreover, these exempli-fications must be, in some sense, *dense.* Since continua (taken in inten-sion) were identified by Peirce with their defining relations, it is also clear why Peirce said not only that continuity is a "higher type" (that is, an ideal type) of that which we know as generality, but also that "it is relational generality." But what did Peirce mean by his claim that all this is "shown by the logic of relations"?

Peirce's full logic of relations included not only the propositional and predicate calculus ("Logic of Relatives"), which he sketched in Lecture Three, but also a form of modal logic. What Peirce was claiming here is clearly not that his analysis of the continuum is itself provable in pure Logic of Relatives, but that that logic (including its modal part, which enabled him to formulate reasoning about potentiality) is rich enough to formalize that analysis and to derive its consequences.[64]

After this remark, Peirce immediately raised the crucial question as to how a continuum could evolve. "Has it for example been put together? Have the separated points become welded, or what?"

In the next ten paragraphs Peirce sketched his answer to this supremely metaphysical question, and in *each* of those paragraphs an additional tremendous ontological claim is added. The first of those paragraphs reveals again Peirce's thorough commitment to an irreversible time, with an absolute "now," a future which is indefinite, and a past which has become definite. "All the evolution we know of proceeds from the vague to the definite." This is connected with the remark that logic "proceeds from the question to the answer, — from the vague to the definite" because Peirce had already hypothesized in Lecture Five that time "is the form under which logical dependence presents itself to intuition." All this convinced Peirce that "however it may be in special cases, then, we must suppose that as a rule the continuum has been derived from a more general continuum, a continuum of higher generality." In other words, every evolutionary development is the realization of one of continuously many possibilities, and therefore, if a continuum is to evolve, *the whole* continuum must itself be one of *continuously many possible continua,* an actualization of one of the potentialities in a "continuum of higher generality."

Those potentialities, the "world of ideas" of which "the existing universe with all its arbitrary secondness" is an offshoot, or "an arbitrary determination," may also be thought of as a logical space, a space of possible worlds (in present-day metaphysical language) of which the actual world is just one. It is not that we look at the impoverished actual world and project the "world of ideas" with "our superior logic" (as we like to imagine), but that the world of ideas was ontologically prior, and our actual world evolved as one of its determinations. And (in the third of our ten paragraphs) Peirce went on to say, "If this be correct we cannot suppose the process of derivation, a process which extends before time and from before logic, we cannot suppose that it began elsewhere than in the utter vagueness of completely undetermined and dimensionless potentiality."

There is more than a hint of German Idealism in this last idea, and indeed Peirce was not unwilling to describe himself as a Schellingian Idealist on occasion,

> I carefully recorded my opposition to all philosophies which deny the reality of the Absolute, and asserted that "the one intelligible theory of the universe is that of objective idealism, that matter is effete mind." This is as much as to say that I am a Schellingian of some stripe . . .[65]

and,

> . . . If you were to call my philosophy Schellingism transformed in the light of modern physics, I should not take it hard.[66]

The claim in the fourth of our ten paragraphs is that "The evolutionary process is, therefore, not a mere evolution of the *existing* universe, but rather a process by which the very Platonic forms themselves have become or are becoming developed." The whole logical space, the whole space of possible worlds, and of possible attributes and relations and possible continua as well, is the product of cosmic evolution!

In the next paragraph we get the next mighty claim, "*This existence* is presumably but a *special* existence. We need not suppose that every form needs for its evolution to emerge into this world, but only that it needs to emerge into *some* theatre of reactions, of which this is one" [emphasis in original]. Like our celebrated present-day metaphysician of possible worlds, David Lewis,[67] Peirce believed in the reality of other "theatres of reaction."

We have already suggested German Idealism as a possible influence, and in the next paragraph (the sixth of our group) we see Peirce using a key term "contradiction" in a Hegelian way, "It must be by a contradiction of the vagueness of that potentiality of everything in general but of nothing in particular that the world of forms comes about."

The seventh paragraph speaks of "the cosmos of sense qualities" (that all Firsts are taken to be sense qualities is further evidence of objective idealism), and says that the ones we now experience are "but the relics of an ancient ruined continuum of qualities, like a few columns standing here and there in testimony that here some old-world forum with its basilica and temples had once made a magnificent *ensemble*." This continuum (which Peirce would have his hearer suppose "in some early stage of being was [as] real as your personal life this minute") was, as required by the whole picture of evolution as going from the vague to the definite, "in an antecedent stage of development a vaguer being, before the relations of its dimensions became definite . . ."

The eighth paragraph repeats the description of Firstness given in Lecture Three (again the example is of a sense quality, this time a "magenta color," as it is in and for itself). "What originally made such a quality of feeling possible?" Peirce asked. "Evidently nothing but itself. It is a First."

The ninth paragraph begins, "Yet we must not assume that the qualities arose separately and came into relation afterward. It was just the reverse. The general indefinite potentiality became limited and heterogeneous." And Peirce went on to say that the idea of a personal God is simply an anthropomorphic metaphor for the springing up of the sense qualities in reaction upon one another, and thus into a kind of existence. "This reaction and this existence [believers in a Divine Creator] call the mind of God."[68]

The tenth and final paragraph of our group goes on to say that "if we are going to regard the universe as a result of evolution at all, we must think that, not merely the existing universe, that locus in the cosmos to which our reactions are limited, but the whole Platonic world which in itself is equally real, is evolutionary in its origin, too." This repeats the claim of the fourth of our group of paragraphs. But Peirce went on to draw an astounding consequence: "And among the things so resulting are time and logic." The vision is that logic itself (and time, which is the form under which logic presents itself to intuition) results from Chance or Spontaneity. (Whether Peirce meant that there could have been a different logic in the sense of a different set of logical laws, or only a different set of properties and relations for the logical laws to operate on, is not clear, but he certainly meant at least the latter.)

The remainder of this concluding lecture consists of an elaboration and illustration of the ideas in these ten paragraphs. Peirce emphasized again that "whatever is First is *ipso facto* sentient," and added "If I make atoms swerve, — as I do, — I make them swerve but very very little, because I conceive they are not absolutely dead." What we know as matter is almost-dead life. (Recall, "matter is effete mind.") Peirce illustrated the whole scheme on the blackboard. The two dimensions of the blackboard represent "a continuum of some indefinite multitude of dimensions." Considerable confirmation for our interpretation of Peirce's theory of the continuum may be found in his illustration, for example, that the blackboard is "a continuum of possible points"; before some discontinuity has been *produced* "there are no points on this blackboard." Lines (representing Firsts) are imagined to spring up by chance. (These are chalk lines, with thickness, not geometric lines. This is what Peirce meant by "it is a plane figure, in Euclid's sense.") Some of these lines spontaneously disappear immediately after spontaneously appearing, but eventually some of them "stick." When enough have stuck here and there, some (by chance) will form envelopes which we will see as further lines (curves).[69]

But why will any line "stick" in the first place? By beginning a *habit*, a "generalizing tendency," Peirce tells us, and "[this habit] must have its origin in the original continuity which is inherent in potentiality. Continuity, as generality, is inherent in potentiality, which is essentially general." Continuing the story, many systems are imagined as springing up in the original continuum—illustrating the origin not of the existing universe but of "a Platonic world, of which we are, therefore, to conceive that there are many, both coördinated and subordinated to one another; until finally out of one of these Platonic worlds is differentiated the particular actual universe of existence in which we happen to be."

We recall that Peirce intended his metaphysics to have testable consequences, and while he could not give his deductions for reasons of time, as he explained, he proceeded to give his audience a few illustrations.

Most of these illustrations involve the notion of a Listing number, which Peirce had defined in the previous mathematical portion of the lecture.

Today there must be very few topologists (if any) who have heard of J. B. Listing, whom Peirce considered to be the discoverer of topology.[70] However, the Listing numbers are perfectly good topological invariants (Peirce's "first Listing number" would today be called "the zero-dimensional Betti number"). And when Peirce called for specification of the Listing numbers of the continua he had been talking about, he was simply asking that we predict their topological properties.

Peirce began with Time. For Peirce, there was no such thing as a line segment without endpoints: as we explained in our account of his theory of the continuum, the very act of isolating a segment in thought constructs endpoints for that segment. Similarly, the very act of conceiving an infinitely long line constructs endpoints, the points at infinity. (This is a happy result for Peirce, since—apart from one place, which we shall shortly mention—he consistently thought of space as having the topology of projective space; that is, he took the "points at infinity" and the "line at infinity" of projective geometry seriously.) Are the endpoints of the infinitely long line distinct? Or does going through the point at infinity on a line, say the x-axis, in the positive direction simply cause one to come back from "minus infinity"? In projective geometry, the latter is the case; any family of parallel lines determines just one point at infinity. (Topologically, projective space is infinite, but a line does not divide the projective plane into two sides, nor does a plane divide projective 3-space into two sides.) In Peirce's view, all this is as it should be; if there were two endpoints, even if they were points at infinity, and one could not continue *beyond* either one of those end-points, that would be a *discontinuity,* and "we have every reason to suppose" time (and space) are not discontinuous. "Your metaphysics must be shaped to accord with that."

Peirce told us that "the first inquiry concerning any general" must be, firstly, into its dimensionality, and, secondly, what the intermediate Listing numbers are. The lowest Listing number must be one, Peirce tells us, and the highest cannot be zero.

To say the "lowest Listing number" of a manifold is one is just to say it consists of one connected piece, for the lowest Listing number is just the number of pieces ("components," in present-day terminology) of the manifold. A single continuum, in Peirce's sense, must have a lowest Listing number of one, regardless of its number of dimensions.

The "highest Listing number" (there are four Listing numbers) in the case of a D-dimensional manifold is "the number of simple places of $D - 3$ dimensions which must be taken away to prevent [the existence of] a noncollapsible solid [that is, a 3-manifold which cannot be continuously shrunk to a point]." In three-dimensional space as ordinarily conceived—that is, without points at infinity—all "solids" are collapsible, including the entire space.[71] Thus the Listing number of space as ordinarily conceived is zero. But the 3-space of projective geometry is not collapsible, although all the bounded manifolds within it are collapsible. However, Peirce incorrectly believed[72] that if we remove just one point from projective 3-space, it becomes collapsible: thus the fourth Listing number of projective space is one according to Peirce [in reality it is infinite], and this is why Peirce said earlier in the lecture that "for all figures in our space [the fourth Listing number] is equal to zero except for the entirety of space itself for which it is 1." For Peirce, space as ordinarily conceived contains "singularities"—because *the absence of points at infinity constitutes a singularity in his view.* All continua without singularities *in Peirce's sense of "singularity"* return on themselves, as he himself had remarked a few moments earlier. It is for this reason that he said that the continua he is describing cannot have a highest Listing number of zero, although the intermediate Listing numbers[73] (the second and third) may be zero "or almost any numbers."

Peirce then looked at some specific continua to determine the value of these intermediate Listing numbers. ("It is one of the great merits of the method of thought that the logic of relatives inculcates that it leads to such definite questions.")

The original continuum of sense qualities which we described earlier ("after this continuum has been so far restricted that the dimensions are distinct"—that is, after it has concretized out of the continuum of possible continua of sense qualities to the extent of having a determinate, possibly transfinite, multitude as its dimensionality) is said to have intermediate Listing numbers whose values are one. Two reasons are given, both of them very metaphysical. The first is that "zero is distinctly a dualistic idea." (Because it is $A - A$, the result of the inverse process of subtraction.) The second is that any continuum whose intermediate Listing numbers are zero can be obtained by pasting together *two* continua whose intermediate Listing numbers are one. (Presumably this is further evidence that such continua are "dualistic," and thus not sufficiently imbued with Thirdness.) Thus, "we must assume that all the Listing numbers of the continuum of sense-qualities are 1."[74] A further piece of evidence Peirce cited is that continua whose intermediate Listing numbers are one admit of coordinate systems[75] in which the coordinate lines are better behaved than the coordinate lines on continua whose intermediate numbers are zero. (Peirce did not justify considering only the values zero and one.)

Lastly, Peirce returned to Space, and here he dropped a bombshell, although one wonders if his audience was aware of the explosion. Peirce wrote, "In my lecture on the subject I pointed out to you how though it is a continuum, and therefore a Thirdness, the whole nature and function of space refers to Secondness. It is the theatre of the reactions of particles, and reaction is Secondness in its purity. For this and other reasons, which I omit for the sake of brevity, we must as our first retroduction assume that the intermediate Listing numbers for space are all *zero*."

What is curious about this is that Peirce, as we have seen, had up to this point written as if space had the topology of projective space and (within the confines of Cayley's absolute) the metric properties associated with Newtonian physics, that is, Euclidean properties. (Although he had remarked in Lecture Seven that "there is no reason whatever to believe that the sum of the angles of a triangle is precisely two right angles," he had not followed this up in any way.) But here just two or three minutes before the end of the series of lectures, he continued,

> When we come to consider the principle of hydrodynamics we find that view confirmed. I cannot enter into details; but the motions of a frictionless incompressible fluid is as though it were composed of interpenetrating parts shot out in straight lines from sources and disappearing into sinks. But that implies that all the straight lines radiating from a single point will meet again in another single point which supposes the [second and third Listing numbers] to be *zero*.

Here what Peirce said implies that space has a geometry (and a topology) with properties like those associated with one version of Riemannian (doubly elliptical) geometry. A two-dimensional example of such a space is the surface of a sphere: any two geodesics (great circles) radiating from a single point on such a two-dimensional manifold will meet in another point, the polar opposite of the first point. Here Peirce's metaphysics led him to make a startling prediction.

Peirce closed the lecture and the series with a moving statement of the difficulty of working on such refractory questions in solitude, and with an expression of gratitude to his listeners.

Reasoning and the Logic of Things

Charles Sanders Peirce

Member, National Academy of Sciences, 1877
Fellow, American Academy of Arts and Sciences, 1867
Member, London Mathematical Society
Member, New York Mathematical Society
A.B., Harvard, 1859, A.M., 1862
B.S., Lawrence Scientific School, Harvard, 1863
Assistant, U.S. Coast and Geodetic Survey, 1867–1891
Lecturer, Harvard, 1864–65, 1869–70
Lecturer, Johns Hopkins, 1880–1884
Lecturer, Lowell Institute, 1866, 1895

ONE

Philosophy and the Conduct of Life

The early Greek philosopher, such as we read about in Diogenes Laertius, is certainly one of the most amusing curiosities of the whole human menagerie. It seems to have been demanded of him that his conduct should be in marked contrast with the dictates of ordinary common sense. Had he behaved as other men are supposed to do his fellow-citizens would have thought his philosophy had not taught him much. I know that historians possessed of "higher criticism" deny all the ridiculous anecdotes about the Hellenic sages. These scholars seem to think that logic is a question of literary taste, and their refined perceptions refused to accept these narratives. But in truth even were taste carried to a point of delicacy exceeding that of the German professor, — which he would think was pushing it quite into that realm of imaginary quantities which lies on the other side of infinity, — it still would not weigh as logic, which is a matter of strict mathematical demonstration wherein opinion is of no weight at all. Now scientific logic cannot approve that historical method which leads to the absolute and confident denial of all the positive testimony that is extant, the moment that testimony deviates from the preconceived ideas of the historian. The story about Thales falling into the ditch while pointing out the different stars to the old woman is told by Plato about two centuries later. But Dr. Edouard Zeller says he knows better, and pronounces the occurrence quite impossible. Were you to point out that the anecdote only attributes to Thales a character common to almost all mathematicians, this would afford him a new opportunity of applying his favorite argument of objection, that the story is "too probable." So the assertion of half a dozen classical writers that Democritus was always laughing and Heraclitus always weeping, "proclaims itself" says Zeller, "an idle fabrication," not withstanding the supports it receives from the fragments. Even Zeller admits that Diogenes of Sinope was a trifle eccentric. Being a contemporary of Aristotle and one of the best known men of Greece, his history cannot well be denied even by Zeller, who has to content himself with averring that the stories are "grossly exaggerated." There was no other philosopher whose conduct according to all testimony was quite so extravagant as that of Pyrrho. The accounts of him seem to come direct from a writing of his devoted pupil, Timon of Phlius, and some of our authorities of whom there are a dozen, profess to use this book. Yet Zeller and the critics do not believe them; and Brandis objects that the citizens of Elis would not have chosen a half insane man high priest, — as if symptoms of that kind would not have particularly recommended him for a divine office. That fashion of writing history is I hope now at last passing away. However, disbelieve the stories if you will; you cannot refuse to admit that they show what kind of a man the narrators expected a philosopher to be, — if they were imaginary legends, all the more so. Now those narrators are a cloud of the sanest and soberest minds of Antiquity, — Plato, Aristotle, Cicero, Seneca, Pliny, Plutarch, Lucian, Elian, and so forth. The Greeks expected philosophy to affect life, — not by any slow process of percolation of forms, as *we* may expect that researches into differential equations, stellar photometry, the taxonomy of echinoderms, and the like will ultimately [affect] the conduct of life, — but forthwith in the person and soul of the philosopher himself rendering him different from ordinary men in his views of right conduct. So little did they separate philosophy from esthetic and moral culture that the *docti furor ardus Lucreti* could clothe [an] elaborate **cosmogony** in noble verse, for the express purpose of influencing men's lives; and Plato tells us in many places how inextricably he considers the study of Dialectic to be bound up with virtuous living. Aristotle, on the other hand, set this matter right. Aristotle was not much of a Greek. That he was of full Greek blood is not likely. That he was not altogether a Greek minded man is manifest. Though he belonged to the school of Plato, yet when he went there he was already a student, perhaps a personal pupil, of Democritus, himself another Thracian; and during his first years in Athens he cannot have had much intercourse with Plato, who was away at Syracuse a large part of the time. Above all Aristotle was an Asclepiades, that is to say he belonged to a line every man of whom since the heroic age had, as a child received a finished training in the dissecting-room. Aristotle was a thorough-paced scientific man such as we see nowadays, except for this, that he ranged over all knowledge. As a man of scientific instinct, he classed metaphysics, in which I doubt not he included logic, as a matter of course, among the sciences, — sciences in *our* sense, I mean, what *he* called theoretical sciences, — along with Mathematics and Natural Science, — natural science embracing what we call the Physical Sciences and the Psychical Sciences, generally. This theoretical science was for him one thing, animated by one spirit and having knowledge of theory as its ultimate end and aim. Æsthetic studies were of a radically different kind; while Morals, and all that relates to the conduct of life, formed a *third* department of intellectual activity, radically foreign in its nature and idea, from both the other two. Now, Gentlemen, it behooves me, at the outset of this course, to confess to you that in this respect I stand before you an Aristotelian and a scientific man, condemning with the whole strength of conviction the Hellenic tendency to mingle Philosophy and Practice.

There are sciences, of course, many of whose results are almost immediately applicable to human life, such as physiology and chemistry. But the true scientific investigator completely loses sight of the utility of what he is about. It never enters his mind. Do you think that the physiologist who cuts up a dog reflects while doing so, that he may be saving a human life? Nonsense. If he did, it would spoil him for a scientific man; and *then* the vivisection would become a crime. However, in physiology and in chemistry, the man whose brain is occupied with utilities, though he will not do much for science, may do a great deal for human life. But in philosophy, touching as it does upon matters which are, and ought to be, sacred to us, the investigator who does not stand aloof from all intent to make practical applications, will not only obstruct the advance of the pure science, but what is infinitely worse, he will endanger his own moral integrity and that of his readers.

In my opinion, the present infantile condition of philosophy, — for as long as earnest and industrious students of it are able to come to agreement upon scarce a single principle, I do not see how it can be considered as otherwise than in its infancy, — is due to the fact that during this century it has chiefly been pursued by men who have not been nurtured in dissecting-rooms and other laboratories, and who consequently have not been animated by the true scientific Eros, but who have on the contrary come from theological seminaries, and have consequently been inflamed with a desire to amend the lives of themselves and others, a spirit no doubt more important than the love of science, for men in average situations, but radically unfitting them for the task of scientific investigation. And it is precisely because of this utterly unsettled and uncertain condition of philosophy at present, that I regard any practical applications of it to Religion and Conduct as exceedingly dangerous. I have not one word to say against the Philosophy of Religion or of Ethics in general or in particular. I only say that for the present it is all far too dubious to warrant risking any human life upon it. I do not say that Philosophical science should not ultimately influence Religion and Morality; I only say that it should be allowed to do so only with secular slowness and the most conservative caution.

Now I may be utterly wrong in all this, and I do not propose to argue the question. I do not ask you to go with me. But to avoid any possible misapprehension, I am bound honestly to declare that I do not hold forth the slightest promise that I have any philosophical wares to offer you which will make you either better men or more successful men.

It is particularly needful that I should say this owing to a singular hybrid character which you will detect in these lectures. I was asked in December to prepare a course of lectures upon my views of philosophy. I accordingly set to work to draw up in eight lectures an outline of one branch of philosophy, namely, Objective Logic. But just as I was finishing one lecture word came that you would expect to be addressed on Topics of Vital Importance, and that it would be as well to make the lectures detached. I thereupon threw aside what I had written and began again to prepare the same number of homilies on intellectual ethics and economics. They were wretched things; and I was glad enough to learn, when three-quarters of my task was done, that it would be desirable that as much as possible should be said of certain philosophical questions[,] other subjects being put in the background. At that time, however, it was too late to write a course which should set before you what I should have greatly desired to submit to your judgement. I could only patch up some fragments partly philosophical and partly practical. Thus, you will find me part of the time offering you Detached Ideas upon Topics of Vital Importance, while part of the time I shall be presenting philosophical considerations, in which you will be able to feel an undercurrent toward that Logic of Things concerning which I shall have an opportunity to interject scarce one overt word.

I shall have a good deal to say about right reasoning; and in default of better, I had reckoned *that* as a Topic of Vital Importance. But I do not know that the theory of reasoning is quite vitally important. That it is absolutely essential in metaphysics, I am as sure as I am of any truth of philosophy. But in the conduct of life, we have to distinguish every-day affairs and great crises. In the great decisions, I do not believe it is safe to trust to individual reason. In everyday business, reasoning is tolerably successful; but I am inclined to think that it is done as well without the aid of a theory as with it. A *Logica Utens*, like the analytical mechanics resident in the billiard player's nerves, best fulfils familiar uses.

In metaphysics, however, it is not so, at all; and the reason is obvious. The truths that the metaphysician infers can be brought to the test of experience, if at all, only in a department of experience, quite foreign from that which furnishes his premises. Thus a metaphysician who infers anything about a life beyond the grave can never find out for certain that his inference is false until he has gone out of the metaphysical business, at his present stand, at least. The consequence is that unless the metaphysician is a most thorough master of formal logic, — and especially of the inductive side of the logic of relatives, immeasurably more important and difficult than all the rest of formal logic put together, — he will inevitably fall into the practice of deciding upon the validity of reasonings in the same manner in which, for example, the practical politician decides as to the weight that ought to be allowed to different considerations, that is to say, by the impressions those reasonings make upon his mind, only with this stupendous difference, that the one man's impressions are the resultant of long experiential training, while with such training the other man is altogether unacquainted. The metaphysician who adopts a metaphysical reasoning because he is impressed that it is sound, might just as well, or better, adopt his conclusions directly because he is impressed that they are true, in the good old style of Descartes and of Plato. To convince yourself of the extent to which this way of working actually vitiates philosophy, just look at the dealings of the metaphysicians with Zeno's objections to motion. They are simply at the mercy of the adroit Italian. For this reason, then, if for no other, the metaphysician who is not prepared to grapple with all the difficulties of modern exact logic had better put up his shutters and go out of the trade. Unless he will do one or the other, I tell him to his conscience that he is not the genuine, honest, earnest, resolute, energetic, industrious, and accomplished doubter that it is his duty to be.

But this is not all, nor half. For after all, metaphysical reasonings, such as they have hitherto been, have been simple enough for the most part. It is the metaphysical concepts which it is difficult to apprehend. Now the metaphysical conceptions, as I need not waste words to show, are merely adapted from those of formal logic, and therefore can only be apprehended in the light of a minutely accurate and thoroughgoing system of formal logic.

But in practical affairs, in matters of Vital Importance, it is very easy to exaggerate the importance of ratiocination. Man is so vain of his power of reason! It seems impossible for him to see himself in this respect, as he himself would see himself if he could duplicate himself and observe himself with a critical eye. Those whom we are so fond of referring to as the "lower animals" reason very little. Now I beg you to observe that those beings very rarely commit a *mistake*, while we —— ! We employ twelve good men and true to decide a question, we lay the facts before them with the greatest care, the "perfection of human reason" presides over the presentment, they hear, they go out and deliberate, they come to a unanimous opinion, and it is generally admitted that the parties to the suit might almost as well have tossed up a penny to decide! Such is man's glory!

The mental qualities we most admire in all human beings except our several selves are the maiden's delicacy, the mother's devotion, manly courage, and other inheritances that have come to us from the biped who did not yet speak; while the characters that are most contemptible take their origin in reasoning. The very fact that everybody so ridiculously overrates his own reasoning, is sufficient to show how superficial the faculty is. For you do not hear the courageous man vaunt his own courage, or the modest woman boast of her modesty, or the really loyal plume themselves on their honesty. What they *are* vain about is always some insignificant gift of beauty or of skills.

It is the instincts, the sentiments, that make the substance of the soul. Cognition is only its surface, its locus of contact with what is external to it.

Do you ask me to prove this? If so, you must be a rationalist, indeed. I can prove it, — but only by assuming a logical principle of the demonstration of which I shall give a hint in the next lecture.[1] When people ask me to prove a proposition in philosophy I am often obliged to reply that it is a corollary from the logic of relatives. Then certain men say, I should like exceedingly to look into this logic of relatives; you must write out an exposition of it. The next day I bring them a MS. But when they see that it is full of A, B, and C, they never look at it again. Such men ... Oh, well. ⟨are intellectual *petit crevés*, nice to have around.⟩ Reasoning is of three kinds. The first is necessary, but it only professes to give us information concerning the matter of our own hypotheses, and distinctly declares that if we want to know anything else, we must go elsewhere. The second depends upon probabilities. The only cases in which it pretends to be of value is where we have, like an insurance company, an endless multitude of insignificant risks. Wherever a vital interest is at stake, it clearly says, "Don't ask me." The third kind of reasoning tries what *il lume naturale,* which lit the footsteps of Galileo, can do. It is really an appeal to instinct. Thus Reason, for all the frills [it] customarily wears, in vital crises, comes down upon its marrow-bones to beg the succour of instinct.

Reason is of its very essence egotistical. In many matters it acts the fly on the wheel. Do not doubt that the bee thinks it has a good reason for making the end of its cell as it does. But I should be very much surprised to learn that its reason had solved that problem of isoperimetry that its instinct has solved. Men many times fancy that they act from reason when, in point of fact, the reasons they attribute to themselves are nothing but excuses which unconscious instinct invents to satisfy the teasing "whys" of the *ego.* The extent of this self delusion is such as to render philosophical rationalism a farce.

Reason, then, appeals to sentiment in the last resort. Sentiment on its side feels itself to be the man. That is my simple apology for philosophical sentimentalism.

Sentimentalism implies Conservatism; and it is of the essence of conservatism to refuse to push any practical principle to its extreme limits, — including the principle of conservatism itself. We do not say that sentiment is *never* to be influenced by reason, nor that under no circumstances would we advocate radical reforms. We only say that the man who would allow his religious life to be wounded by any sudden acceptance of a philosophy of religion or who would precipitately change his code of morals, at the dictate of a philosophy of ethics, — who would, let us say, hastily practise incest, — is a man whom we should consider *unwise.* The regnant system of sexual rules is an instinctive or Sentimental induction summarizing the experience of all our race. That it is abstractly and absolutely infallible we do not pretend; but that it is practically infallible for the individual, — which is the only clear sense the word "infallibility" will bear, — in that he ought to obey it and not his individual reason, *that* we do maintain.

I would not allow to sentiment or instinct any weight whatsoever in theoretical matters, not the slightest. Right sentiment does not demand any such weight; and right reason would emphatically repudiate the claim, if it were made. True, we are driven oftentimes in science to try the suggestions of instinct; but we only *try* them, we compare them with experience, we hold ourselves ready to throw them overboard at a moment's notice from experience. If I allow the supremacy of sentiment in human affairs, I do so at the dictation of reason itself; and equally at the dictation of sentiment, in theoretical matters I refuse to allow sentiment any weight whatever. Hence, I hold that what is properly and usually called *belief*, that is, the adoption of a proposition as a κτημα ἐσ ἀεί [a possession for all time], to use the energetic phrase of Dr. Carus, has no place in science at all. We *believe* the proposition we are ready to act upon. *Full belief* is willingness to act upon the proposition in vital crises, *opinion* is willingness to act upon it in relatively insignificant affairs. But pure science has nothing at all to do with *action*. The propositions it accepts, it merely writes in the list of premises it proposes to use. Nothing is *vital* for science; nothing can be. Its accepted propositions, therefore, are but opinions, at most; and the whole list is provisional. The scientific man is not in the least wedded to his conclusions. He risks nothing upon them. He stands ready to abandon one or all as soon as experience opposes them. Some of them, I grant, he is in the habit of calling *established truths;* but that merely means propositions to which no competent man today demurs. It seems probable that any given proposition of that sort will remain for a long time upon the list of propositions to be admitted. Still, it may be refuted tomorrow; and if so, the scientific man will be glad to have got rid of an error. There is thus no proposition at all in science which answers to the conception of belief.

But in vital matters, it is quite otherwise. We must act in such matters; and the principle upon which we are willing to act is a *belief*.

Thus, pure theoretical knowledge, or science, has nothing directly to say concerning practical matters, and nothing even applicable at all to vital crises. Theory is applicable to minor practical affairs; but matters of vital importance must be left to sentiment, that is, to instinct.

Now there are two conceivable ways in which right sentiment might treat such terrible crises; on the one hand, it might be that while human instincts are not so detailed and featured as those of the dumb animals yet they might be sufficient to guide us in the *greatest* concerns without any aid from reason, while on the other hand, sentiment might act to bring the vital crises under the domain of reason by rising under such circumstances to such a height of self abnegation as to render the situation insignificant. In point of fact, we observe that a healthy natural human nature does act in both these ways.

The instincts of those animals whose instincts are remarkable present the character of being chiefly, if not altogether, directed to the preservation of the stock and of benefitting the individual, very little, if at all, except so far as he may happen as a possible procreator to be a potential public functionary. Such, therefore, is the description of instinct that we ought to expect to find in man, in regard to vital matters; and so we do. It is not necessary to enumerate the facts of human life which show this, because it is too plain. It is to be remarked, however, that individuals who have passed the reproductive period, are more useful to the propagation of the human race than to any other. For they amass wealth, and teach prudence, they keep the peace, they are friends of the little ones, and they inculcate all the sexual duties and virtues. Such instinct does, as a matter of course, prompt us, in all vital crises, to look upon our individual lives as small matters. It is no extraordinary pitch of virtue to do so; it is the character of every man or woman that is not despicable. Somebody during the Reign of Terror said: Tôut le monde croit qu'il est difficile de mourrir. Je le crois comme les autres. Cependant je vois que [quand] on est là chacun s'en tire. [Everyone believes that it is difficult to die. I believe it too. However, I see that when the time comes, each of us manages to get the job done.] It is less characteristic of the woman because her life is more important to the stock, and her immolation less useful.

Having thus shown how much less vitally important reason is than instinct, I next desire to point out how exceedingly desirable, not to say indispensable it is, for the successful march of discovery in philosophy and in science generally, that practical utilities, whether low or high, should be **put out of sight** by the investigator.

The point of view of utility is always a narrow point of view. How much more we should know of chemistry today if the most practically important bodies had not received excessive attention; and how much *less* we should know, if the rare elements and the compounds which only exist at low temperatures had received only the *share* of attention to which their *utility* entitled them.

It is notoriously true that into whatever you do not put your whole heart and soul in that you will not have much success. Now, the two masters, *theory* and *practice*, you cannot serve. That perfect balance of

attention which is requisite for observing the system of things is utterly
lost if human desires intervene, and all the more so the higher and
holier those desires may be.

In addition to that, in philosophy we have prejudices so potent that
it is impossible to keep one's *sang-froid* if we allow ourselves to dwell
upon them at all.

It is far better to let philosophy follow perfectly untrammeled a
scientific method, *predetermined* in advance of knowing to what it will
lead. If that course be honestly and scrupulously carried out, the results
reached, even if they be not altogether true, even if they be grossly
mistaken, cannot but be highly serviceable for the ultimate discovery of
truth. Meantime, sentiment can say "Oh well, philosophical science has
not by any means said its last word yet; and meantime I will continue
to believe *so and so.*"

No doubt a large proportion of those who now busy themselves
with philosophy will lose all interest in it as soon as it is forbidden to
look upon it as susceptible of practical applications. We who continue
to pursue the theory must bid adieu to them. But so we must in any
department of pure science. And though we regret to lose their company, it is infinitely better that men devoid of genuine scientific curiosity
should not barricade the road of science with empty books and embar-
rassing assumptions.

I *repeat* that a great many people think they shape their lives according to reason, when it is really just the other way. But as for the
man who should in truth allow his moral conduct to be vitally changed
by an ethical theory, or his religious life by a philosophy of religion, I
should need a strong word to express my view of his unwisdom.

I would classify the sciences upon the general principle set forth by
Auguste Comte, that is, in the order of abstractness of their objects, so
that each science may largely rest for its principles upon those above it
in the scale while drawing its data in part from those below it. At their
head I would place Mathematics, for this irrefutable reason, that it is
the only one of the sciences which does not concern itself to inquire
what the actual facts are, but studies hypotheses exclusively. It is merely
because it did not become clear to mathematicians themselves before
modern times that they do study nothing but hypotheses without as
pure mathematicians caring at all how the actual facts may be, — a
principle perfectly established today, — that Plato and Aristotle and
the whole host of philosophers made Philosophy more abstract than
Mathematics. But there is this criticism to be made upon almost all

philosophic systems beginning with Plato's doctrine of ideas. Plato before he went to Socrates had been a student of the Heraclitean Cratylus. And the consequence of that accidental circumstance is that almost every philosopher from that day to this has been infected with one of the two great errors of Heraclitus, namely with the notion that Continuity implies Transitoriness. The things of this world, that seem so transitory to philosophers, are *not* continuous. They are composed of discrete atoms, no doubt Boscovichian points. The really continuous things, Space, and Time, and Law, are eternal. The dialogue of the Sophistes, lately shown to belong to Plato's last period, — when he had, as Aristotle tells us, abandoned Ideas and put Numbers in place of them, — this dialogue, I say, gives reasons for abandoning the Theory of Ideas which imply that Plato himself had come to see, if not that the Eternal Essences are continuous, at least, that there is an order of affinity among them, such as there is among Numbers. Thus, at last, the Platonic Ideas became Mathematical Essences, not possessed of Actual Existence but only of a Potential Being quite as *Real,* and his maturest philosophy became welded into mathematics.

Next under mathematics I would place Philosophy, which has the following characteristics:

1st, it differs from mathematics in being a search for real truth;

2nd, it consequently draws upon experience for premises and not merely, like mathematics, for suggestions[;]

3rd, it differs from the special sciences in not confining itself to the reality of existence, but also to the reality of potential being;

4th, the phenomena which it uses as premises, are not special facts, observable with a microscope or telescope, or which require trained faculties of observation to detect; but they are those universal phenomena which saturate all experience through and through so that they cannot escape us;

5th, in consequence at once of the universality of the phenomena upon which philosophy draws for premises, and also of its extending its theories to potential being, the conclusions of metaphysics have a certain necessity, — by which I do not mean that we cannot help accepting them, or a necessity of form, — I mean a necessity of matter, in that they inform us not merely how the things are but how from the very nature of being they *must* be.

Philosophy seems to consist of two parts, Logic and Metaphysics. I exclude Ethics,[2] for two reasons. In the first place, as the science of the end and aim of life [ethics] seems to be exclusively psychical, and there-

fore to be confined to a special department of experience, while philosophy studies experience in its universal characteristics. In the second
place, in seeking to define the proper aim of life, ethics seems to me to
rank with the arts, or rather with the theories of the arts, which of all
theoretical sciences I regard as the most concrete, while what I mean by
philosophy is the most abstract of all the real sciences.

Logic is the science of thought, not merely of thought as a psychical
phenomenon but of thought in general, its general laws and kinds.
Metaphysics is the science of being, not merely as given in physical
experience, but of being in general, its laws and types. Of the two
branches of philosophy Logic is somewhat more affiliated to psychics,
metaphysics to physics.

As I have already said, it seems to me one of the least doubtful of
propositions that metaphysics must take as the guide of its every step
the theory of logic.

On the other hand, I hold that logic is guided by mathematics, in
a sense which is not true of any other science. Every science has its
mathematical part, in which certain results of the special science are
assumed as mathematical hypotheses. But it is not merely in this way
that logic is mathematical. It *is* mathematical in that way, and to a far
greater extent than any other science; but besides that it takes the proceedings of mathematics in all their generality and founds upon them
logical principles.

All necessary reasoning is strictly speaking mathematical reasoning[,] that is to say, it is performed by *observing* something equivalent
to a mathematical Diagram; but mathematical reasoning *par excellence*
consists in those peculiarly intricate kinds of reasoning which belong to
the logic of relatives. The most peculiarly mathematical of these are
reasonings about continuity of which geometrical Topics, or Topology,
and the theory of functions offer examples. In my eighth lecture I shall
hope to make clear my reasons for thinking that metaphysics will never
make any real advance until it avails itself of mathematics of this kind.

Metaphysics recognizes an inner and an outer world, a world of
time and a world of space. The special sciences, all that follow after
metaphysics divide themselves into Psychics and Physics. In each of
these branches of inquiry, there are first, Nomological Sciences which
formulate the laws of psychology on the one hand[,] of dynamics on
the other. Next there are Classificatory Sciences, such as linguistics and
anthropology on the psychical side[,] chemistry on the physical side.
The aim of these sciences is from the known laws made out by the

nomological investigations, and the fundamental differences which are mathematically possible to deduce all the properties of the different classes of mental products on the one hand, of kinds of matter on the other hand. Finally there are the Descriptive Sciences in Psychics and Physics. History generally speaking on the psychical side, Geology, Astronomy, Geography, Hydrology, Metrology, etc. on the physical side. The aim of these sciences is to explain special phenomena by showing that they are the results of the general Laws ascertained by the Nomological Sciences applied to the special kinds discovered by the Classificatory Sciences together with certain accidental arrangements. Last of all psychics and physics reunite in the applied sciences or arts. Of these I have made a list not at all intended to be exhaustive but only to serve as examples from which to get some idea of the relations of these sorts of science. This list contains upwards of 300 different sciences ranging from such general psychical sciences as Ethics, Religion, Law to Goldbeating, Cooking, Charcoal burning, and so forth.

It has been an unfortunate accident of our century that philosophy has come to be set off from the other sciences as if it were foreign and almost hostile to them. In the early years of the Century men like Hegel fancied that their philosophical methods [were] so strong that they could afford to rather emphasize the contrast. They fancied they were able to run the inductive sciences down, to outstrip them altogether. They had been educated in Theological Seminaries and they only knew Natural Science in a Popular Way from the outside. Pride must have a fall, generally involving more or less injustice; and the natural result of this Hegelian Arrogance has been a mistaken notion that Metaphysics, in general, not this or that system of it, but all Metaphysics is necessarily idle subjective and illogical stuff. This is a very serious accusation. It is not to be treated lightly on the one side or the other. The question is, can we find anything in metaphysics, not which shall contrast with other science now put beyond all peradventure, but falling in with it as in inward harmony with it, obeying its logic, and serving its turn.

Having thus presented to you a schedule of all the sciences, a very imperfect one, I dare say, but such a schedule as my acquaintance with the different branches of science enables me to draw up, we come to the question, what is the general upshot of all these sciences, what do they all come to? Now in minor particulars I am hostile to Plato. I think it most unfortunate that he should in his most brilliant works have eviscerated his Ideas of those two elements which especially render ideas valuable. But in regard to the general conception of what the ultimate purpose and importance of science consists in, no philosopher who ever lived, ever brought that out more clearly than this early scientific philosopher. Aristotle justly finds fault with Plato in many respects. But all his criticisms leave unscathed Plato's definitive philosophy, which results from the correction of that error of Heraclitus which consisted in holding the Continuous to be Transitory and also from making the Being of the Ideas potential. Aristotle for example justly complains that of the four kinds of causes Plato only recognizes the two internal ones[,] Form and Matter[,] and loses sight of the two external ones, the Efficient Cause and the End. Though in regard to final causes this is scarcely just, it is more than just in another respect. For not only does Plato only recognize internal causes, but he does not even recognize matter as anything positive. He makes it mere negation, mere non-Being, or Emptiness, forgetting or perhaps not knowing that that which produces positive effects must have a positive Nature. Although Plato's whole philosophy is a philosophy of Thirdness, — that is to say, it is a philosophy which attributes every thing to an action which rightly analyzed has Thirdness for its capital and chief constituent, he himself only recognizes Quality, and makes himself an apostle of Dichotomy, — which is a misunderstanding of himself. To overlook second causes is only a special case of the common fault of all metaphysicians that they overlook the *Logic of Relatives*. But when he neglects External Causes, it is Secondness itself that he is overlooking. This self-misunderstanding this failure to recognize his own conceptions marks Plato throughout. It is a characteristic of the man that he sees much deeper into the Nature of Things than he does into the Nature of his own Philosophy. And it is a trait to which we cannot altogether refuse our esteem.

If you ask me why I drag in the name of Plato so often in this lecture on the relation of philosophy to the conduct of life, I reply that it is because Plato who upon many subjects is at once more in the wrong and yet more in the right [than] other philosophers, upon this question [he] outdoes himself in this double *rôle*. There is no philosopher of any age who mixes poetry with philosophy with such effrontery as Plato. Is Robert Browning within a mile of doing so? As for our philosophic poets, so called, Alexander Pope, Falke Greville, Baron Brooke of Beauchamp Court, Sir John Davies, I am sure nobody ought to complain that they mingle too much sentiment with their philosophy. They do not err more in regard to the practicality of philosophy than the majority of prose philosophers. Plato, on the other hand, is more extravagant than anybody else in this respect. Only having committed the error of making the value and motive to philosophy consist mainly in its moral influence, he surprises his reader by balancing this error by the opposite one of making the whole end and aim of human life to consist in making the acquaintance of pure ideas. In saying that one of these errors counterbalances the other, I do not mean that taken together they do justice at all to those who live simple lives without at all thinking of philosophy, or that they give any just view of right conduct even for the philosopher. For undoubtedly each person ought to select some definite duty that clearly lies before him and is well within his power as the special task of his life. But what I mean is that the two propositions taken together do express a correct view of the ultimate end of philosophy and of science in general.

As a general proposition, the history of science shows every science growing into a more abstract science, one higher in our scale.

The art of medicine grows from the Egyptian book of formulas into physiology. The study of the steam-engine gave birth to modern thermodynamics. Such is the historical fact. The steam engine made mechanical precision possible and needful. Mechanical precision rendered modern observational precision possible, and developed it. Now every scientific development is due to some new means of improved observation. So much for the tendency of the arts. Can any man with a soul deny that the development of pure science is the great end of the arts? Not indeed for the individual man. He uses them, just as [he] uses the deer, which yesterday I saw out of my window; and just as in writing this lecture I am burning great logs in a fireplace. But we are barbarious to treat the deer and the forest trees in that fashion. They have ends of their own, not related to my individual stomach or skin. So, too, man looks upon the arts from his selfish point of view. But they, too, like the beasts and the trees, are living organisms, none the less so for being parasitic to man's mind; and their manifest internal destiny is to grow into pure sciences.

Next consider the descriptive sciences. The proverb that History is philosophy teaching by examples, is another way of saying that the descriptive science of history tends to grow into a classificatory science of kinds of events of which the events of history are specimens. In like manner astronomy under the hands of Sir William Herschel rose from the *tiens état* of a descriptive science to the rank of a classificatory science. Physical geography is more or less following the same course. So likewise is geology. Galton, de Candolle, and others have endeavored to elevate biography into a classificatory science.

Next look at the classificatory sciences. Linguistics is becoming more and more nomological. Anthropology is tending that same way. On the physical side of the schedule Zoölogy and Botany have made long strides toward nomology during the last half century. The wonderful law of Mendeléef and the development of Williamson's ideas go toward accomplishing the same result for chemistry. To become nomological is manifestly the destiny of such sciences.

Now let us proceed to the Nomological Sciences, general psychics, or psychology, on the one hand, general physics on the other. Both of these branches are surely developing into parts of metaphysics. That is their aim. We are far enough from that goal yet. Nevertheless, all the world plainly sees it before us in distance, "sparkling in the monstrous hill."

Metaphysics in its turn is gradually and surely taking on the character of a logic. And finally logic seems destined to become more and more converted into mathematics.

Thus, all the sciences are slowly but surely converging to that centre.

There is a lesson there.

And now whither is mathematics tending? Mathematics is based wholly upon hypotheses, which would seem to be entirely arbitrary. It is very rare, too, to find a mathematical investigator who covers the whole field. Cayley evidently made it a point to do so, as far as he could; and yet, for all that marvellous insight which produced his famous Fifth Memoir on Quantics with its theory of the Absolute and the doctrine that geometrical metrics was only a special case of geometrical optics, or optical geometry, which produced his Memoir on Matrices, and his Memoir on Absolute Geometry, he showed himself downright stupid about Multiple Algebra and about Quaternions, and he did nothing important either in geometrical Topics, or Topical Geometry, or in the Theory of Numbers proper. Even he, therefore, was unable to embrace the whole of mathematics. Even Klein, whose studies have brought the most widely separated subjects into connection, has his limitations. The host of men, who achieve the bulk of each year's new discoveries, are mostly confined to narrow ranges. For that reason you would expect the arbitrary hypotheses of the different mathematicians to shoot out in every direction into the boundless void of arbitrariness. But you do not find any such thing. On the contrary, what you find is that men working in fields as remote from one another as the African Fields are from the Klondike, reproduce the same forms of novel hypotheses.

Riemann had apparently never heard of his contemporary Listing. The latter was a naturalistic Geometer, occupied with the shapes of leaves and birds' nests, while the former was working upon analytical functions. And yet that which seems the most arbitrary in the ideas created by the two men, are one and the same form. This phenomenon is not an isolated one; it characterizes the mathematics of our times, as is, indeed, well-known. All this crowd of creators of forms for which the real world affords no parallel, each man arbitrarily following his own sweet will, are, as we now begin to discern, gradually uncovering one great Cosmos of Forms, a world of potential being. The pure mathematician himself feels that this is so. He is not indeed in the habit of publishing any of his sentiments nor even his generalizations. The fashion in mathematics is to print nothing but demonstrations, and the reader is left to divine the workings of the man's mind from the sequence of those demonstrations. But if you enjoy the good fortune of talking with a number of mathematicians of a high order, you will find that the typical Pure Mathematician is a sort of Platonist. Only, he is Platonist who corrects the Heraclitan error that the Eternal is not Continuous. The Eternal is for him a world, a cosmos, in which the universe of actual existence is nothing but an arbitrary locus. The end that Pure Mathematics is pursuing is to discover that real potential world.

Once you become inflated with that idea *vital importance* seems to be a very low kind of importance, indeed.

But such ideas are only suitable to regulate another life than this. Here we are in this workaday world, little creatures, mere cells in a social organism itself a poor and little thing enough, and we must look to see what little and definite task circumstances have set before our little strength to do. The performance of that task will require us to draw upon all our powers, reason included. And in the doing of it we should chiefly depend not upon that department of the soul which is most superficial and fallible, — I mean our reason, — but upon that department that is deep and sure, — which is instinct. Instinct is capable of development and growth, — though by a movement which is slow in the proportion in which it is vital; and this development takes place upon lines which are altogether parallel to those of reasoning. And just as reasoning springs from experience, so the development of sentiment arises from the soul's Inward and Outward Experiences. ⟨such as meditation, on the one hand, and adversity on the other⟩ Not only is it of the same nature as the development of cognition; but it chiefly takes place through the instrumentality of cognition. The soul's deeper parts can only be reached through its surface. In this way the eternal forms, that mathematics and philosophy and the other sciences make us acquainted with will by slow percolation gradually reach the very core of one's being, and will come to influence our lives; and this they will do, not because they involve truths of merely vital importance, but because they [are] ideal and eternal verities.

TWO

Types of Reasoning

I fear you got little good from the conversation at the end of the last lecture; for I am long dishabituated to talking philosophy. But upon my side I found it very delightful to be assured of so intelligent and critical an auditory.

I am truly vexed to find myself obliged this evening to plunge into the dry and dreary subject of formal logic. But you know as well as I do that there is a part of the philosophical world whose unlucky convictions force them to base metaphysics upon formal logic. To that unfortunate party I appertain. We have at our head three men of might, Aristotle, Duns Scotus, and Kant. Among our most redoubtable antagonists there were in the ancient world Pythagoras and Epicurus, and in the modern world Descartes, Locke, and I must add Hegel. The general question of which party is right I shall not argue. The scheme of classification of the sciences which I laid before you last time serves to define my position that metaphysics must draw its principles from logic, and that logic must draw its principles neither from any theory of cognition nor from any other philosophical position but from mathematics. The defence of this view must rest upon the fruits that it can exhibit.

In order to enliven the deathly dullness of Formal Logic, I will throw what I have to say in the form of a narration of my own mental history, so that you may at least see how a man might keep up a lively interest in this subject during many years. Besides, it will perhaps not be altogether unprofitable for young thinkers to contemplate the picture of an unusually sustained train of thought along a narrow path way, and to note the advantages and disadvantages of such systematized thinking. For that it has both advantages and disadvantages is I think not to be denied. At the same time I shall take care not to weary you by overaccuracy of autobiographical detail, the main thing being to sketch the formal logic, using the narrative form merely for embellishment.

Having been bred in a highly scientific circle, I entered upon the study of philosophy, not at all for the sake of its teachings about God, Freedom, and Immortality, concerning the practical value of which I was very dubious from the outset, but moved rather by curiosity in regard to Cosmology and Psychology. In the early sixties I was a passionate devotee of Kant, at least, of that part of his philosophy which appears in the Transcendental Analytic of the Critic of the Pure Reason. I believed more implicitly in the two tables of the Functions of Judgment and the Categories than if they had been brought down from Sinai. But even then it seemed to me that formal logic ought not to be made to rest upon psychology. For the question whether a given conclusion follows from given premises is not a question of what we are able to think, but of whether such a state of things as that set forth in the premises was able to be true without the state of things related to it as that set forth in the conclusion is to that set forth in the premises being true likewise.

But Kant, as you may remember, calls attention to sundry relations between one category and another. I detected some additional relations between the categories, *all but* forming a regular system, yet not quite so. Those relations seemed to point to some larger list of conceptions in which they might form a regular system of relationship. After puzzling over these matters very diligently for about two years, I rose at length from the problem certain that there was something wrong with Kant's formal logic.

Thereupon I fell to reading every book on logic that I could procure. At first, I had a senseless prepossession in favor of German books; but I soon found myself forced away from it. The German logics, for example, since Kant, are almost unanimous in dividing propositions into the categorical, the conditional (which they wrongly call the hypothetical) and the disjunctive. This was a division introduced by Kant because he rightly or wrongly imagined that the traditional one would spoil his table of categories. The traditional definition of hypothetical, that is, of compound, propositions was into the conditional, the disjunctive, and the copulative.[1] As an example of a copulative proposition, take this: It lightens *and* it thunders. But in truth, conditional propositions merely form a special variety of disjunctive propositions. Thus, "You will either take care where you tread or you will wet your feet" is disjunctive. "If you march equably, you will wet your feet" is a conditional proposition which comes to the same effect. But you will find it impossible to express the same idea in a copulative form. Thus, hypotheticals are in truth either disjunctive or copulative. The same thing is equally true of categoricals. The universal propositions are disjunctive, the particular propositions are copulative. Thus, to say that every man who is without sin may fire a stone is as much as to say of any man you may select that he is either sinful or is at liberty to stone the person. On the other hand to say that some swan is black, is the same as to say that an object can be found of which it is true that it is a swan *and* that it is black.

Cicero informs us that in his time there was a famous controversy between the logicians, Philo and Diodorus, as to the signification of conditional propositions. Philo held that the proposition "if it is lightening it will thunder" was true if it is not lightening or if it will thunder and was only false if it is lightening but will not thunder. Diodorus objected to this. Either the ancient reporters or he himself failed to make out precisely what was in his mind, and though there have been many virtual Diodorans since, none of them have been able to state their position clearly without making it too foolish. Most of the strong logicians have been Philonians, and most of the weak ones have been Diodorans. For my part, I am a Philonian; but I do not think that justice has ever been done to the Diodoran side of the question. The Diodoran vaguely feels that there is something wrong about the statement that the proposition "If it is lightening it will thunder," can be made true merely by its not lightening.

Duns Scotus, who was a Philonian, as a matter of course, threw considerable light upon the matter by distinguishing between an ordinary *consequentia,* or conditional proposition, and a *consequentia simplex de inesse.* A *consequentia simplex de inesse* relates to no range of possibilities at all, but merely to what happens, or is true, *hic et nunc.* But the ordinary conditional proposition asserts not merely that here and now either the antecedent is false or the consequent is true, but that in each possible state of things throughout a certain well-understood range of possibility either the antecedent is false or the consequent true. To understand the proposition "If it lightens it will thunder" means that on each occasion which could arise consistently with the regular course of nature, either it would not lighten or thunder would shortly follow.

Now this much may be conceded to the Diodoran, in order that we may fit him out with a better defence than he has ever been able to construct for himself, namely, that in our ordinary use of language we always understand the range of possibility in such a sense that in some possible case the antecedent shall be true. Consider, for example, the following conditional proposition: If I were to take up that lampstand by its shaft and go brandishing the lamp about in the faces of my auditors it would not occasion the slightest surprise to anybody. Everybody will say that it is false; and were I to reply that it was true because under no possible circumstances should I behave in that outrageous manner, you would feel that I was violating the usages of speech.

I would respectfully and kindly suggest to the Diodoran that this way of defending his position is better than his ordinary stammerings. Still, should he accept my suggestion I shall with pain be obliged to add that the argument is the merest *ignoratio elenchi* which ought not to deceive a tyro in logic. For it is quite beside the question what ordinary language means. The very idea of formal logic is, that certain *canonical forms* of expression shall be provided, the meanings of which forms are governed by inflexible rules; and if the forms of speech are borrowed to be used as *canonical forms of logic* it is merely for the mnemonic aid they afford, and they are always to be understood in logic in strict technical senses. These forms of expression are to be defined, just as zoölogists and botanists define the terms which they invent, that is to say, without the slightest regard for usage but so as to correspond to natural classifications. That is why I entitled one of the first papers I published, "On the Natural Classification of Arguments."[2] And by a *natural* classification, we mean the most *pregnant* classification, pregnant that is to say with implications concerning what is important from a strictly logical point of view.

Now I have worked out in MS. the whole of syllogistic in a perfectly thoroughgoing manner both from the Philonian and from the Diodoran point of view. But although my exposition is far more favorable to the Diodoran system even than that of DeMorgan in his *Syllabus of Logic*, which is much the best presentation of the Diodoran case ever made by an adherent of it, yet I find that the Philonian system is far the simpler, — almost incomparably so. You would not wish me to take you through all those details. This general statement is all that is appropriate for this brief course of lectures.

Be it understood, then, that in logic we are to understand the form "If A, then B" to mean "Either A is impossible or in every possible case in which it is true, B is true likewise," or in other words it means "In each possible case, either A is false or B is true."

That being granted, I say that there is no logical difference between a categorical and a hypothetical proposition. A universal categorical is a disjunctive hypothetical and a particular categorical is a copulative hypothetical. This is my position today just as it was in 1867. If any distinction could be admitted, it would be necessary to declare that categorical propositions are of more complicated structure than hypotheticals. Indeed, the most convenient order of exposition will be to begin by asserting provisionally that this is the case, making afterwards the slight correction that is necessary to establishing the perfect identity between the categoricals and hypotheticals. I say, then, that but for a consideration of secondary importance, a categorical proposition is of an essentially more complex structure than a hypothetical proposition.

This sounds like a paradox. A hypothetical proposition is by definition a compound proposition. Of what, then, is it compounded? To that question I reply that it may be compounded of simple propositions that for the present may be regarded as non-categorical. But no matter of what it be compounded[,] my point is that categorical propositions are equally compound; only they are not *merely* compound, but are affected by a peculiar complication from which hypotheticals may for the present be regarded as free.

The truth is that the appearance of paradox is due merely to the preconceptions which we imbibe from the European languages. These languages do not represent the nature of thought in general, nor even that of human thought. They form one small class among half a dozen large classes, and in many respects are quite exceptional. In other respects, the Indo-European and Shemitic languages taken together are exceptional. The idea that a categorical proposition such as "All men are rational animals," is so simple is an idea suggested by a language in which the *common noun* is a distinct part of speech. Now *Proper names* must, of course, exist in all languages. But the common noun seems to be nowhere else developed as it is in the Indo-European languages. In the Shemitic languages common nouns are met with; but by far the greater part are mere verbal inflections. They are not felt as independent words, nor for the most part entered in the vernacular dictionaries. The other languages of mankind, that is to say the great bulk of human speech are almost devoid of [that] part of speech. Take, for example, a language with which in these days of tourists a good many people acquire some smattering, I mean the Ancient Egyptian. I believe there is no such thing in that language as a word which can only be used as a common noun and cannot be used as a verb. A language in which the noun is as fully developed as in our own certainly cannot express the idea, that "Every man is a rational animal" without the verb *is*. But even in a language so closely allied to ours as Greek this verb may be omitted, — a fact which shows that even so near home as that, the common nouns still retain some verbal life. Outside of the Indo-European branch, a language which requires an *is* in such a sentence is a distinct rarity. The Old Egyptian often uses a copula, it is true; but what is the nature of that copula? According to ??LePay Renouf?? and I think ??Brujsch?? it is not a verb at all; it is a *pronoun* whose function is to show that the man and the rational animal refer to the same object.

We thus see that the truth of the matter is this. There are in the first place certain propositions, such as *fulgurat* and *pluviet*, which can be expressed by a single word. Those propositions are certainly not distinctively categorical. They express no inherence, no character of any object. They do not convey any definite idea of a *thing*. In the second place, these propositions or any propositions may be *denied*. In the third place, any propositions may be logically compounded either by way of disjunction or by way of conjunction. Thus, we get *hypotheticals*. In the fourth place, to these last there may be attached as in Egyptian relative pronouns; or other linguistic devices may be employed to signify that the objects to which the different clauses refer are identical. It is this last complication which makes a proposition distinctly *categorical*.

Thus far, the categorical proposition appears as something more complex than the hypothetical. Thus, Every man is a rational animal means, under a Philonian interpretation, If there be a man, then *he* feels and thinks. It is the identifying pronoun "he" that distinguishes this proposition as categorical. If you object that the categorical proposition asserts the existence of men, I reply that this is a Diodoran interpretation. But now it is time to *correct* the view that categoricals are more complex than hypotheticals by showing that hypotheticals equally involve something equivalent to the pronoun. In my paper of 1867 on the Natural Classification of Arguments, I had already reached the knowledge of the perfect identity of Categoricals and Hypotheticals; but I could not then have given the account of the matter which I am now about to borrow from my long subsequent studies of the logic of relatives. We must in the first place consider such propositions as these: "This is beautiful, — I thirst, — The sky is blue.["] In "This is beautiful," we have the pronoun, but it does not identify two common nouns; it only identifies beautiful with the object which the pronoun *This* directly points out. The demonstrative and personal pronouns, *this, that, I, you, we,* etc. have very peculiar powers. They enable us to convey meanings which words alone are quite incompetent to express; and this they do by stimulating the hearer to look about him. They refer to an experience which is or may be common to speaker and hearer, to deliverer and interpreter. They are thus quite *anti-general*, referring to a *hic et nunc*. The proper name "the sky" is of similar effect. It is that which if you look up, you will see. Any proper name is of the same nature. "The Bible" could not mean to a Japanese what it means to us. In order to discuss with an Afghan the character of George Washington, you must begin by making him partake in some of the experience you have yourself. It is not the same thing when you talk to the man blind from birth about colors. It is no *definite experience* in that case that is lacking, but only a power of imagining. In the case of George Washington, the experience is not *quite* definite in its outlines; still it is approximately so.

Allow me just here to make a parenthetical observation. It is far more true to say that such a name as George Washington is a feeble substitute for a *this* or *that* which should spread the very experience referred to before the interpreter's eyes, than it is to say that "*this*" and "*that*" are *pronouns, or substitutes for nouns.* They are not substitutes for nouns at all; they are *stimulants to looking*, like the bicyclist's bell, or the driver's "hi! there," or "mind your eyes." Duns Scotus clearly saw this and composed a new definition of a pronoun which was accepted by all grammarians down to the time of the reformation of the universities in the 16th century. Then, the hatred of the reformers for the Dunces was such that they reverted to the absurd old definition; and this was continued down to our times. But I see that of late years the new edition of Allen and Greenough and some other grammars have substantially returned once more to the Scotistic definition.

Of a somewhat different nature, yet involving the same element of haecceity, are the selective pronouns, *some, any, every, whoever,* etc. Boole imagined that the proposition "Some swan is black" could be represented by writing, "An undefined kind of swan is black." The very first paper on logic I ever published corrected this error. It is *in any case* true that "Some kind of a swan is black," namely, "every black swan is black"; but that is not what the proposition "Some swan is black" asserts. It declares that here in this actual world *exists* a black swan. There is a reference to a *here and a this;* only the interpreter is not told precisely where among *this here* vast collection of swans the one referred to is to be found. "*Every*" or "*any*" is of a similar nature. When I say "every man dies," I say you may pick out your man for yourself and provided he belongs to *this here* world you will find he will die. The "some" supposes a selection from "this here" world to be made by the *deliverer* of the proposition, or made in his interest. The "every" *transfers* the function of selection to the *interpreter* of the proposition, or to anybody acting in his interest.

Now then, in the sense in which the words "some" and "every" are demonstrative, that is refer to an examination of an experience common to the deliverer and interpreter, in that sense the same element is to be found even in hypotheticals. "If it lightens, it will thunder," means: select from *this here* range of possibility any case *you* like, and *either* it will *not* be a case of present lightening or else it *will* be a case of thunder shortly following. So "It may lighten without thundering," means: *I* could find you in *this here* range of possibilities, a case in which there *should be* lightening *without* any thunder.

Having thus satisfied ourselves of the perfect logical equivalence of categorical and hypothetical propositions, we may for the sake of convenience speak of them as expressed in categorical form. The copula, understood as it must be according to this analysis, is called the *copula of inclusion*. It is opposed to the *copula of identity* which is employed by those who advocate the quantification of the predicate, if any such logicians still linger on the scene after their doctrine has been thoroughly exploded.[3]

There are various other modes of logically analyzing propositions which are equally exact. Two of them are exemplified in the papers by Mrs. Franklin and Prof. Mitchell in the Johns Hopkins Studies in Logic.[4] So there are innumerable different systems of coördinates in geometry all equally correct. And there are different modes of space-measurement, the elliptic, the parabolic, and the hyperbolic, all equally correct. But of all the different kinds of geometrical coördinates, *rectangular point-coördinates alone* correspond to the *principles of mechanics;* and consequently this kind of coördinates must be taken as the *basic coördinates* in the study of mechanics. So it is with the different kinds of space-measurement. The *parabolic alone* corresponds to the principles of *Euclidean geometry;* and nobody would dream of using any other, unless he intended to suppose Euclidean geometry to be false. In complete analogy with these illustrations, of all the methods in which propositions *may be* analyzed and analyzed correctly, *that one* which uses the copula of inclusion *alone* corresponds to the *theory of inference.* And *this* it does, inasmuch as it makes the relation of subject to predicate of a categorical proposition, *precisely the same* as the relation of antecedent to consequent of a conditional proposition; for this latter is manifestly no other relation than that of a premise to its conclusion. The greatest scholastic doctors, who were unquestionably the most exact reasoners there have ever been *except* the mathematicians, always called the minor premise the antecedent and the conclusion the consequent.

In my paper on the Classification of Arguments, I made use of this scholastic doctrine of the *Consequentia* in order to get a πoῦ στῶ [a place where I might stand] from which to start a doctrine of inference. I reasoned in this way. Suppose we draw a conclusion. Whether it be necessary or probable I do not care. Let **S** is **P** represent this conclusion. Now we certainly never can be warranted in drawing any conclusion about **S** from a premise, or set of premises, which does not relate in any way to **S**. If the inference is drawn from more than one premise, let all the premises be colligated into one copulative proposition. Then this single premise must relate to **S**; and in that sense, it may be represented thus: **S** is **M**. I do not, of course, mean that **S** need appear formally in this premise as a subject, far less as the sole subject. I only mean that "**S** is **M**" may in a general sense stand for any proposition which virtually relates to **S**. The inference, then, appears in this form

> *Premise*   **S** is **M**
>
> *Conclusion*   **S** is **P**.

But, *whenever we draw a conclusion,* we have an idea, more or less definite, that the inference we are drawing is only an example of a whole class of possible inferences, in each of which from a premise more or less similar to the actual premise there would be a sound inference of a conclusion analogous to the actual conclusion. And not *only* is this idea present to our consciousness, — as is shown by our thinking that the premise *leads to* the conclusion, — but, what is still more important, there is a principle *actually operative* in the depths of our minds, — a *habit,* natural or acquired, by virtue of which we really *should* draw that analogous conclusion in each of those possible cases. This operative principle I call, after the logician Fries,[5] the *leading principle* of the inference. But now *logic* supposes that reasonings are *criticised;* and as soon as the reasoner asks himself what *warrant* he has for concluding from **S** is **M** that **S** is **P**, he is driven to *formulate* his leading principle. Now in a very general sense we may write as representing that formulation, **M** is **P**. I write **M** is **P** instead of **P** is **M** because the inference takes place from **M** to **P**, that is **M** is antecedent while **P** is consequent. So that the reasoner in consequence of his self criticism reforms his argument and substitutes in place of his original inference, this *complete* argument:

$$\text{Premises} \quad \begin{cases} \textbf{M} \text{ is } \textbf{P} \\ \textbf{S} \text{ is } \textbf{M} \end{cases}$$

Conclusion   **S** is **P.**

I do not mean that the formulation of the leading principle necessarily takes the form *M is P* in any *narrow sense*. I only mean that it must express some general relation between **M** is **P**, which not merely in reference to the special subject, **S**, but in all analogous cases will warrant the passage from a premise similar to **S** is **M** to a conclusion analogous to **S** is **P**.

This second argument has certainly itself a leading principle, although it is a far more abstract one than the leading principle of the original argument. But you might ask, why not express this *new* leading principle as a premise, and so obtain a *third argument* having a leading principle *still more* abstract? If, however, you try the experiment, you will find that the third argument so obtained has no more abstract a leading principle than the second argument has. Its leading principle is indeed precisely *the same* as that of the second argument. This leading principle has therefore attained a *maximum degree* of abstractness; and a leading principle of maximum abstractness may be termed a *logical principle*.

It is thus proved that *in an excessively general sense* every complete argument, i.e. every argument having a leading principle of maximum abstractness, is an argument in the form of *Barbara*.

The purpose of this whole investigation was to ascertain what the principal types of reasoning were; and my plan of proceeding was this. Since all reasoning is in an excessively general sense of the form of *Barbara*, if I could only find a kind of reasoning which should be of the same form of *Barbara* in a more special sense, and yet not in so special a sense as to prevent my discerning clearly its different species, then I might try whether reasoning in general being compared to that kind of reasoning would not show itself to be divided into *analogous classes*.

The first figure of syllogism is of the form of *Barbara* in a special sense; but the difficulty was that its four moods appear to be mere accidental variations of essentially the same kind of inference. But demonstrative syllogism *in general* may be considered as belonging to the

form of *Barbara.* For every mood of such syllogism can be reduced to
the first figure by the aid of immediate inferences which seem to be
inferences in form only, — mere transformations of statements. Thereupon, the question arose whether any differences in the mode of reasoning in demonstrative syllogism could be detected with certainty. Kant in
his brochure *Über die falsche Spitzfindigkeit der vier syllogistischen Figuren*
had maintained that there were no such differences. But then Kant had
had in mind substantial differences, and was not on the lookout for
mere *forms* of difference, which might nevertheless be quite unmistakable. Moreover, Kant had seriously tripped in his reasoning in that little
book in *two particulars, not to mention* less important errors. In the first
place, he had argued that because the second, third, and fourth figures
might be resolved into reasonings in the first figure together with immediate inferences, as indeed all logicians since Aristotle had *fully explained,*
therefore those figures *must* be regarded as so compounded, which was
very much as if he had argued that because a force could be resolved
into two components therefore it could not be regarded as really composed in any other way. In the second place, Kant had never thought
of inquiring what the *nature* of those *immediate inferences* might be; but
had hidden the question from himself by a verbal device consisting in
calling them *Folgerungen* and denying to them the title of *Schlüsse.* The
immediate inferences in question are in principle two, one being the
inference

   No **M** is **P**

   ∴ No **P** is **M,**

while the other is the inference

   Some **S** is **M**

   ∴ Some **M** is **S.**

Now it is quite true that No **M** is **P** and No **P** is **M** are nothing more
than different expressions for the same fact; so that *in substance* there is
no inference at all; and the same thing is true of Some **S** is **M** and Some
M is **S.** But *then,* I bethought me that it frequently happens *in geometry*
that we have to distinguish between two forms which in *themselves considered* are *just alike,* but which differ *toto caelo* when we consider each as a
limiting case of a continuous series of other forms. For example, we say

that two coincident straight lines cross one another at two points, which may be any two points on their length. What is the sense in saying that, or how can two coincident lines differ from a single line? The answer is that if we draw different conics having their vertices at the same two points on a straight line,

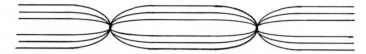

the nearer those conics come to the line, the nearer will the tangents to the conics from any given point in the plane come to passing through those two fixed points. Is there, then, I asked myself, any distinction at all analogous to this between No **M** is **P** and No **P** is **M** [?] Suppose that instead of saying absolutely No **M** is **P** and absolutely No **P** is **M**, we talk of excessively small proportions. It is one thing to say that of men who start writing poetry an excessively small proportion will turn out to have powers like those of Dante; but it is quite another thing to say that of men with powers like those of Dante an excessively minute proportion will ever start to write poetry.

To cut a long matter short, I found that each of those immediate inferences could be thrown into syllogistic form. Namely the mood *Cesare* of the second figure runs thus:

> No **M** is **P**
>
> Any **S** is **P**
>
> ∴ No **S** is **M**.

Now change the **S** to **P**, and this becomes

> No **M** is **P**
>
> Any **P** is **P**
>
> ∴ No **P** is **M**.

And here is the inference from No **M** is **P** to No **P** is **M**. So likewise the mood *Datisi* of the third figure runs thus:

> Any **S** is **P**
>
> Some **S** is **M**
>
> ∴ Some **M** is **P**.

Now change the **P** to **S** and this becomes

> Any **S** is **S**
>
> Some **S** is **M**
>
> ∴ Some **M** is **S**.

Here is the immediate inference from Some **S** is **M** to Some **M** is **S**.

Now I *found*, that the reduction of the Second Figure *always requires that immediate inference* which thus shows itself to be of the form of the second figure, and requires no other; while the reduction of the third figure always requires that immediate inference which shows itself to be of the form of the third figure and requires no other. As to the fourth figure, that turned out to be of a mixed character.

Confining ourselves then to the first three figures, their forms are as follows:

1st Figure

Any M is / is not P

Any / Some S is M

Any / ∴ Some S is / is not P

2nd Figure

Any M is / is not P

Any / Some S is not / is P

Any / ∴ Some S is not M

3rd Figure

Some / Any S is / is not P

Any / Some S is M

∴ Some M is / is not P

It will be seen that the Second Figure is derived from the first by interchanging the minor premise and conclusion while changing them both from affirmative to negative or *vice versa;* while the third figure is derived from the first by interchanging the major premise and conclusion while changing both from universal to particular [or] *vice versa.*

This does not include the two moods *Darapti* and *Felapton* because these are not valid in the Philonian system.

Having thus established this real, although merely formal, distinction between the three figures of syllogism, the *next* question was, whether I might not find that this corresponded to a *more substantial* distinction between three types of inference in general, just as we *usually find in* geometry that merely *nominal* differences in *degenerate* forms correspond to highly *important* distinctions between the genuine forms of which those degenerate forms are the *limiting cases*.

Demonstrative inference is the *limiting case* of probable inference. Certainty *pro* is probability 1. Certainty *con* is probability 0. Let us start, then, with probable syllogism in the first figure. This runs as follows:

> The proportion r of the **M**s possess π as a haphazard character;
>
> These **S**s are *drawn at random* from the **M**s;
>
> ∴ *Probably and approximately,* the proportion r of the **S**s possess π.

Four explanatory remarks are here called for:

1st, The phrase "probably and approximately" in the conclusion, means, loosely speaking, that the probability of the proportion approximating to the value r is *greater* the *wider* the limits of approximation are chosen. Were the conditions of the premises *exactly fulfilled,* the phrase "probably and approximately" would imply agreement with the law of the *probability curve*. Those conditions need not, however, be *exactly fulfilled* and that law has to be modified accordingly. I might occupy a whole lecture on this point.

2nd, The proportion, r, has not necessarily any *precise* numerical value. It may stand for "more than half," or for "nearly all or none" or for "near any simple ratio," and so forth. In short, we are simply to conceive that all possible values from 0 to 1 are distributed in any way whatever into two parcels, and that the statement is that the value of the ratio is contained in a specified parcel.

3rd, The condition that the **S**'s shall be "taken at random" means *nearly enough* at random; and the more nearly the closer will the approximation be. But the nearer the proportion r approaches *all* or *none* the less important is the randomness of the selection, until when r is *quite* all or none, the randomness becomes *altogether indifferent*. It remains to define perfect randomness, which is very important. The **S**'s are drawn *quite at random* provided they are drawn according to a method such that if the drawing were continued indefinitely no **M** would escape getting drawn. But this cannot be, if the multitude of **M**'s exceeds that of the whole numbers, — as does for example, the whole section of real irrational numbers. In regard to such a collection it is impossible directly to reason in this way. I complete the definition of this condition by noting that it is only requisite that the **S**'s should be random with respect to π, that is, that the **S**'s that are π and the **S**'s that are not π should be drawn with the same relative frequencies.

4th, The condition that π must be taken *haphazard* is analogous to the condition that the **S**'s must be taken *at random*. Qualities, however, are *innumerable,* and consequently cannot be taken strictly at random. Yet an object may be said to be taken *haphazard* from a collection, when we so far exert our wills that the object taken shall belong to the collection, while refraining from any further interference, we leave it to the *course of experience* to determine what particular object presents itself. In the case of qualities, this course of experience is not the course of outward experience but is the course of our inward thoughts. If the course of experience should not present any general character, as we hope it will, the effect will, *not* be to vitiate the reasoning, but merely to prevent any conclusions from being drawn. Should the course of experience approximate toward the fulfillment of a general rule but not *precisely* fulfil any rule, the effect will be that we shall never be able to conclude any quite precise proposition. It is to be noted that every quality like every mechanical force, is resolvable into innumerable others in innumerable ways. Hence it is that I have written π in the singular number; for in any event it will have innumerable elements. According to the present requirement, π must be composed of elements which the course of thought, left to itself, naturally throws together. It must not be a recondite or artificially composed character. It must not be suggested by the manner in which instances are presented, nor by the characters of those instances. The safest way will be to insist that π shall be settled upon before the **S**'s are examined.

This is so *important* a rule of reasoning and is so *frequently violated,* that I think I had better give illustrations of the effect of neglecting it. Here is one example:

> The immense majority of small objects which fall to the bottom of the deep sea will never be seen by mortal eye;
>
> Here are some specimens of Challenger Expedition dredgings drawn at random from small objects that had fallen to the bottom of the deep sea;

∴. Probably the immense majority of these specimens will never be seen by mortal eye.

Such reasoning is manifestly absurd. Here is another example. I wish to draw at random a few names of eminent persons. In order that the randomness of the selection may be above suspicion I have simply taken the first name on those pages of Phillip's Great Index of Biography whose numbers end in two zeros, preceded by an odd number, that is on pages 100, 300, 500, 700, 900. Here are the names:

Francis Baring	Born 1740	Died 1810 Sep 12
Vicomte de Custine	1760	1794 Jan 3
Hippostrates	(of uncertain age)	
Marquis d'O	1535	1594 Oct 24
Theocrenus	1480	1536 Oct 18.

Now suppose we reason in disregard of the present rule.

One man in every ten is born in a year ending in a cipher, and therefore probably not more than one of these men. In fact, all but 1.

One man in four dies in autumn.
Probably therefore about one of these. In fact, all but one.
One man in three dies on a day of the month divisible by 3.
Probably therefore 1 or 2 of these. In fact every one.
One man in ten dies in such a year that its number doubled and increased by 1 gives a number whose last figure is the figure in the ten's place of the date itself.
Probably therefore not more than one of these. In fact, every one.

I have not stated these four rules with the utmost possible accuracy but only with so much accuracy as I thought you might be able to carry away from a single lecture. The subject ought to be spread over a number of lectures. But it is necessary for the development of what I have to say later that I should sketch it out as best I may. We see here the first figure of probable reasoning which were the rules stated accurately would be seen to embrace all necessary reasoning as a special case under it. It is in fact Deduction.

I next proceed to form the 3rd figure of probable reasoning. This is derived from the first by interchanging the major premise and conclusion, while denying both. You will remember that r merely means that the true ratio is in one or other of two parcels. Let ζ denote any ratio contained in the parcel to which r does not belong. Then the denial of the proposition

$$\text{The proportion } r \text{ of the } \left\{ \begin{matrix} \mathbf{Ms} \\ \mathbf{Ss} \end{matrix} \right\} \text{ have the character } \pi$$

will be

$$\text{The proportion } \zeta \text{ of the } \left\{ \begin{matrix} \mathbf{Ms} \\ \mathbf{Ss} \end{matrix} \right\} \text{ have the character } \pi.$$

The *form* of the denial is the same as that of the assertion. Hence, the third figure will be

These **Ss** are drawn at random from the **Ms**;

Of these **Ss** the proportion ζ have the haphazard character π;

∴ Probably and approximately, the proportion ζ of the **Ms** have the character π.

This is the formula of Induction. I first gave this theory in 1867. Subsequently, I remarked that it was substantially Aristotle's theory. Since [then], many logicians have expounded it. The word *inductio* is Cicero's imitation of Aristotle's term ἐπαγωγή. It fails to convey the full significance of the Greek word, which implies that the examples are arrayed and brought forward in a mass. Aristotle in one place calls the reasoning ἡ ἀπὸ τῶν καθ᾽ ἕκαστον ἐπὶ τὰ καθόλου ἔφοδος, the assault upon the generals by the singulars.

Induction, then, is probable reasoning in the Third Figure. This theory is distinguished from all others by two attributes, 1st, it derives the rules of induction as necessary corollaries from the definition of Induction, and 2nd, the rules so derived are much more stringent than those of any other theory. For example, Mill and others quite overlook the necessity of the rule that the character π must not be suggested by an examination of the sample itself.

It follows as a consequence of this rule that induction *can never make a first suggestion*. All that induction can do is *to infer the value of a ratio*, and that only approximately. If the **M**'s are infinite in number, the proportion of **M**'s that are **P** may be strictly as 1 to 1, and *still* there may be exceptions. But we shall see later that in fact induction *always* relates to infinite classes, — though never to such as exceed in multitude the whole numbers. Consequently, induction can never afford the *slightest reason to think that a law is without exception.* I may remark that this result is admitted to be true by Mill.

I will refrain from a minute and tedious formalistic discussion of what the Second Figure of probable reasoning will be, but will content myself with informing you that such a discussion would lead to the following result, namely that the second figure reads:

>   Anything of the nature of **M** would have the character π, taken haphazard;
>
>   **S** has the character π
>
> ∴ Provisionally, we may suppose **S** to be of the nature of **M**.

Still more convenient is the following conditional form of statement:

>   If μ were true, π, π′, π″ would follow as miscellaneous consequences.
>
>   But π, π′, π″ are in fact true;
>
> ∴ Provisionally, we may suppose that μ is true.

This kind of reasoning is very often called *adopting a hypothesis for the sake of its explanation of known facts.* The explanation is the *modus ponens*

>   If μ is true, π, π′, π″ are true
>
>   μ is true
>
> ∴ π, π′, π″ are true.

This probable reasoning in the second figure is, I apprehend, what Aristotle meant by ἀπαγωγή. There are strong reasons for believing that in the chapter on the subject in the Prior Analytics, there occurred one of those many obliterations in Aristotle's MS due to its century long exposure to damp in a cellar, which the blundering Apellicon, the first editor, filled up with the wrong word. Let me change but one word of the text, and the meaning of the whole chapter is metamorphosed in such a way that it no longer breaks the continuity of the train of Aristotle's thought, as in our present text it does[,] so as to bring it into parallelism with another passage, and to cause the two examples, like the generality of Aristotle's examples, to represent reasonings current at his time, instead of being, as our text makes them, the one utterly silly and the other nearly as bad. Supposing this view to be correct, ἀπαγωγή should be translated not by the word *abduction,* as the custom of the translators is, but rather by reduction or *retroduction.* In these lectures I shall generally call this type of reasoning *retroduction.*

I first gave this theory in 1867, improving it slightly in 1868. In 1878 I gave a popular account of it in which I rightly insisted upon the radical distinction between Induction and Retroduction. In 1883, I made a careful restatement with considerable improvement. But I was led away by trusting to the perfect balance of logical breadth and depth into the mistake of treating Retroduction as a kind of Induction.[6] Nothing I observe is so insidious as a tendency to suppose symmetry to be exact. The first anatomist must have been surprised to find the viscera were not as symmetrical as the hands and features. In 1892 I gave a good statement of the rationale of Retroduction but still failed to perceive the radical difference between this and Induction, although earlier it had been clear enough to my mind. I do not regard the present lecture, into which I have been obliged to cram too much matter, as a formal restatement; but it suffices to indicate that I am now ready to make such a fresh restatement which shall correct some former errors and I hope will stand as satisfactory for a good many years.

For the sake of brevity I have abstained from speaking of the argument from analogy, which Aristotle terms παράδειγμα. I need hardly say that the word *analogy* is of mathematical provenance. This argument is of a mixed character being related to the others somewhat as the Fourth Figure of syllogism is related to the other three.

Now let us remove the scaffolding of syllogistic forms which has served as our support in building up this theory and contemplate our erection without it. We see three types of reasoning. The first figure embraces all Deduction whether necessary or probable. By means of it we predict the special results of the general course of things, and calculate how often they will occur in the long run. A definite probability always attaches to the Deductive conclusion because the mode of inference is necessary. The third figure is Induction by means of which we ascertain how often in the ordinary course of experience one phenomenon will be accompanied by another. No definite probability attaches to the Inductive conclusion, such as belongs to the Deductive conclusion;

but we can calculate how often inductions of a given structure will attain a given degree of precision. The second figure of reasoning is Retroduction. Here, not only is there no definite probability to the conclusion, but no definite probability attaches even to the mode of inference. We can only say that the Economy of Research prescribes that we should at a given stage of our inquiry try a given hypothesis, and we are to hold to it provisionally as long as the facts will permit. There is no probability about it. It is a mere suggestion which we tentatively adopt. For example, in the first steps that were made toward the reading of the cuneiform inscriptions, it was necessary to take up hypotheses which nobody could have expected would turn out true, — for no hypothesis positively likely to be true could be made. But they had to be provisionally adopted, — yes, and clung to with some degree of tenacity too, — as long as the facts did not absolutely refute them. For that was the system by which in the long run such problems would quickest find their solutions.

[Exordium for Lecture Three]

Before beginning my lecture this evening I wish to add a few words in further reply to that question which after the last lecture took the uppermost place, namely, the question concerning logic being entirely independent of psychology. The reason I wish to return to this matter is that it is a most elementary point without a perfectly clear understanding of which it is impossible to take one step in logic without danger of setting your foot into mud. My proposition is that logic, in the strict sense of the term, has nothing to do with how you think. The word logic is ambiguous. It is at once the name of a more general science and of a specific branch of that science. What I am saying of its independence of psychology is *true* of logic in both senses; but all that I care to *insist upon* at this stage of the business, is that it is true of logic in the narrower sense. Logic in the narrower sense is that science which concerns itself primarily with distinguishing reasonings into good and bad reasonings, and with distinguishing probable reasonings into strong and weak reasonings. Secondarily, logic concerns itself with all that it must study in order to draw those distinctions about reasoning, and with nothing else. Now the question of whether a deductive argument is true or not is simply the question whether or not the *facts* stated in the premises could be true in any sort of a universe no matter what be *true* without the *fact* stated in the conclusion being *true* likewise. Take, for example, the following argument:

A certain insurance company receives money only from persons to every one of whom it pays back more than the principal sum that person paid into its treasury *plus* the accumulations of that principal.

Therefore, that insurance company is paying out more than it is receiving.

Take another example:

A vast collection of gamesters each provided with unlimited funds sit down to play against a bank with unlimited funds at a game in which the chances of any single bet are equally divided between the bank and the player. Each player bets one franc at each bet and continues to play until he has netted a gain of one franc, when he rises from the table and yields his place to a new player who does the same thing. Now since according to the doctrine of chances each player must sooner or later net a gain of one franc, the question is whether it does not necessarily follow that the bank loses money.

Those are examples, — very easy ones, of course, — of the sort of problems with which deductive logic has to deal. And you will have seen that both the two consequences are unsound. Now I say that any man who imagines that the solution of such questions can be facilitated by asking whether the premises and conclusion are thought under categorical forms or hypothetical forms is wandering far away from the point. The forms of statement are not of the slightest consequence except so far as they distinguish between the state of things supposed in the premises to be true and other states of things; and the sole question is whether the state of things supposed in the premises leave any possibility open for the falsity of the state of things concluded.

Thus, it is plain, that the question of whether any deductive argument, be it necessary or probable, is sound is simply a question of the mathematical relation between the matter of one hypothesis and the matter of another hypothesis; and the consideration of the ways in which the thinking of that matter is done is no more germane to the logical question, than it would be to inquire whether the propositions were written in the English or the Hungarian language. The distinction between categoricals and hypotheticals is a mere linguistic distinction which happens to take great prominence in the Indo European languages owing to the accidental circumstance that in those languages the common noun is developed into a perfectly distinct part of speech.

It is true that the propositions must be expressed *somehow;* and for this reason formal logic, in order to disentangle itself completely from linguistic, or psychical, considerations, invents an artificial language of its own, of perfectly regular formation, and declines to consider any proposition under any other form of statement than in that artificial language. That language affords a way of expressing any hypothesis. Owing to the imperfection of everything that man achieves, every variety of logical language yet constructed affords two or more ways of expressing some hypotheses. That is not because two propositions true and false under precisely the same circumstances can really be logically different, but is simply because our logical language has not reached its last degree of perfection. As for the business of translating from ordinary speech into precise logical forms, — with which for example Georg ⟨Hoppe⟩ in his treatise so much [occupies] himself, — that is a matter of applied logic if you will; that is to say, it is the logical part of the science of the particular language in which the expressions analyzed occur.

So much for Deductive Reasoning. It would be idle to contend that any other thinkers can compare with the mathematicians as deductive reasoners. Yet the mathematicians neither know, nor pretend to know, nor care, by what psychological machinery their hypotheses were thought. It would be a strange thing that they should combine this ignorance and indifference with so high a degree of skill if it were really essential to the solution of questions in deductive logic to consider how we think. I would not believe it until some man showed that by such consideration he could advance the reasoning of the mathematicians in an eminent degree.

As for the other two types of inference Induction and Retroduction, I have shown that they are nothing but apagogical transformations of deduction and by that method the question of the value of any such reasoning is at once reduced to the question of the accuracy of a Deduction. Hence, if the consideration of how we think is not pertinent to Deductive logic, no more is it to Inductive and Retroductive logic.

THREE

The Logic of Relatives

When in 1866, Gentlemen, I had clearly ascertained that the three types of reasoning were Induction, Deduction, and Retroduction, it seemed to me that I had come into possession of a pretty well-rounded system of Formal Logic. I had, it is true, a decided suspicion that there might be a logic of relations; but still I thought that the system I had already obtained ought to enable me to take the Kantian step of transferring the conceptions of logic to metaphysics.[1] My formal logic was marked by triads in all its principal parts. There are three types of inference Induction, Deduction, and Retroduction each having three propositions and three terms. There are three types of logical forms, the term, the proposition, and the inference. Logic is itself a study of signs. Now a sign is a thing which represents a second thing to a third thing, the interpreting thought. There are three ways in which signs can be studied, first as to the general conditions of their having any meaning, which is the *Grammatica Speculativa* of Duns Scotus, secondly, as to the conditions of their truth, which is logic, and thirdly, as to the conditions of their transferring their meaning to other signs. The Sign, in general, is the third member of a triad; first a thing as thing, second a thing as reacting with another thing; and third a thing as representing another to a third. Upon a careful analysis, I found that all these triads embody the same three conceptions, which I call after Kant, my Categories. I first named them Quality, Relation, and Representation. I cannot tell you with what earnest and long continued toil I have repeatedly endeavored to convince myself that my notion that these three ideas are of fundamental importance in philosophy was a mere deformity of my individual mind. It is impossible; the truth of the principle has ever reappeared clearer and clearer. In using the word *relation*, I was not aware that there are relations which cannot be analyzed into relations between pairs of objects. Had I been aware of it, I should have preferred the word *Reaction*. It was also perhaps injudicious to stretch the meaning of the word Representation so far beyond all recognition as I did.[2] However, the words Quality, Reaction, Representation, might well enough serve to name the conceptions. The *names* are of little consequence; the point is to apprehend the conceptions. And in order to avoid all false associations, I think it far the best plan to form entirely new scientific names for them. I therefore prefer to designate them as *Firstness, Secondness,* and *Thirdness.* I will endeavor to convey to you some idea of these conceptions. They are ideas so excessively general, so much more general than ordinary philosophical terms, that when you first come to them they must seem to you vague.

Firstness may be defined as follows: It is the mode in which anything would be for itself, irrespective of anything else, so that it would not make any difference though nothing else existed, or ever had existed, or could exist. Now this mode of being can only be apprehended as a mode of feeling. For there is no other mode of being which we can conceive as having no relation to the possibility of anything else. In the second place, the First must be without parts. For a part of an object is something other than the object itself. Remembering these points, you will perceive that any color, say *magenta,* has and is a positive mode of feeling, irrespective of every other. Because, Firstness is all that it is, for itself, irrespective of anything else, when viewed *from without* (and therefore no longer in the original fullness of firstness) the firstnesses are all the different possible sense-qualities, embracing endless varieties of which all we can feel are but minute fragments. Each of these is just as simple as any other. It is impossible for a sense quality to be otherwise than absolutely simple. It is only complex to the eye of comparison, not in itself.

A *Secondness* may be defined as a modification of the being of one subject, which modification is *ipso facto* a mode of being of quite a distinct subject, or, more accurately, secondness is that in each of two absolutely severed and remote subjects which pairs it with the other, not for my mind nor for, or by, any mediating subject or circumstance whatsoever, but in those two subjects alone; so that it would be just the same if nothing else existed, or ever had existed, or could exist. You see that this Secondness in each subject must be secondary to the inward Firstness of that subject and does not supersede that firstness in the least. For were it to do so, the two subjects would, in so far, become one. Now it is precisely their twoness all the time that is most essential to their secondness. But though the secondness is secondary to the firstness, it constitutes no limitation upon the firstness. The two subjects are in no degree one; nor does the secondness belong to them taken together. There are two Secondnesses, one for each subject; but these are only aspects of one Pairedness which belongs to one subject in one way and to the other in another way. But this pairedness is nothing different from the secondness. It is not mediated or brought about; and consequently it is not of a comprehensible nature, but is absolutely blind. The aspect of it present to each subject has no possible *rationale*. In their *essence,* the two subjects are not paired; for in its essence anything is what it is, while its secondness is that of it which is another. The secondness, therefore, is an accidental circumstance. It is that a blind reaction takes place between the two subjects. It is that which we experience when our will meets with resistance, or when something obtrudes itself upon sense. Imagine a magenta color to feel itself and nothing else. Now while it slumbers in its magenta-ness let it suddenly be metamorphosed into pea green. Its experience at the moment of transformation will be secondness.

The idea of Thirdness is more readily understood. It is a modification of the being of one subject which is a mode of a second so far as it is a modification of a third. It might be called an inherent reason. The dormitive power of opium by virtue of which the patient sleeps is more than a mere word. It denotes, however indistinctly, some reason or regularity by virtue of which opium acts so. Every law, or general rule, expresses a thirdness; because it induces one fact to cause another. Now such a proposition as, Enoch is a man, expresses a firstness. There is no reason for it; such is Enoch's nature, — that is all. On the other hand the result that Enoch dies like other men, as result or effect, expresses a Secondness. The necessity of the conclusion is just the brute force of this Secondness. In Deduction, then, Firstness by the operation of Thirdness brings forth Secondness. Next consider Induction. The people born in the last census-year may be considered as a sample of Americans. That *these* objects should be Americans has no reason except that that was the condition of my taking them into consideration. There is Firstness. Now the Census tells me that about half those people were males. And that this was a necessary result is almost guaranteed by the number of persons included in the sample. There, then, I assume to be

Secondness. Hence we infer the *reason* to be that there is some virtue, or occult regularity, operating to make one half of all American births male. There is Thirdness. Thus, Firstness and Secondness following have risen to Thirdness.

There are my three categories. I do not ask you to think highly of them. It would be marvelous if young students in philosophy should be able to distinguish these from a flotsam and jetsam of the sea of thought that is common enough. Besides, I do not ask to have them distinguished. All thought both correct and incorrect is so penetrated with this triad, that there is nothing novel about it, and no merit in having extracted it. I do not at present make any definite assertion about these conceptions. I only say, here are three ideas, lying upon the beach of the mysterious ocean. They are worth taking home, and polishing up, and seeing what they are good for.

I will only say this, there is a class of minds whom I know more intimately probably than many of you do, in whose thought, if it can be called thought, Firstness has a relative predominance. It is not that they are particularly given to hypothetic inference, though it is true that they are so given; but that all their conceptions are relatively detached and sensuous. Then there are the minds whom we commonly meet in the world, who cannot at all conceive that there is anything more to be desired than power. They care very little for inductions, as such. They are nominalists. They care for the things with which they react. They do reason, so far as they see any use for it; and they know it is useful to read. But when it comes to a passage in which the reasoning employs the letters A,B,C they skip that. Now the letters A,B,C are pronouns indispensable to thinking about Thirdness; so that the mind who is repelled by that sort of thought, is simply a mind in which the element of Thirdness is feeble. Finally, there is the geometrical mind, who is quite willing that others should snatch the power and the glory so long as he can be obedient to that great world-vitality which is bringing out a cosmos of ideas, which is the end toward which all the forces and all the feelings in the world are tending. These are the minds to whom I offer my three Categories as containing something valuable for their purpose.

These Categories manifest themselves in every department of thought; but the advantage of studying them in formal logic is, that there we have a subject which is very simple and perfectly free from all doubt about its premises, and yet is not like pure mathematics confined entirely to purely hypothetical premises. It is the most abstract and sim-

ple of all the positive sciences, and the correct theory of it is quite indispensable to any true metaphysics.

Having in 1867 made out the three categories,[3] various facts proved
to me beyond a doubt that my scheme of formal logic was still incom-
plete. For instance, I found it quite impossible to represent in syllogism
any course of reasoning in geometry or even any reasoning in algebra
except in Boole's Logical algebra. I had already ascertained that Boole's
algebra was inadequate to the representation of ordinary syllogisms of
the third figure; and though I had invented a slight enlargement of
it to remedy this defect, yet it was of a make-shift character, plainly
foreshadowing something yet unseen more organically connected with
the part of the algebra discovered by Boole. In other directions, Boole's
system strongly suggested its own imperfection. Pondering over these
things, my note-book shows that I soon came out upon the logic of
relatives, and had so complemented the Boolian algebra as to give it
power to deal with all dyadic relations[.] I learned from the great memoir of Prof. DeMorgan, dated [1860], which he now sent me, that the
same ground had already been considerably explored by him, though
by a different route, starting from his own line of logical thought as
expounded in his work *Formal Logic.*

It is now time to explain to you this Logic of Relatives.[4] I will first
give a chronology of the most important papers. I shall not mention
any that are not quite fundamental. Relation was recognized as a part
of the subject matter of logic by Aristotle and all ancient and medieval
logicians. There is a tractate *De Relativis* probably dating from the 11th
century appended to the *Summulae of Petrus Hispanus.* Ockham and Pau-
lus Venetus treat of it in their extended treatises on logic. Leslie Ellis
made a single obvious remark on the application of Algebra to it which
Professor Halsted thinks makes him the author of the logic of relatives.
The remark is really fundamental. Yet it was exceedingly obvious; and
was not followed out. Next came DeMorgan's Memoir. Then in 1870
[came] my first mode of extending Boole's Logical algebra to relatives.
In 1883 I gave what I call the *Algebra of Dyadic Relatives,* which Schröder
has fallen in love with. In the same volume O. H. Mitchell, in one of
the most suggestive chapters that the whole history of logic can show,
gave a method of treating a logical universe of several dimensions, which
I soon after showed amounted to a new algebraic method of treating
relatives generally. I call it the *General Algebra of Logic.* I think this the
best of the algebraic methods. In 1890, Mr. A. B. Kempe published an
extended memoir on *Mathematical Form* which is really an important

contribution to the logic of relatives. Schröder's third volume treats of the subject at great length, but in the interest of algebra rather than in that of logic. Finally about two years ago, I developed two intimately connected graphical methods which I call Entitative and Existential Graphs.

I shall here treat the subject by means of Existential Graphs, which is the easiest method for the unmathematical. Still, I shall not attempt to set this forth at all. I shall not even trouble you with the statement of its nine fundamental rules; far less with the score of others with which it is necessary to familiarize oneself in order to practice the method. But I shall describe in a confused, illogical fashion every essential feature of the system.

Let us pretend to assert anything we write down on the black board. As long as the board remains blank, whatever we may opine, we assert nothing. If we write down

You are a good girl

we assert that. If we write

You are a good girl
You obey mamma

we assert both. This is therefore a copulative proposition. When we wish to assert something about a proposition without asserting the proposition itself, we will enclose it in a lightly drawn oval, which is supposed to fence it off from the field of assertions. Thus

and again

This last assertion that a proposition is false is a *logical* statement about it; and therefore in a logical system deserves special treatment. It

is also by far the commonest thing we have occasion to say of propositions without asserting them. For those reasons, let it be understood
that if a proposition is merely fenced off from the field of assertion
without any assertion being explicitly made concerning it, this shall be
an elliptical way of saying that it is false.

> **You are a good girl**

Accordingly

> **You are a good girl**

You obey mamma

is the copulative proposition "you are not a good girl, but you obey
mamma." The denial of a copulative proposition is a *disjunctive* proposition. Thus

> **You are a good girl**
> **You obey mamma**

which denies that you are both a good girl and obey mamma, asserts
that you are either not a good girl *or* you do not obey mamma. So

> **You are a good girl**
> **You obey mamma**

asserts that you are either a good girl or do not obey mamma, that is,
"If you obey mamma you are a good girl." This is a *conditional* proposition. It is a species of disjunctive proposition. Copulative and disjunctive
propositions are the two kinds of *Hypothetical* Propositions; and are generally recognized as such. Kant had a purpose in endeavoring to wrench
this plain division into another form, or thought he had; and Kantian
Logicians have been too feeble minded to dispute their master.

Now there remains only one little bit of a feature to complete the description of the system. But this little feature is everything. Namely, we will use a heavy line to *assert the identity of its extremities.* Thus

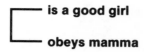

shall mean there *exists* something that is a good girl and is identical with something that obeys mamma. That is Some existing good girl obeys mamma. Or we can better express this thus

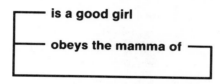

That is, Some existing good girl obeys the mamma of *her.* Now as long as there is but one such line of identity, whether it branches or not, the forms of inference are just the same as if there were no such line. But the moment there are two or more such lines, new forms of inference, unknown to ordinary logic, become possible. For example, let us write

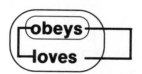

That means, there is something which whoever loves obeys. For it says, there is something of which it is not true that somebody loves it and yet does not obey it. From this we can infer, by a very simple principle

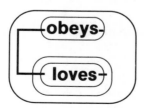

which means "whoever loves everything obeys something." For it denies that there is something of which it is not true that there is something that it does not love and yet of which it is not true that there is something that it obeys. You will find it impossible to express this simple inference syllogistically.

There is all the mathematics with which I intend to burden your poor heads. I hope you will not suffer from the effects of it. I will try to give you a rest now, by passing to something easier. But mind, you certainly miss very important revelations concerning the question of nominalism and realism by being shut out from that great world of logic of which I have just given you one momentary glimpse as I whisk you by it in our railway journey through the forms of reasoning.

Any part of a graph which only needs to have lines of identity attached to it to become a complete graph, signifying an assertion, I call a *verb*. The places at which lines of identity can be attached to the verb I call its *blank subjects*. I distinguish verbs according to the numbers of their subject blanks, as *medads, monads, dyads, triads,* etc. A *medad,* or impersonal verb, is a complete assertion, like "it rains," "you are a good girl." A *monad,* or neuter verb, needs only one subject to make it a complete assertion, as

━━ obeys mamma

you obey ━━

A *dyad,* or simple active verb, needs just two subjects to complete the assertion as

━━ obeys━━

━━━━ or ━━ is identical with ━━

A *triad,* needs just three subjects as

━━ gives ┓ to ━━

━━ obeys both ┓ and ━━

Now I call your attention to a remarkable theorem. Every polyad higher than a triad can be analyzed into triads, though not every triad can be analyzed into dyads. Thus, [the tetrad]

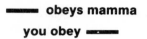

━━ sells ┓ to ┛ for the price ━━

[can be analyzed into these triads]

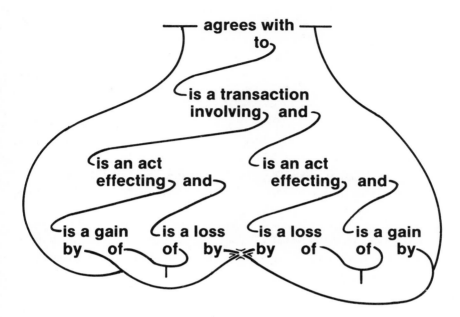

From this theorem we see that our list of categories is complete.[5] I do not say there is no conception of Fourthness. We know that the tetrad was most sacred with the Pythagoreans. Of that, however, I believe I have the secret. If so, it argues nothing. But the fourthness in melody for example is indisputable. It contains however no peculiar intellectual element not found in Firstness, Secondness, and Thirdness. Let me say again that the connection of my categories with the numbers 1,2,3, although it affords a convenient [designation] of them, is a very trivial circumstance.

In the system of graphs may be remarked three kinds of signs of very different natures. First, there are the verbs, of endless variety. Among these is the line signifying identity. But, second[,] the ends of the lines of identity (and *every* verb ought to [be] conceived as having such loose ends) are signs of a totally different kind. They are demonstrative pronouns, indicating existing objects, not necessarily material things, for they may be *events,* or even *qualities,* but still objects, merely designated as *this* or *that.* In the third place the writing of verbs side by side, and the ovals enclosing graphs not asserted but subjects of assertion which last is continually used in mathematics and makes one of the great difficulties of mathematics, constitute a third, entirely different kind of sign. Signs of the first kind represent objects in their firstness, and give the significations of the terms. Signs of the second kind represent objects as existing, — and therefore as reacting, — and also in their reactions. They contribute the *assertive* character to the graph. Signs of the third kind represent objects as representative, that is in their Thirdness, and upon them turn all the inferential processes. In point of fact, it was considerations about the categories which taught me how to construct the system of graphs.

Although I am debarred from showing anything in detail about the logic of relatives, yet this I may remark, that where ordinary logic considers only a single, special kind of relation, that of similarity, — a relation, too, of a particularly featureless and insignificant kind, the logic of relatives imagines a relation in general to be placed. Consequently, in place of the *class*, — which is composed of a number of individual objects or facts brought together in ordinary logic by means of their relation of similarity, the logic of relatives considers the *system*, which is composed of objects brought together by any kind of relations whatsoever. For instance, ordinary logic recognizes such reasoning as this:

> A does not possess any shade of grey
>
> B does possess a shade of grey
>
> ∴ A is not B

But the logic of relatives sees that the quality grey here plays no part that any object might not play. Nor does the relation of possessing as a character differ in its logical powers from any other dyadic relation. It therefore looks upon that inference as but a special case of one like the following

> A loves everybody of the name of Grey
>
> B has a servant of the name of Grey
>
> ∴ A loves a servant of B

But there *are* inferences in the logic of relatives which have not so much resemblance to anything in ordinary logic. Among the classes which ordinary logic recognizes, *general* classes are particularly important. These general classes are composed not of real objects, but of possibilities, and hence it is that the nominalist for whom (though he be so mild a nominalist as Hegel was) a mere possibility which is not realized is nothing but what they call an "abstraction," and little better, if at all, than a fiction. It will be instructive, therefore, to inquire what it is in the logic of relatives which takes the logical position occupied in ordinary logic by "generality," or in medieval language by the *universal*.

Let us see, then, what it is that, in the logic of relatives, corresponds to generality in ordinary logic. From the point of view of Secondness, which is the pertinent point of view, the most radical difference between systems is in their multitudes. For systems of the same multitude can be transformed into one another by mere change of Thirdness, which is not true of systems of different multitude. A system of multitude *zero* is no system, at all. That much must be granted to the nominalists. It is not even a quality, but only the abstract and germinal possibility which antecedes quality. It is at most being *per se*. A system of multitude unity is a mere First. A system of the multitude of two is like the system of truth and falsity in necessary logic. A system of the multitude of three is the lowest perfect system. The finite multitudes are all marked by this character that if there be a relation in which every individual in such a system stands to some other but in which no third stands to that other, then to every individual of the system some other individual stands in that relation. We next come to the multitude of all possible different finite multitudes, that is to the multitude of the whole numbers. A system of this multitude, which I call the *denumeral* multitude, is characterized by this, that though finite, yet its individuals have what I call *generative relations*. These are dyadic relations of relate to correlate such that, taking any one of them, whatever character belongs to the correlate of that relation wherever it belongs to the relate, and which also belongs to a certain individual of the system, which may be called the *origin* of the relation, belongs to every individual of the system. For example, in the system of cardinal numbers from *zero* up, the relation of being next lower in the order of magnitude is a generative relation. For every character which is such that if it belongs to the number next lower than any number also belongs to the number itself, and which also belongs to the number *zero* belongs to every number of the system. The next multitude is that of all possible collections of different finite collections [of finite multitudes]. This is the multitude of irrational quantities. I term it the *first abnumeral* multitude. The next multitude is that of all possible collections of collections of finite multitudes. I call it the *second abnumeral multitude*. The next is the multitude of all possible collections of collections of collections of finite multitudes. There will be a denu-

meral series of such abnumeral multitudes. I prove that these are all
different multitudes in the following way. In the first place, I say, that
taking any such collection, which we may designate as the collection of
A's, if each individual A has an identity distinct from all other A's, then
it is manifestly true that each collection of A's has an identity distinct
from all other collections of A's; for it is rendered distinct by containing
distinctly different individuals. But the individuals of a denumeral collection, such as all the whole numbers, have distinct identities. Hence,
it follows that the same is true of all the abnumeral multitudes. But this
does not prove that those multitudes are all different from one another.
In order to prove that, I begin by defining, after Dr. Georg Cantor,
what is meant by saying that one collection of distinct objects, say the
B's, is greater in multitude than another multitude of distinct objects,
say the A's. Namely, what is meant is that while it is possible that every
A should have a distinct B assigned to it exclusively, and not to any
other A, yet it is not possible that every B should have a distinct A
assigned to it exclusively and not to any other B. Now then suppose the
A's to form a collection of any abnumeral multitude, then all possible
collections of different A's will form a collection of the next higher
abnumeral multitude. It is evidently possible to assign to each A a distinct collection of A's for we may assign to each the collection of all the
other A's. But I say that it is impossible to assign to every collection of
A's a distinct A. For let there be any distribution of collections of A's
which shall assign only one to each A, and I will designate a collection
of A's which will not have been assigned to any A whatever. For the A's
may be divided into two classes, the first containing every A which is
assigned to a collection containing itself, the second containing every A
to which is assigned a collection not containing itself. Now, I say that
collection of A's which is composed of all the A's of the second class and
none of the first has no A assigned to it. It has none of the first class
assigned to it for each A of that class is assigned to but one collection
which contains it while this collection does not contain it. It has none of
the second class assigned to it for each A of this class is assigned only
to one collection which does not contain it, while this collection does
contain it. It is therefore absurd to suppose that any collection of distinct
individuals, as all collections of abnumeral multitudes are, can have a
multitude as great as that of the collection of possible collections of its
individual members.

   .   But now let us consider a collection containing an individual for
every individual of a collection of collections comprising a collection of

every abnumeral multitude. That is, this collection shall consist of all finite multitudes together with all possible collections of those multitudes, together with all possible collections of collections of those multitudes, together with all possible collections of collections of collections of those multitudes, and so on *ad infinitum.* This collection is evidently of a multitude as great as that of all possible collections of its members. But we have just seen that this cannot be true of any collection whose individuals are distinct from one another. We, therefore, find that we have now reached a multitude so vast that the individuals of such a collection melt into one another and lose their distinct identities. Such a collection is *continuous.*

Consider a line which returns into itself, — a ring.

That line is a collection of points. For if a particle occupying at any one instant a single point, moves until it returns to its first position, it describes such a line, which consists only of the points that particle occupied during that time. But no point in this line has any distinct identity absolutely discriminated from every other. For let a point upon that line be marked.

Now this mark is a discontinuity; and therefore I grant you, that this point is made by the marking distinctly different from all other points. Yet cut the line at that point,

and where is that marked point now? It has become two points. And if those two ends were joined together so as to show the place, — they would become one single point. But if the junction ceased to have any distinguishing character, that is any discontinuity, there would not be any distinct point there. If *we* could not distinguish the junction it would not appear distinct. But the line is a mere conception. It is nothing but that which it can show; and therefore it follows that if there were no discontinuity there would *be* no distinct point there, — that is, no point absolutely distinct in its being from all others. Again going back to the line with two ends, let the last point of one end burst away.

Still there is a point at the end still, and if the isolated point were put back, they would be one point. The end of a line might burst into any discrete multitude of points whatever, and they would all have been one point before the explosion. Points might fly off, in multitude and order like all the real irrational quantities from 0 to 1; and they might all have had that order of succession in the line and yet all have been at one point. Men will say this is self-contradictory. It is not so. If it be so prove it. The apparatus of the logic of relatives is a perfect means of demonstrating anything to be self-contradictory that really is so; but that apparatus not only absolutely refuses to pronounce this self-contradictory but it demonstrates, on the contrary, that it is not so. Of course, I cannot carry you through that demonstration. But it is no matter of *opinion*. It is a matter of plain demonstration. Even although I should have fallen into some subtle fallacy about the series of abnumeral multitudes, which I must admit possible in the sense in which it is possible that a man might add up a column of five figures in all its 120 different orders and always get the same result, and yet that result might be wrong, yet I say, although all my conclusions about abnumerals were brought to ruin, what I now say about continuity would stand firm. Namely, a continuum is a collection of so vast a multitude that in the whole universe of possibility there is not room for them to retain their distinct identities; but they become welded into one another. Thus the continuum is all that is possible, in whatever dimension it be continuous. But the general or universal of ordinary logic also comprises whatever of a certain description is possible. And thus the *continuum* is that which the Logic of Relatives shows the *true* universal to be. I say the *true* universal; for *no* realist is so foolish as to maintain that universal is a fiction.

Thus, the question of nominalism and realism has taken this shape: Are any continua real? Now Kant, like the faithful nominalist, that Dr.

Abbot[6] has shown him to be, says no. The continuity of Time and Space are merely subjective. There is nothing of the sort in the real thing-in-itself. We are therefore not quite to the end of the controversy yet; though I think very near it.[7]

What is reality? Perhaps there isn't any such thing at all. As I have repeatedly insisted, it is but a retroduction, a working hypothesis which we try, our one desperate forlorn hope of knowing anything. Again it may be, and it would seem very bold to hope for anything better, that the hypothesis of reality though it answers pretty well, does not perfectly correspond to what is. But if there is any reality, then, so far as there is any reality, what that reality consists in is this: that there is in the being of things something which corresponds to the process of reasoning, that the world *lives,* and **moves**, and **HAS ITS BEING**, in [a] logic of events. We all think of nature as syllogizing. Even the mechanical philosopher, who is as nominalistic as a scientific man can be, does that. The immutable mechanical law together with the laws of attraction and repulsion form the major premise, the instantaneous relative positions and velocities of all the particles whether it be "at the end of the sixth day of creation," — put back to an infinitely remote past if you like, though that does not lessen the miracle, — or whether it be at any other instant of time is the minor premise, the resulting accelerations form the conclusion. That is the very way the mechanical philosopher conceives the universe to operate.

I have not succeeded in persuading my contemporaries to believe that Nature also makes inductions and retroductions. They seem to think that her mind is in the infantile stage of the Aristotelian and Stoic philosophers. I point out that Evolution wherever it takes place is one vast succession of generalizations, by which matter is becoming subjected to ever higher and higher Laws; and I point to the infinite variety of nature as testifying to her Originality or power of Retroduction. But so far, the old ideas are too ingrained. Very few accept my message.

I will submit for your consideration the following metaphysical principle which is of the nature of a retroduction: Whatever unanalyzable element *sui generis seems* to be in nature, although it be not really where it seems to be, yet must *really* be in nature somewhere, since nothing else could have produced even the false appearance of such an element *sui generis.* For example, I may be in a dream at this moment, and while I think I am talking and you are trying to listen, I may all the time be snugly tucked up in bed and sound asleep. Yes, that may be; but still the very semblance of my feeling a reaction against my will and against my senses, suffices to prove that there really is, though not in this dream, yet somewhere, a reaction between the inward and outward worlds of my life.

In the same way, the very fact that there seems to be Thirdness in the world, even though it be not where it seems to be, proves that real Thirdness there must somewhere be. If the continuity of our inward and outward sense be not real, still it proves that continuity there really be, for how else should sense have the power of creating it?

Some people say that the sense of time is not in truth continuous, that we only imagine it to be so. If that be so, it strengthens my argument immensely. For how should the mind of every rustic and of every brute find it simpler to imagine time as continuous, in the very teeth of the appearances, — to connect it with by far the most difficult of all the conceptions which philosophers have ever thought out, — unless there were something in their real being which endowed such an idea with a simplicity which is certainly in the utmost contrast to its character in itself. But this something must be something in some sense *like* continuity. Now nothing can be like an element so peculiar except that very same element itself.

Of all the hypotheses which metaphysicians have ever broached, there is none which quarrels with the facts at every turn, so hopelessly, as does their favorite theory that continuity is a fiction. The only thing that makes them persist in it is their notion that continuity is self-contradictory, and *that* the logic of relatives when you study it in detail will explode forever. I *have* refuted it before you, in showing you how a multitude carried to its greatest possibility necessarily becomes continuous. Detailed study will furnish fuller and more satisfying refutations.

The extraordinary disposition of the human mind to think of everything under the difficult and almost incomprehensible form of a continuum can only be explained by supposing that each one of us is in his own real nature a continuum. I will not trouble you with any disquisition on the extreme form of realism which I myself entertain that every true universal, every continuum, is a living and conscious being, but I will content myself with saying that the only things valuable, even here in this life, are the continuities.

The *zero* collection is bare, abstract, germinal possibility. The continuum is concrete, developed possibility. The whole universe of true and real possibilities forms a continuum, upon which this Universe of Actual Existence is, by virtue of the essential Secondness of Existence, a discontinuous mark—like a line figure drawn on the area of the blackboard.

There is room in the world of possibility for any multitude of such universes of Existence. Even in this transitory life, the only value of all the arbitrary arrangements which mark actuality, whether they were introduced once for all "at the end of the sixth day of creation" or whether as I believe, they spring out on every hand and all the time, as the act of creation goes on, their only value is to be shaped into a continuous delineation under the creative hand, and at any rate their only use for us is to hold us down to learning one lesson at a time, so that we may make the generalizations of intellect and the more important generalizations of sentiment which make the value of this world. Whether when we pass away, we shall be lost at once in the boundless universe of possibilities, or whether we shall only pass into a world of which this one is the superficies and which itself is discontinuity of higher dimensions, we must wait and see. Only if we make no rational working hypothesis about it we shall neglect a department of logical activity proper for both intellect and sentiment.

Endeavors to effectuate continuity have been the great task of the Nineteenth Century. To bind together ideas, to bind together facts, to bind together knowledge, to bind together sentiment, to bind together the purposes of men, to bind together industry, to bind together great works, to bind together power, to bind together nations into great natural, living, and enduring systems was the business that lay before our great grandfathers to commence and which we now see just about to pass into a second and more advanced stage of achievement. Such a work will not be aided by regarding continuity as an unreal figment, it cannot but be helped by regarding it as the really possible eternal order of things to which we are trying to make our arbitrariness conform.

As to detached ideas, they are of value only so far as directly or indirectly, they can be made conducive to the development of systems of ideas. There is no such thing as an absolutely detached idea. It would be no idea at all. For an idea is itself a continuous system. But of ideas those are most suggestive which detached though they seem are in fact fragments broken from great systems.

Generalization, the spilling out of continuous systems, in thought, in sentiment, in deed, is the true end of life. Every educated man who is thrown into business ought to pursue an avocation, a side-study, although it may be well to choose one not too remote from the subject of his work. It must be suited to his personal taste and liking, but whatever it is, it ought, unless his reasoning power is decidedly feeble, to involve some acquaintance with modern mathematics, at least with modern geometry, including topology, and the theory of functions. For in those studies there is such a wealth of forms of conception as he will seek elsewhere in vain. In addition to that, these studies will inculcate a strong dislike and contempt for all sham-reasoning, for all thinking made easy, for all attempts to reason without clothing conceptions in diagrammatic forms.

FOUR

The First Rule of Logic

There are several methods of mathematical computation which present this peculiarity that if any mistakes are made, we have only to keep right on and they will correct themselves. Suppose for example that I wish to find the cube root of 2. I set down any three numbers one below another. I add the last two numbers of the column and to the tripled sum add in the number next above those two in the column and set down the result at the bottom of the column. I go on doing that the longer the better, and then the last number but one divided by the last will be one less than the cube root of two. [See table on following page.]

If you sit down to solve *ten* ordinary linear equations between ten unknown quantities, you will receive materials for a commentary upon the infallibility of mathematical processes. For you will almost infallibly get a wrong solution. I take it as a matter of course that you are not an expert professional computer. He will proceed according to a method which will correct his errors if he makes any.

This calls to mind one of the most wonderful features of reasoning, and one of the most important philosophemes in the doctrine of science, of which however you will search in vain for any mention in any book I can think of, namely, that reasoning tends to correct itself, and the more so the more wisely its plan is laid. Nay, it not only corrects its conclusions, it even corrects its premises. The theory of Aristotle is, that necessary conclusion is just equally as certain as its premises, while a probable conclusion somewhat less so. Hence, he was driven to his strange distinction between what is better known to Nature and what is better known to us. But were every probable inference less certain than

Error							0			10					1		
			1				0			0					4		
	18		2				1									20	60
15		54	3	5	15		1	4	3	-1	-1	-3		16		20	60
15	71	213	16	19	57		3	15	12	7	6	18		61		77	231
56	272	826	59	75	225		12	58	45	18	25	75		235		296	888
216	1047	3011	228	287	861		46	223	174	74	92	276		904		1139	3417
831	4028	3084	877	1105	3315		177	858	669	283	357	1071		3478		4382	9146
3197			3374	4251	12753		681		2574	1089	1372	4116		13381		16859	50567
12300			12981				2620			4190				51471			
1.259919			1.259918				1.259924			1.259905							

correct $\sqrt[3]{2} - 1 = .259921$

its premises, science, which piles inference upon inference, often quite deeply, would soon be in a bad way. Every astronomer, however, is familiar with the fact that the catalogue place of a fundamental star, which is the result of elaborate reasoning, is far more accurate than any of the observations from which it was deduced.

That Induction tends to correct itself, is obvious enough. When a man undertakes to construct a table of mortality upon the basis of the Census, he is engaged in an inductive inquiry. And lo, the very first thing that he will discover from the figures, if he did not know it before, is that those figures are very seriously vitiated by their falsity. The young find it to their advantage to be thought older than they are, and the old to be thought younger than they are. The number of young men who are just 21 is altogether in excess of those who are 20, although in all other cases the ages expressed in round numbers are in great excess. Now the operation of inferring a law in a succession of observed numbers, is, broadly speaking, inductive; and therefore we see that a properly conducted Inductive research corrects its own premises.

That the same thing may be true of a Deductive inquiry our arithmetical example has shown. *Theoretically*, I grant you, there is no possibility of error in necessary reasoning. But to speak thus "theoretically," is to use language in a Pickwickian sense. In practice and in fact, mathematics is not exempt from that liability to error that affects everything that man does. Strictly speaking, it is not certain that twice two is four. If on an average in every thousand figures obtained by addition by the average man there be one error, and if a thousand million men have each added 2 to 2 ten thousand times, there is still a possibility that they have all committed the same error of addition every time. If everything were fairly taken into account, I do not suppose that twice two is four is more certain than Edmund Gurney held the existence of veridical phantasms of the dying or dead to be. Deductive inquiry, then, has its errors; and it corrects them, too. But it is by no means so sure, or at least so swift to do this as is Inductive science. A celebrated error in the *Mécanique Céleste* concerning the amount of theoretical acceleration of the moon's mean motion deceived the whole world of astronomy for more than half a century. Errors of reasoning in the first book of Euclid's Elements, the logic of which book was for two thousand years subjected to more careful criticism than any other piece of reasoning without exception ever was or probably ever will be, only became known after the non-Euclidean geometry had been developed. The certainty of mathematical reasoning, however, lies in this, that once an error is suspected, the whole world is speedily in accord about it.

As for Retroductive Inquiries, or the Explanatory Sciences, such as Geology, Evolution, and the like, they always have been and always must be theatres of controversy. These controversies do get settled, after a time, in the minds of candid inquirers. Though it does not always happen that the protagonists themselves are able to assent to the justice of the decision. Nor is the general verdict always logical or just.

So it appears that this marvellous self-correcting property of Reason, which Hegel made so much of, belongs to every sort of science, although it appears as essential, intrinsic, and inevitable only in the highest type of reasoning which is induction. But the logic of relatives shows that the other types of reasoning, Deduction and Retroduction are not so thoroughly unlike Induction as they might be thought, and as Deduction, at least, always has been thought to be. Stuart Mill, alone among the older logicians in his analysis of the *Pons Asinorum* came very near to the view which the logic of relatives forces us to take. Namely in the logic of relatives, treated let us say, in order to fix our ideas, by means of those existential graphs of which I gave a slight sketch in the last lecture, begins a Deduction by writing down all the premises. These different premises are then brought into one field of assertion, that is are *colligated,* as Whewell would say, or joined into one copulative proposition. Thereupon, we proceed attentively to observe the graph. It is just as much an operation of *Observation* as is the observation of bees.[1] This observation leads us to make an *experiment* upon the Graph. Namely, we first, duplicate portions of it; and then we erase portions of it, that is, we put out of sight part of the assertion in order to see what the rest of it is. We observe the result of this experiment, and that is our deductive conclusion. Precisely those three things are all that enter into the Experiment of any Deduction, — Colligation, Iteration, Erasure. The rest of the process consists of Observing the result. It is not, however, in every Deduction that all the three possible elements of the Experiment take place. In particular, in ordinary syllogism the iteration may be said to be absent. And that is the reason that ordinary syllogism can be worked by a machine. There is but one conclusion of any consequence to be drawn by ordinary syllogism from given premises. Hence, it is that we fall into the habit of talking of *the* conclusion. But in the logic of relatives there are conclusions of different orders, depending upon how much iteration takes place. What is *the* conclusion deducible from the very simple first principles of number? It is ridiculous to speak of *the* conclusion. *The* conclusion is no less than the aggregate of all the theorems of higher arithmetic that have been discovered or that ever will be discovered. Now let us turn to Induction. This mode of reasoning also begins by a colligation. In fact it is precisely the colligation that gave induction its name, ἐπαγάγειν with Socrates, συναγωγή with Plato, ἐπαγωγή with Aristotle. It must by the rule of predesignation be a deliberate Experiment. In ordinary induction we proceed to observe something about each instance. Relative induction is illustrated by the process of making out the law of the arrangement of the scales of a pine-cone. It is necessary to mark a scale taken as an instance, and counting in certain directions to come back to the marked scale. This double observation of the same instance corresponds to Iteration in deduction. Finally, we erase the particular instances and leave the class or system sampled directly connected with the characters[,] relative or otherwise, which have been found in the sample of it.

We see, then, that Induction and Deduction are after all not so very unlike. It is true that in Induction we commonly make many experiments and in Deduction only one. Yet this is not always the case. The chemist contents himself with a single experiment to establish any qualitative fact. True, he does this because he knows that there is such a uniformity in the behavior of chemical bodies that another experiment would be a mere repetition of the first in every respect. But it is precisely such a knowledge of a uniformity that leads the mathematician to content himself with one experiment. The inexperienced student in mathematics will mentally perform a number of geometrical experiments which the veteran would regard as superfluous before he will permit himself to come to a general conclusion. For example, if the question is, how many rays can cut four rays fixed in space, the experienced mathematician will content himself with imagining that two of the fixed rays intersect and that the other two likewise intersect. He will see, then, that there is one ray through the two intersections and another along the intersection of the two planes of pairs of intersecting fixed rays, and will unhesitatingly declare thereupon that but two rays can cut four fixed rays, unless the fixed rays are so situated that an infinite multitude of rays will cut them all. But I dare say many of you would want to experiment with other arrangements of the four fixed rays, before making any confident pronouncement. A friend of mine who seemed to have difficulties in adding up her accounts was once counselled to add each column five times and adopt the mean of the different results. It is evident that when we run a column of figures down as well as up, as a check, or when we review a demonstration in order to look out for any possible flaw in the reasoning, we are acting precisely as when in an induction we enlarge our sample for the sake of the self-correcting effect of induction.

As for retroduction, it is itself an experiment. A retroductive research is an experimental research; and when we look upon Induction and Deduction from the point of view of Experiment and Observation, we are merely tracing in those types of reasoning their affinity to Retroduction. It begins always with colligation, of course, of a variety of separately observed facts about the subject of the hypothesis. How remarkable it is, by the way, that the entire army of logicians from Zeno to Whateley should have left it to this mineralogist to point out Colligation as [a] generally essential step in reasoning.[2] To return to Retroduction, then, it begins with Colligation. Something corresponding to Iteration may or may not take place. And then comes an Observation. Not, however, an External observation of the objects as in Induction, nor yet an Observation made upon the parts of a Diagram, as in Deduction; but for all that just as truly an observation. For what is observation? What is experience? It is the enforced element in the history of our lives. It is that which we are constrained to be conscious of by an occult force residing in an object which we contemplate. The act of observation is the deliberate yielding of ourselves to that *force majeure,* — an early surrender at discretion, due to our foreseeing that we must whatever we do be borne down by that power, at last. Now the surrender which we make in Retroduction, is a surrender to the Insistence of an Idea. The hypothesis, as The Frenchman says, *c'est plus fort que moi.* It is irresistible; it is imperative. We must throw open our galis and admit it, at any rate for the time being.[3]

Thus it is that inquiry of every type, fully carried out, has the vital power of self-correction and of growth. This is a property so deeply saturating its inmost nature that it may truly be said that there is but one thing needful for learning the truth, and that is a hearty and active desire to learn what is true. If you really want to learn the truth, you will, by however devious a path, be surely led into the way of truth, at last. No matter how erroneous your ideas of the method may be at first, you will be forced at length to correct them so long as your activity is moved by that sincere desire. Nay, no matter if you only half desire it, at first, that desire would at length conquer all others could experience continue long enough. But the more voraciously truth is desired at the outset, the shorter by centuries will the road to it be.

In order to demonstrate that this is so, it is necessary to note what is essentially involved in The Will to Learn. The first thing that the Will to Learn supposes is a dissatisfaction with one's present state of opinion. There lies the secret of why it is that our American Universities are so miserably insignificant. What have they done for the advance of civilization? What is the great idea or where is [a] single great man who can truly be said to be the product of an American University? The English universities, rotting with sloth as they always have, have nevertheless in the past given birth to Locke and to Newton, and in our time to Cayley, Sylvester and Clifford. The German universities have been the light of the whole world. The medieval University of Bologna gave Europe its system of law. The University of Paris, and that despised Scholasticism took Abelard and made him into Descartes. The reason was that they were institutions of learning while ours are institutions for teaching. In order that a man's whole heart may be in teaching he must be thoroughly imbued with the vital importance and absolute truth of what he has to teach; while in order that he may have any measure of success in learning he must be penetrated with a sense of the unsatisfactoriness of his present condition of knowledge. The two attitudes are almost irreconcilable. But just as it is not the self-righteous man who brings multitudes to a sense of sin, but the man who is most deeply conscious that he is himself a sinner, and it is only by a sense of sin that men can escape its thraldom; so it is not the man who thinks he knows it all, that can bring other men to feel their need of learning, and it is only a deep sense that one is miserably ignorant that can spur one on in the toilsome path of learning. That is why, to my very humble apprehension, it cannot but seem that those admirable pedagogical methods for which the American teacher is distinguished are of little more consequence than the cut of his coat, that they surely are as nothing compared with that fever for learning that must consume the soul of the man who is to infect others with the same apparent malady. Let me say that of the present condition of Harvard I really know nothing at all except that I know the leaders of the Department of philosophy to be all true scholars, particularly marked by eagerness to learn and freedom from dogmatism. And in every age, it can only be the philosophy of that age, such as it may be, which can animate the special sciences to any work that shall really carry forward the human mind to some new and valuable truth. Because the valuable truth is not the detached one, but the one that goes toward enlarging the system of what is already known.

The Inductive Method springs directly out of dissatisfaction with existing knowledge. The great rule of predesignation which must guide it is as much as to say that an induction to be valid must be prompted by a definite doubt or at least an interrogation; and what is such an interrogation but 1st, a sense that we do not know something, 2nd, a desire to know it, and 3rd, an effort, — implying a willingness to labor, — for the sake of seeing how the truth may really be. If that interrogation inspires you, you will be sure to examine the instances; while if it does not, you will pass them by without attention.[4]

I repeat that I know nothing about the Harvard of today but one of the things which I hope to learn during my stay in *Cambridge* is the answer to this question, whether the Commonwealth of Massachusetts has set up this University to the end that such young men as can come here may receive a fine education and may thus be able to earn handsome incomes, and have a canvas-back and a bottle of Clos de Vougeot for dinner, whether this is what she is driving at, — or whether it is, that, knowing that all America looks largely to Sons of Massachusetts for the solutions of the most urgent problems of each generation, she hopes that in this place something may be studied out which shall be of service in the solutions of those problems. In short, I hope to find out whether Harvard is an educational establishment or whether it is an institution for learning what is not yet thoroughly known. Whether it is for the benefit of the individual students or whether it is for the good of the country and for the speedier elevation of man onto that rational animal of [which] he is the embryonic form.[5]

There is one thing that I am sure a Harvard education cannot fail to do, because it did that much even in my time, and for a very insouciant student, I mean that it cannot fail to disabuse the student of the popular notion that modern science is so very great a thing as to be commensurate with Nature and indeed to constitute of itself some account of the universe, and to show him that it is yet, what it appeared to Isaac Newton to be, a child's collection of pebbles gathered upon the beach, — the vast ocean of Being lying there unsounded.

It is not merely that in all our gropings we bump up against problems which we cannot imagine how to attack, why space should have but three dimensions, if it really has but three, why the Listing numbers which define its shape should all equal one, if they really do, or why some of them should be zero, as Listing himself and many geometers think they are, if that be the truth, of why forces should determine the second derivative of the space rather than the third or fourth, of why matter should consist of about seventy distinct kinds, and all those of each kind apparently exactly alike, and these different kinds having masses nearly in arithmetical progression and yet not exactly so, of why atoms should attract one another at a distance in peculiar ways, if they really do, or if not what produced such vortices, and what gave the vortices such peculiar laws of attraction, of how or by what kind of influence matter came to be sifted out, so that the different kinds occur in considerable aggregations, of why certain motions of the atoms of certain kinds of protoplasm are accompanied by sensation, and so on through the whole list. These things do indeed show us how superficial our science still is; but its littleness is made even more manifest when we consider within how narrow a range all our inquiries have hitherto lain. The instincts connected with the need of nutrition have furnished all animals with some virtual knowledge of space and of force, and made them applied physicists. The instincts connected with sexual reproduction have furnished all animals at all like ourselves with some virtual comprehension of the minds of other animals of their kind, so that they are applied psychists. Now not only our accomplished science, but even our scientific questions have been pretty exclusively limited to the development of those two branches of natural knowledge. There may for aught we know be a thousand other kinds of relationship which have as much to do with connecting phenomena and leading from one to another, as dynamical and social relationships have. Astrology, magic, ghosts, prophecies, serve as suggestions of what such relationships might be.

Not only is our knowledge thus limited in scope, but it is even more important that we should thoroughly realize that the very best of what we, humanly speaking, know [we know] only in an uncertain and inexact way.[6] Nobody would dream of contending that because the sun has risen and set every day so far, that afforded any reason at all for supposing that it would go on doing so to all eternity. But when I say that there is not the very slightest reason for thinking that no material atoms ever go out of existence or come into existence, there I fail to carry the average man with me; and I suppose the reason is, that he dimly conceives that there is some reason other than the pure and simple induction for holding matter to be ingenerable and indestructible. For it is plain that if it be a mere question of our weighings or other experiences, all that appears is that not more than one atom in million or ten million becomes annihilated before the deficiency of mass is pretty certain to be balanced by another atom's being created. Now when we are speaking of atoms, a million or ten million is an excessively minute quantity. So that as far as purely inductive evidence is concerned we are very very far from being entitled to think that matter is absolutely permanent. If you put the question to a physicist his reply will probably be, as it certainly ought to be, that physicists only deal with such phenomena as they can either directly or indirectly observe, or are likely to become able to observe until there is some great revolution in science, and to that he will very likely add that any limitation upon the permanence of matter would be a purely gratuitous hypothesis without anything whatever to support it. Now this last part of the physicist's reply is, in regard to the order of considerations which he has in mind, excellent good sense. But from an absolute point of view, I think it leaves something out of account. Do you believe that the fortune of the Rothschilds will endure forever? Certainly not; because although they may be safe enough as far as the ordinary causes go which engulph fortunes, yet there is always a chance of some revolution or catastrophe which may destroy all property. And no matter how little that chance may be, as far as this decade or this generation goes, yet in limitless decades and generations, it is pretty sure that the pitcher will get broken, at last. There is no danger however slight which in an indefinite multitude of occasions does not come as near to absolute certainty as probability can come. The existence of the human race, we may be as good as sure, will come to an end at last. For not to speak of the gradual operation of causes of which we know, the action of the tides, the resisting medium, the dissipation of energy, there is all the time a certain danger that the earth may be struck by a meteor or wandering star so large as to ruin it, or by some poisonous gas. That a purely gratuitous hypothesis should turn out to be true is, indeed, something so exceedingly improbable that we cannot be appreciably wrong in calling it zero. Still, the chance that out of an infinite multitude of gratuitous hypotheses an infinitesimal proportion, which may itself be an infinite multitude should turn out to be true, is zero multiplied by infinity, which is absolutely indeterminate. That is to say we simply know nothing whatever about it. Now that any single atom should be annihilated is a gratuitous hypothesis. But there are, we may suppose, an infinite multitude of atoms, and a similar hypothesis may be made for each. And thus we return to my original statement that as to whether any finite number or even an infinite number of atoms are annihilated *per* year, that is something of which we are simply in a state of blank ignorance, unless we have found out some method of reasoning altogether superior to induction. If, therefore, we should detect any general phenomenon of nature which could very well be explained, not by supposing any definite breach of the laws of nature, for that would be no explanation at all, but by supposing that a continual breach of all the laws of nature, every day and every second, was itself one of the laws or habitudes of nature, there would be no power in induction to offer the slightest logical objection to that theory. But as long as we [are] aware of no such general phenomena tending to show such continual inexactitude in law, then we must remain absolutely without any rational opinion upon the matter *pro* or *con!*

There are various [ways] in which the natural cocksuredness and conceit of man struggles to escape such confession of total ignorance. But they seem to be all quite futile. One of the commonest and at the same time the silliest is the argument [that] God would for this or that excellent reason never act in such an irregular manner. I think all the men who talk like that must be near-sighted. For to suppose that any man who could see the moving clouds and survey a wide expanse of landscape and note its wonderful complexity, and consider how unimaginably small it all was in comparison to the whole face of the globe, not to speak of the millions of orbs in space, and who would not presume to predict what move Morphy or Steinitz might make in so simple a thing as a game of chess, should undertake to say what God would do, would seem to impeach his sanity. But if instead of its being a God, after whose image we are made, and whom we can, therefore, begin to understand, it were some metaphysical principle of Being, even more incomprehensible, whose action the man pretended to compute, that would seem to be a pitch of absurdity one degree higher yet.[7]

People talk of the hypothesis where there is a *vera causa*. But in such cases the inference is not hypothetic but inductive. A *vera causa* is a state of things known to be present and known partially at least to explain the phenomena, but not known to explain them with quantitative precision. Thus, when seeing ordinary bodies round us accelerated toward the earth's centre and seeing also the moon, which both in its *albedo* and its [volcanic] appearance altogether resembles stone, to be likewise accelerated toward the earth, and when finding these two accelerations are in the inverse duplicate ratios of their distances from that centre, we conclude that their nature, whatever it may be, is the same, we are inferring an analogy, which is a type of inference having all the strength of induction and more, besides. For the sake of simplicity, I have said nothing about it in these lectures; but I am here forced to make that remark. Moreover, when we consider that all that we infer about the gravitation of the Moon is a continuity between the terrestrial and lunar phenomena, a continuity which is found throughout physics, and when we add to that the analogies of electrical and magnetical attractions, both of which vary inversely as the square of the distance, we plainly recognize here one of the strongest arguments of which science affords any example. Newton was entirely in the right when he said, *Hypotheses non fingo*. It is they who have criticized the dictum whose logic is at fault. They are attributing an obscure psychological signification to *force*, or *vis insita*, which in physics only connotes a regularity among accelerations. Thus inferences concerning *verae causae* are inductions not retroductions, and of course have only such uncertainty and inexactitude as belong to induction.

When I say that a retroductive inference is not a matter for belief at all, I encounter the difficulty that there are certain inferences which scientifically considered are undoubtedly hypotheses and yet which practically are perfectly certain. Such for instance is the inference that Napoleon Bonaparte really lived at about the beginning of this century, a hypothesis which we adopt for the purpose of explaining the concordant testimony of a hundred memoirs, the public records of history, tradition, and numberless monuments and relics. It would surely be downright insanity to entertain a doubt about Napoleon's existence. A still better example is that of the translations of the cuneiform inscriptions which began in mere guesses, in which their authors could have had no real confidence. Yet by piling new conjectures upon former conjectures apparently verified, this science has gone on to produce under our very eyes a result so bound together by the agreement of the readings with one another, with other history, and with known facts of linguistics, that we are unwilling any longer to apply the word *theory* to it. You will ask me how I can reconcile such facts as these with my dictum that hypothesis is not a matter for belief. In order to answer this question I must first examine such inferences in their scientific aspect and afterward in their practical aspect. The only end of science, as such, is to learn the lesson that the universe has to teach it. In Induction it simply surrenders itself to the force of facts. But it finds, at once, — I am partially inverting the historical order, in order to state the process in its logical order, — it finds I say that this is not enough. It is driven in desperation to call upon its inward sympathy with nature, its instinct for aid, just as we find Galileo at the dawn of modern science making his appeal to *il lume naturale*. But insofar as it does this, the solid ground of fact fails it. It feels from that moment that its position is only provisional. It must then find confirmations or else shift its footing. Even if it does find confirmations, they are only partial. It still is not standing upon the bedrock of fact. It is walking upon a bog, and can only say, this ground seems to hold for the present. Here I will stay till it begins to give way. Moreover, in all its progress, science vaguely feels that it is only learning a lesson. The value of *Facts to it*, lies only in this, that they belong to Nature; and Nature is something great, and beautiful, and sacred, and eternal, and real, — the object of its worship and its aspiration. It therein takes an entirely different attitude toward facts from that which Practice takes. For Practice facts are the arbitrary forces with which it has to reckon and to wrestle. Science when it comes to understand itself regards facts as merely the vehicle of eternal truth, while for Practice they remain the obstacles which it has to turn, the enemy of which it is determined to get the better. Science feeling that there is an arbitrary element in its theories, still continues its studies confident that so it will gradually become more and more purified from the dross of subjectivity; but practice requires something to go upon, and it will be no consolation to it to know that it is on the path to objective truth, — the actual truth it must have, or when it cannot attain certainty must at least have high probability, that is must know that though a few of its ventures may fail the bulk of them will succeed. Hence the hypothesis which answers the purpose of theory may be perfectly worthless for Art. After a while, as Science progresses, it comes upon more solid ground. It is now entitled to reflect, this ground has held a long time without showing signs of yielding. I may hope that it will continue to hold for a great while longer. This reflection, however, is quite aside from the purpose of science. It does not modify its procedure in the least degree. It is extra-scientific. For Practice, however, it is vitally important, quite altering the situation. As practice apprehends it, the conclusion no longer rests upon mere retroduction, it is inductively supported. For a large sample has now been drawn from the entire collection of occasions in which the theory comes into comparison with fact, and an overwhelming proportion, in fact all the cases that have presented themselves, have been found to bear out the theory. And so, says Practice, I can safely presume that so it will be with the great bulk of the cases in which I shall go upon the theory, especially as they will closely resemble those which have been well tried. In other words there is now reason to believe in the theory, for belief is the willingness to risk a great deal upon a proposition. But this belief is no concern of science which has nothing at stake on any temporal venture, but is in pursuit of eternal verities, not semblances to truth, and looks upon this pursuit, not as the work of one man's life, but as that of generation after generation, indefinitely. Thus those retroductive inferences which at length acquire such high

degrees of certainty, so far as they are so probable are not pure retroductions and do not belong to science, as such, while so far as they are
scientific and are pure retroduction have no true probability and are
not matters for belief. We call them in science established truths, that
is, they are propositions into which the economy of endeavor prescribes
that for the time being further inquiry shall cease.[8]

An eminent religious teacher, Dr. Carus, seems to think that I do
not regard with sufficient horror the doctrine that the conception of
truth is ambiguous. For in an article in which he holds up several other
of my moral failings to public reprobation, he caps the climax by saying
that I admire Duns Scotus who was a man who held that a proposition
might be false in philosophy yet true in religion, and names the volumes
and pages in the works of Duns Scotus of two passages, which the reader
infers would enunciate that position. One of the pages is substantially
blank and the other contains nothing remotely bearing on the subject.
Duns Scotus may possibly have said something of the kind; but if he did
I cannot imagine where it can be hidden away. This however I do know,
that that doctrine was the distinguishing tenet of the followers of Averrhoes. Now I know of but one place in all my reading of Duns in which
he speaks unkindly of any opponent, and that one is where he alludes
to Averrhoes as "Iste damnatus Averrhoes." This hardly looks as if he
followed him in his main position. But whether the word truth has two
meanings or not, I certainly do think that *holding for true* is of two kinds;
the one is that practical holding for true which alone is entitled to the
name of Belief, while the other is that acceptance of a proposition which
in the intention of pure science remains always provisional. To adhere
to a proposition in an absolutely definitive manner, supposing that by
this is merely meant that the believer has personally wedded his fate to
it, is something which in practical concerns, say for instance in matters
of right and wrong, we sometimes cannot and ought not to avoid; but
to do so in science amounts simply to not wishing to learn: Now he who
does not wish to learn cuts himself off from science altogether.

Upon this first, and in one sense this sole, rule of reason, that in
order to learn you must desire to learn and in so desiring not be satisfied
with what you already incline to think, there follows one corollary which
itself deserves to be inscribed upon every wall of the city of philosophy.[9]

Do not block the way of inquiry.

Although it is better to be methodical in our investigations, and to
consider the Economics of Research,[10] yet there is no positive sin against
logic in *trying* any theory which may come into our heads, so long as it

is adopted in such a sense as to permit the investigation to go on unimpeded and undiscouraged. On the other hand, to set up a philosophy which barricades the road of further advance toward the truth is the one unpardonable offence in reasoning, as it is also the one to which metaphysicians have in all ages shown themselves the most addicted.

Let me call your attention to four familiar shapes in which this venomous error assails our knowledge:

The first is the shape of absolute assertion. That we can be sure of nothing in science is an ancient truth. The Academy taught it. Yet science has been infested with over-confident assertion, especially on the part of the third rate and fourth rate men, who have been more concerned with teaching than with learning, at all times. No doubt some of the geometries still teach as a self-evident truth the proposition that if two straight lines in one plane meet a third straight line so as to make the sum of the internal angles on one side less than two right angles those two lines will meet on that side if sufficiently prolonged. Euclid, [whose] logic was more careful, only reckoned this proposition as a *Postulate*, or arbitrary Hypothesis. Yet even he places among his axioms the propositions that a part is less than its whole, and falls into several conflicts with our most modern geometry in consequence. But why need we stop to consider cases where some subtlety of thought is required to see that the assertion is not warranted when every book which applies philosophy to the conduct of life lays down as positive certainty propositions which it is quite as easy to doubt as to believe.

The second bar which philosophers often set up across the roadway of inquiry lies in maintaining that this, that, and the other never can be known. When Auguste Comte was pressed to specify any matter of positive fact to the knowledge of which no man could by any possibility attain, he instanced the knowledge of the chemical composition of the fixed stars; and you may see his answer set down in the *Philosophie positive*. But the ink was scarcely dry upon the printed page before the spectroscope was discovered and that which he had deemed absolutely unknowable was well on the way of getting ascertained. It is easy enough to mention a question the answer to which is not known to me today. But to aver that that answer will not be known tomorrow is somewhat risky; for oftentimes it is precisely the least expected truth which is turned up under the ploughshare of research. And when it comes to positive assertion that the truth never will be found out, that, in the light of the history of our time, seems to me more hazardous than the venture of Andree.

The third philosophical stratagem for cutting off inquiry consists in maintaining that this, that, or the other element of science is basic, ultimate, independent of aught else, and utterly inexplicable, — not so much from any defect in our knowing as because there is nothing beneath it to know. The only type of reasoning by which such conclusion could possibly be reached is *retroduction*. Now nothing justifies a retroductive inference except its affording [an] explanation of the facts. It is, however, no explanation at all of a fact to pronounce it *inexplicable*. That therefore is a conclusion which no reasoning can ever justify or excuse.

The last philosophical obstacle to the advance of knowledge which I intend to mention is the holding that this or that law or truth has found its last and perfect formulation; — and especially that the ordinary and usual course of nature never can be broken through. "Stones do not fall from heaven" said Laplace, although they had been falling upon inhabited ground every day from the earliest times. But there is no kind of inference which can lend the slightest probability to any such absolute denial of an unusual phenomenon.

FIVE

Training in Reasoning

Since the vogue in this country of the Herbartian pedagogy, which I hope is far weaker where it touches such sciences as I happen to be acquainted with than anywhere else, — though it seems strange that of a philosophy not altogether distinguished for sobriety in its theoretical departments this practical part should alone remain in high favor, — the old ideas which used to cluster about the phrase *Liberal Education* have become scattered. One of those ideas was that the matter of instruction in the common education was of less concern than the training of men's powers. The pedagogists of today sneer at this as an antiquated and crude conception. But for my part I continue to believe that the welfare of the commonwealth depends far less on the assent of all the citizens to any definite propositions, — such, we will say, as the doctrine of the independence of the executive, legislative, and judiciary functions, which, after all are easily made handles for bosses, than it does in the power of recognizing the sort of thought and the sort of methods in which it will be well for the government and public opinion to put their trust. In the last analysis it comes to this, that the very focus and centre of common education should be placed in the art of thinking, *ad omnium methodorum principia viam habens* [which contains a path to the principles of all methods]. I do not know why a man should not devote himself to the training of his reasoning powers with as much assiduity as to corporal athletics.

There [are] a good many books that bear upon the subject. Some of the *Logics* pay attention to this matter, such as *L'Art de Penser* of the Port Royalists, Beneke's *Logik,* and *Dresslor's* two treatises. Then there are irregular logical essays, the *Regles de l'esprit* of Descartes and the first book of the *Novum Organum.* There are special works devoted to the consideration of the matter. The *Medicina Mentis* promises what it fails to perform. But Locke's *Conduct of the Understanding,* Watts's *Improvement of the Mind,* "a work in the highest degree useful and pleasing" remarked Johnson, Senebier's *Art d'Observer,* and many others might be mentioned. In addition there are various books of exercises, more or less trivial, more or less calculated to inculcate machine made discussions, the ready logic of the English leader-writer, a vicious habit fatal to all living and healthy reasoning. I will not say, however, that a moderate use of such books is altogether useless. I would not absolutely condemn even Jevons's *Studies in Deductive Logic* although the author shows in his own person how very unadroit a reasoner a man of real ability may be.

But neither reading books nor working exercises, — whether they be trivial or serious, — will suffice to develop the reasoning powers. An analytical method of procedure is requisite which shall perfect one by one our performance of the different mental operations that enter into the business of inquiry. Now the mental operations concerned in reasoning are three. The first is Observation; the second is Experimentation; and the third is Habituation.

Observation consists of two parts which though theoretically they have much in common yet practically are of almost contrary natures. The first is a sort of subconscious induction, by which upon repeatedly reviewing an object of perception a certain element of it acquires great associational potency, — that is, has a magnified tendency to call up other ideas. For example, I cast my eyes let us say upon an impressionist marine picture, one of those things in which the wet pastels are affixed in blotches nearly as large as the end of your little finger. It has a very disagreeable look and seems very meaningless. But as I gaze upon it I detect myself sniffing the salt-air and holding up my cheek to the sea breeze. That subconscious element of observation is I am strongly inclined to think the very most important of all the constituents of practical reasoning. The other part of observation consists in moulding in the upper consciousness a more or less skeletonized idea until it is felt to respond to [the] object of observation. This last element is quite indispensable if one is trying to form a theory of the object in hand, or even to describe it in words; but it goes a long way toward breaking down, denying, and pooh-poohing away, all the fineness of the subconscious observation. It is, therefore, a great art to be able to suppress it and put it into its proper place in cases where it attempts impertinent intermeddling. Do not allow yourself to be imposed upon by the egotism and conceit of the upper consciousness.

Observation may also be divided into three nearly independent genera according to the different natures of the elements observed. Namely, it may be directed to the qualities of objects or to experiential facts of relation, or to the relations between the parts of an image one's own phantasy has created. These are all observations, composed of the two elements I have mentioned. Nevertheless, they are so far different that in training one kind you do not necessarily strengthen either of the others in any sensible measure. It consequently becomes necessary to train each of these three modes of observation separately.

The qualities which we observe may, in the first place, be sensible qualities, colors, sounds, sizes, shapes, etc. Or, in the second place, they may be secondary, or emotional, qualities, such as the esthetic qualities. A training in discrimination of sensible qualities will affect the power of discriminating emotional qualities in no inconsiderable measure, and *vice versa*. Thirdly, there is observational discrimination of mental states, which in my experience has been found associated with sense-discrimination much more frequently than I should have anticipated that it would be.

All these powers are most important in reasoning; and I need hardly say that just as a person who has not frequented a gymnasium or its equivalent can in a single month amazingly bring up the strength of a given set of muscles by means of systematic exercise, so a person whose powers of observational discrimination have been neglected can by analogous exercises attain results quite as surprising.

I am sure that I need not tell you how much education for the power of discrimination there is in practice with a photometer or color-box. But, perhaps, you may be surprised that I should put such stress upon such exercises as contributing to the cultivation of the reasoning powers. I have certainly known men great in their powers of observational discrimination who nevertheless showed lamentable defects as reasoners. But I never knew a man whose sagacity as a reasoner compelled my admiration without finding in him a considerably cultivated discrimination. Perhaps the same ardent desire to learn which causes a man to become a good reasoner also causes him to cultivate his senses. I have known an ardent votary to truth to place himself under the tutelage of the *sommelier* of some famous cellars, until he could not only tell at once what class of Bordeaux he was tasting, but also the precise vintage within certain limits of time. He held, himself, that there was something of a rational education in it. Nor did he become a mere Sybarite, but continued with the great poet of Nature to prefer

> A *cru* that's not too high and good
> For human nature's daily food.

It needed a great poet to make a rhyme like that.[1]

I will not say that every wine-taster is a man of sense; but I will say that a man who like an acquaintance of mine, can tell by smelling the *percentage* of real attar in attar of roses with a probable error of 2 *per cent* will probably be a man whose acquaintance is worth making.

If it was superfluous for me to speak of the intellectual benefit to be derived from the cultivation of sensuous discrimination, it is ten times more so to speak of training in esthetic discrimination.

Of psychical discrimination there ought to be still less to be said, for its practical utility is too obvious. When I read Theophrastus, — whose great strength, by the way, lay in his power of discrimination whether he was writing upon logic, or psychology, or botany, or what, — or when I read *La Bruyère,* and other French delineators of character down to Maupassant, or when I read George Eliot (I will except Lavater), I must confess I am not half so much struck with the extraordinary fineness of their discriminations as I am with the comparative obviousness of the remarks they have thought worthy of registry. I have met with incomparably subtler observers. But then it is to be remembered that the first and most genuine element of observation, — the subconscious observation, — was not the principal task of those literary artists. What they mainly had to do was to translate observations into words, — and to draw character sketches which the not too fine reader would recognize as agreeing with his own subconscious impressions.

The art of looking at a man and reading what lies in his heart depends I am sure on no extraordinary faculty; but it can be carried to such perfection that its results seem miraculous. Lavater's *Essais de physionomie* are well worth careful study and comparison with the book of nature. One of the themes to which he constantly recurs is that the higher consciousness must not be allowed to obtrude itself between the observer and his object. For that reason comparatively little weight is to be allowed to his propositions in physiognomy. When he tells you that he judges by the shape of a man's nose, that you must remember, is only his theory of a process which in his own mind takes place behind a curtain which he is never able to lift. His personal judgments were said to be often very wonderful. Such a man as Goethe considered them to be so, I believe. But he tells us that his greatest successes have been impressions, unstudied, instantaneous, irresistible. On the other hand, he openly confesses to having committed the most ridiculous blunders, which he details in the frankest candour. For example, he tells us how on one occasion when, expecting to receive a portrait of the poet Herder, that which he actually received was a sketch of a ferocious and stupid murderer, before reading the letter of explanation, he went into rhapsodies over the sublime and noble inclinations which he fancied he detected in the head. Such errors are very instructive. When you desire to increase the sensitiveness of a balance, you raise the centre of gravity of the beam. Fine balances are provided with a weight on a vertical screw over the fulcrum for this purpose. In your extreme effort after sensitiveness, you screw the centre of gravity up till it is higher than the fulcrum; and then what happens is that [the] next wrong weight you try will upset your balance as the phrase is and the error of weighing may go to almost any length. It is just so with the fine observer when he screws himself up too fine. He is thrown off his balance, — and then the great wine taster will mistake sherry for madeira, the connoisseur of pictures will mistake Rembrandt for a Franz Hals, or the physiognomist will mistake a murderer for a moralist. The moral of it is that you must not judge of delicate discriminations by their occasional gross errors but by the proportion of their eminent successes.

This applies for example to *clair-voyance*. If you choose to set it down as a humbug without examination, I for one shall applaud your good sense. For life is altogether too short to permit any person with business to do to investigate every monstrous story that is told him. But once you have made up your mind to enter upon the investigation, you cannot logically come to a negative conclusion because you discover your *clairvoyante* to be a liar. You knew from the first she was in an abnormal condition of nerves; and everybody whose nerves are not in perfect adjustment does lie. So that was what you had to expect from the outset.[2]

So far we have considered Discrimination of characters. Now we come to Observation proper, that is to say, observation of the relations of real objects and parts of objects external to us. Of all the varieties of this observation proper it seems to me that the easiest must be that of objects of Natural History using the term in so wide a sense as to include for example the examination of banknotes, — in short, the observation of *things*. For you generally have in the first place an assortment of specimens. Then you can handle a thing, turn it over, view it from different sides, and even avail yourself of instrumental aids to observation. Yet everybody knows that even this kind of observation requires professional training. To observe an event, especially one which is not repeated, is necessarily far more difficult. The whole art of the prestigiator [prestidigitator?] depends on that difficulty. In the life of Robert Houdin, there is an account of the exercizes which he and his son went through in learning the Second Sight Trick. It is a good hint. Next, we may consider observations of character which is an altogether different thing, by the way, from discrimination between qualities of character. One of the keenest observers I ever knew had this habit. He saw that I had an inkling of it; and so he took me into his confidence, thinking that would bind me not to betray him. Whenever he went into a large gathering of able men, which frequently happened, he would before hand carefully select one topic upon which to converse with a number of men separately. As soon as he had learned the sentiments of any man on that subject, you might see him take out his tablets in a semidistracted manner, make a single mark and put them up again. When he got home, he would not lay his head on his pillow until all those men's relative sentiments had been assiduously posted in a ledger. By relative sentiments, I mean, upon any given man's page of the ledger would be written, "Tendency to think so and so somewhat above the average." The result of this was that in the course of a few years he could tell accurately how any important man would feel about any given matter.

I would not advise a man to devote much time to observations of oneself. The great [thing] is to become emancipated from oneself. [Γνῶθι] σεαυτόν [know thyself], make your own acquaintance, does not mean Introspect your soul. It means See yourself as others would see you if they were intimate enough with you. Introspection[,] I mean a certain kind of fascinated introspection[,] on the contrary, is looking at yourself as nobody else will ever look at you, from a narrow, detached, and illusory point of view. Of course, a man must search his heart somewhat. It is highly needful. Only don't make a pursuit of it.

There remains still another kind of power of observation which ought to be trained; and that is the power of observing the objects of our own creative fancy. In such objects, there are three different elements to which observation may be particularly directed. The first is the sensuous element, the second is the relations between different parts of the object, whether as coordinate parts or as governing one another, and the third is the system, the form, and the idea of the whole. In regard to the vividness of sensuous imagination the differences between different persons [are] astonishing. Some men, myself among the number, are almost entirely destitute of this power. I can match colors from memory with a degree of precision quite beyond the average lady's, unless she be a Parisian. And yet when I look at a red thing, and then shut my eyes, I cannot *see* anything in the least like the vision. You will here and there meet with a psychological writer who utterly denies that there is any power of reproducing a peripheral sensation; and I thought so too, until conversation with accurate observers convinced me that it was merely an idiosyncrasy of my own. You will see an artist put himself to some trouble to get a dark place by the side of his picture where he can project the image he is copying without its colors being modified by the actual ones upon which they are superimposed.[3] I am now satisfied, after a good deal of scepticism that the power of observing the sensuous element of the image is conducive to good reasoning on the whole.[4] Among exercises for strengthening the power of accurate dealing with the relations of parts of an image may be mentioned chess-playing and the solution of the mathematical problems in The Educational Times. The English, who have proved themselves to be in some respects the best educated people in Europe, notwithstanding their artistic insensibility, pay much more attention than any others to practice with mathematical puzzles; and this is a practice that ought to be imitated.

The highest kind of observation is the observation of systems, forms, and ideas. No other exercise I know of is half so good for strengthening this faculty as the study of pure mathematical theories, and practice in making ourselves such theories. I would not advise any man to go without reading Hegel's *Phänomenologie des Geistes;* but in my opinion as a discipline for the mind it is almost immeasurably inferior to the study of mathematics.

So much for the first of the three psychological operations involved in reasoning. The second is experimentation. In observation, the most essential condition is passivity, the inhibition of the natural tendency to meddle, to conjecturally emend, the dicta of Nature. In experimentation, on the contrary, the most essential ingredient is energy, perseverance, in short, strong work of the will, both external and internal. In the dialect of the medieval writers on occult science, *laborare* means to make experiments. We now, for instance, perform abstraction, that is, we seize upon transient elements of thought and pin them down as subjects of thought. Accordingly, it is a fact beyond all doubt, that whatever strengthens the will power, strengthens the powers of reasoning. I used to find it a salutary practice to lift a thousand pounds dead weight three times a week.[5] Do that and you will not dread this or that line of thinking as too difficult and mathematical.

A certain amount of contrivance is also called for in experimentation. It is nothing extraordinary. The chief qualities that this contrivance requires are, first, an agility of creative imagination which is a will-power that nothing can fatigue but is always begging for a harder task, second, a *flair* which abridges the work by enabling the man to pick out the suggestions probably best worth study, and third perseverance, in tracing out different suggestions and tracing them out into sufficient detail to make sure of their advantages and disadvantages. The solution of chess problems makes a tolerably good practice in contrivance.

Detached experiments, like detached thoughts or detached soldiers, are of little account. It is when they are massed into squads, and companies, and battalions, and regiments, and brigades, and divisions, and armies that they become strong and stronger. There are plenty of experiments that are easy to make and which in systematized masses are potent instruments of learning. An active mind ought always to be carrying on some systematic experimentation.

An indispensable condition of systematization of any kind is *systematic records*. Everything worth notice is worth recording; and those records should be so made that they can readily be arranged, and particularly so that [they] can be *rearranged*. I recommend slips of stiff smooth paper of this exact size. By ordering 20000 at a time, you get them cheap; and 20000 will last an industrious student a year. For you won't average more than 60 a day and there will be, one way and another a month of idleness in the year. Upon these slips you will note every disconnected fact that you see or read that is worth record. Besides that, you want a book of the same size containing 30–40 pages, for nearly every day. A gross of such books only costs a dollar or two. Each book is a connected record of some little investigation. At the end of a year, you have 10000 to 20000 slips which you have arranged in bands, in envelopes, and in drawers or boxes; and you have near a gross of books. There is *that* part of your year's experience. After thirty years of systematic study, you have every fact at your fingers' ends. Think what a treasure you will have accumulated. There will not be a man or any subject of interest that you ever had dealings with, whose whole character you will not be able to survey at pleasure. Other records that ought to be systematically made I shall mention in a few moments.

Experimentation is of three kinds, that which is made upon images of our own creation, that which is made upon outward things, and that which is made upon persons. But I have already said enough about them under the head of observation. Exercises for training in Observation and in Experimentation will differ mainly in this that the former

class are chosen for the difficulty of the passive element of the performance while the latter are chosen for the difficulty of the active part.

The third of the psychological operations involved in reasoning is
Habituation, — the power of readily taking habits and of readily throwing them off. There is no habit more useful [than] this habit of easily
taking up and easily throwing off mental habits. Let me briefly outline
what I conceive to be the logical significance of habit. I have already
said that from a logical point of view generality is continuity. A continuous curve, that is one whose differential coefficients are continuous[,] is
one which can be described in general terms, that is, has an equation.
True the curve may have singularities, which are no doubt discontinuities. In reply to this objection, I shall at present content myself with
remarking that the only kinds of point-singularities a curve can have
are *crunodes,* or points of crossing,

cusps,

and *acnodes,* or isolated points. Now crunodes and cusps are not strictly
discontinuities of the point, but only of its differential coefficient. As
for an *acnode,* the way in which it arises is this. The curve has two
branches.

There is no breach of discontinuity here; but mere plurality. Now one
of those branches shrinks to a point

and that gives the acnode. The rest of the curve is continuous and the acnode presents of itself no *break*. The two together are merely a curve with two branches. Thus in no case is there a pure point-discontinuity, such as an extremity would be

or furcation.

Those genuine discontinuities are impossible. But in my appended lecture, I shall take up this objection again and answer it much more thoroughly, explaining fully how it is that such singularities arise as do occur and demonstrating that they fully bear out and confirm the identity of continuity and generality. For I grant that my present reply to the objection is not entirely satisfactory, the acnode, at any rate, being undoubtedly an *exceptional* point, and therefore a breach of generality. But even taking it so, the puzzle is how a perfectly general description, like an equation, can intrinsically involve an exceptional case. My full reply will show that in truth it *cannot* do so; that the exception arises not out of the general description but at an attempt to reconcile two mutually contradictory hypotheses.

Generality, then, is logically the same as continuity. But continuity is Thirdness in its full entelechy. Now Firstness, Secondness, and Thirdness are all-pervasive categories, and appear in psychology with great clearness. Feeling-quality, or Immediate Consciousness, is First; for the first is that which is whatever it is in and for itself. The sense of Reaction between the Inward and the Outward, which takes the two forms of Exertion and the shock of Experience, is Second, for the second is that which is as it is in the accident of something else. Now I hold with Reid that both in Exertion and in Experience, which really differ only in degree, we are directly conscious of an Ego and an Other. This is no hypothesis to explain a *datum*. It is a *datum*, as much and in the same sense as any other result of introspective analysis is properly called a *datum*. In addition to these elements there is a direct consciousness of habit-forming, or learning, equally a *datum,* which particularly appears in our consciousness of the flow of time; for a *Tertium*, which as you are aware is a synonym of *Medium,* is defined as that which is as it is in the pairing of two other things, that is, in the bringing of them into relation with one another. Now the consciousness of the formation of mental habit, or association of ideas, is the consciousness of something coming to pass within us whereby a certain quality of Experience will be connected with a certain quality of Effort. You may object that this is not a direct *datum* of consciousness but rather of the nature of an inference. Could you establish that proposition you would only bring the Thirdness, and the radical contrast with both Feeling-quality and the Sense of Reaction, into stronger prominence. And that there is an Inferential character to it, I admit. That is the nature of Thirdness. Nevertheless, I contend that it is impossible to escape the fact that the flow of time for instance is a direct datum of consciousness. It may be urged that the evidence is that consciousness oscillates up and down across the limen, at the rate of 30 waves a second; so that we really have no such direct consciousness of a flow. I will grant you *that,* for the sake of argument, but every such objection only strengthens the conclusion. For how then do we get this idea of a flow[?] If there is nothing like it in sense, you must think it a sort of Kantian form of sense, an innate hypothesis which we inevitably apply even in the very teeth of the data. But this is only making it all the more a direct *datum.* You are supposing a consciousness behind the sense-consciousness which sees the gaps in the sense-consciousness. In no other way could the atoms of consciousness get synthesized. To talk of its being untrue would be simply to forget what truth means, as Kant virtually says. That is to say, authentic Kantism and Reidism come to the same thing, at last. The consciousness of inferring is in a sense inferential; but in being inferential it is a direct *datum*[,] because it is the consciousness of the operation in its actual operation and as it really is. In short, the more objections you raise, the more thoroughly you are led to see that this consciousness of learning is a peculiar element of consciousness different from feeling-quality and from the sense of reaction. If you say that this analysis of consciousness into three elements is merely a logical analysis, I reply that it is so utterly logical that it belongs not merely to subjective logic but to the logic of being. However, we have not time now to dwell further upon this point.

The operation of acquiring associations is the third of the psychological operations involved in reasoning. It is a sort of generalization by which, for example, the middle term is dropped. Perfect readiness to assimilate new associations implies perfect readiness to drop old ones. It is the plasticity of childhood, which if a man is going to become a teacher, or an exponent of a fixed idea, or a mechanic at any immovable trade, or a settled man in any respect, it is just in so far best that he should outgrow. But so far as a man is to be a learner, a *philo* - sopher, it is most essential that he should preserve; and to do so he has to battle against a natural law of growth. To be a philosopher, or a scientific man, you must be as a little child, with all the sincerity and simple-mindedness of the child's vision, with all the plasticity of the child's mental habits.

What are the exercises conducive to this? Extensive reading to begin with. A hundred volumes a year or $3^2/3$ days per volume does not sound like hard work. Fifty volumes are easily read, if you can find so many good books. Real reading consists in putting oneself into the author's position, and assimilating his ways of thinking. Conversation with all sorts of people whom we do not altogether understand, freshens the mind; but then interesting people are as hard to find as interesting books. As a corrective to all that a suitable dose of rumination and solitude is indicated; provided that it be not idling, but intense and systematic activity of the most definite and diagrammatic thought.[6]

In order to make thought systematic it should be recorded. The record should be brief and almost tabular. No laconism is to be permitted in the record. It should have the style of the obelisk which sets forth that which [it] has to express completely, clearly, and purely. Carry your train of thought to its terminus, and draw up the schedule of it in a copy book devoted to it, in such shape that thirty years after, if you wish to recur to it, the force and good sense and unity of the idea may compel you to say, "After all, I wasn't such a fool in respect to what I did see, however much I may have failed to see."[7]

There are three kinds of exercises which seem to be particularly suited to strengthen the power of habituation. Exercises in divisions and classifications, exercises in definitions and the logical analysis of ideas, and exercises in compacting theories or trains of reasoning.

Now let me conclude this review of the best means of improving our reasoning powers by noticing the three fallacies which according to my experience are most apt to delude thinkers. I mean the positive fallacies; for not to have thought deeply enough and not to have carried out your thought to its extreme consequences, although these are the worst and commonest of all defects of thought [they] do not imply any positive error. I will say parenthetically, however, that while in practical matters nothing is more unwise than to carry an idea to extreme lengths, yet in speculative thought, this is the greatest of locomotives for advancing upon the road to truth. Indeed, it is the extreme cases which alone, teach you anything new.

But I wish to notice one fallacy each in retroduction, in deduction, and in induction. The commonest fallacy of retroduction, as it seems to me, is the idea that the most probable hypothesis is the best. If you consult almost any treatise on logic you will find it laid down after Aristotle, that a hypothesis should be more antecedently probable than the facts which it serves to explain; and on the same principle a most probable hypothesis is superior to a less probable one. There is some reason in this, too. If you really can find an explanation having sufficient probability to be worth consideration, you escape in great measure from reposing upon retroduction and make your inference inductive. But probability in that sense of the term in which it is of value, is some positive information you possess. It is not mere seeming and not mere ignorance. The difficulty is that in most cases where resort is had to retroduction you know nothing about any factual probability. A much more useful maxim is, be upon your guard against assuming anything to be true because it seems likely or a matter of course; for that is the great source of delusions. All the most admirable rules of retroduction are more or less allied to this; such as that of Bentley, of various readings of good MSS prefer the most difficult. Still better is the modern formula, Adopt that reading which though it be not found in any MS best accounts for the readings that are found. This, you will remark, is sure to lead to the adoption of a reading not at all to be expected antecedently. You have to remember that any hypothesis is merely provisional. It will be sure to be corrected by and by. But you want to begin with the one which while it synthesizes the known facts can at the outset be most conveniently tested by comparison with observations you are most nearly ready to make. I regret I have not time to give an example of the fallacy I speak of; because any good example would require long discussion. But you can find examples in abundance in a work of ancient history by one of the masters of the modern method of internal criticism, whose results the still more modern archaeological method has treated so cruelly. *Hultsch's Griechische und Römische Metrologie* is such a pagoda erected on quicksand. More in your line is *Zeller's* History of Ancient Philosophy. See the way he treats Pythagoras. He seems to think that because all our chief witnesses about Pythagoras are extremely untrustworthy therefore the safest way is to disbelieve everything they say.

He makes a feeble attempt in the right direction when he disbelieves them most when what they all testify would in all probability have happened. When you have to rely entirely upon testimony, no matter what liars your witnesses may be, the best way to begin with is to accept what they say as far as you can believe them all, and where you cannot do that to adopt the simplest hypothesis which will account for their testifying as they do. It is possible in this way to get a conception of Pythagoras which explains every item of testimony remarkably well. It may not be altogether true, probably [it] is not; but it is the most rational hypothesis that we can at present frame.

The worst fallacy of deductive reasoning consists in not reasoning at all, but only going by the rule of thumb. That is to say, the *soi-disant* reasoner has been in the habit of inferring in a certain way which in his experience has worked well; and he now roundly asserts its absolute necessity. The commonest form that this fallacy takes is that of treating every collection as if it were finite, and every sequence as if it must have a last or first, an assumption destitute of all shadow of reason and resting on brute habit merely. It is astonishing how many men go through the world successfully enough whose rational part seems altogether abortive. Somewhat more subtle forms of this fallacy are Euclid's assumption that every whole is greater than its part, and that reasoning of the doctrine of limits which thinks it proves a quantity to be zero by saying, if not, let E be its value, and goes on to show that the value is less than E. What this does prove is that the value of the quantity is less than that of any quantity chosen as E has been chosen, generally as a finite quantity. [The] proposition really proved is *less* than the truth, even though the proposition supposed to be proved is *more* than the truth.

The most dangerous fallacy of inductive reasoning consists in examining a sample, finding some recondite property in it and concluding at once that it belongs to the whole collection, instead of definitely determining what the property to be tested is and then drawing a sample and testing the property with that sample. As an illustration of this fallacy, I shall take a paper by Dr. Carus on the relations between the distances of the orbits of the planets. Dr. Carus states that the law he expounds is an "established fact." Considering that an established fact is one which all competent men admit, this is strong language. After some prefatory matter which need not be noticed, we come to the statement of the law in the following words: "The theory is that twice the time of one planet's revolution is equal to the sum of its two neighbors." This is an awkward way of saying that the times of revolution of the successive planets are in arithmetical progression. "Thus," — I quote the exact words, — "Thus, twice the period of the circuit of Venus, which is 450 days, is approximately equal to the revolution of Mercury, its interior neighbor, and that of the earth its exterior." Suppose we make a little table.

		Periodic Times Days	Δ
☿	[Mercury]	87.97	
			136.73
♀	[Venus]	224.70	
			140.56
⊕	[Earth]	356.26	

This does nicely. Now Mars is

♂	[Mars]	686.98	
			321.72

But how is this? Let us see what Dr. Carus says to this. He says, "Again doubling this number (he means doubling twice the period of Venus) we have the sum [of] the revolutions of Venus and Mars." This is [a way] of saying that the period of Mars is thrice that of Venus, which makes the period of Mars depend exclusively on that of *one* and that one not a neighbor of it.

$$\frac{\begin{array}{r} 224.70 \\ 3 \end{array}}{674.10}$$

The relation

$$3\ ♀\ =\ ♂$$

is however not 2 per cent out. Now what about the asteroids? Their periodic time varies from 3¼ to 6½ years, or say from 1200 to 2400 days. Dr. Carus on this subject says, "Again, this number doubled (he means 1⅓ times the period of Mars doubled), is about equal to the revolution of the Earth and one of the asteroids." Now 2⅔ ♂ = 1832 days. Subtracting 365 days we have 1467 for his Asteroid period. He gives us no idea at all what the law prescribes the period of ♃, ♄, and ♅ shall be. And I am sure I cannot guess. The numbers are

		Δ
[♂ Mars]	687	
		780
Ast[eroids]	1467	
		2865
♃ [Jupiter]	4332 days	
		6428
♄ [Saturn]	10760 days	
		19929
♅ [Uranus]	30689 "	
		29499
♆ [Neptune]	60188	

I am sure they are not in arithmetical progression. But as to Neptune whose period is 60188 he does tell us that ♄ ♅ ♆ are in arithmetical progression. I think he probably made some little slip, however, in saying that. After displaying this wonderful demonstration of the law, Dr. Carus [said] that instead of using the number 2, it would have been more exact to use 2.03. Now 2.03 is the square root of the cube of 1.61 which [is] $\frac{1}{2}(1 + \sqrt{5})$. The numbers are not quite right[;] 2.06 is the square root of the square of $\frac{1}{2}(1 + \sqrt{5})$. But this will do as a model of bad induction.

SIX

Causation and Force

Those who make causality one of the original *uralt* elements in the universe or one of the fundamental categories of thought, — of whom you will find that I am not one, — have one very awkward fact to explain away. It is that men's conceptions of a Cause are in different stages of scientific culture entirely different and inconsistent. The great principle of causation which we are told, it is absolutely impossible not to believe, has been one proposition at one period of history and an entirely disparate one [at] another and is still a third one for the modern physicist. The only thing about it which has stood, to use my friend Carus's word, a κτῆμα ἐς ἀεί, — *semper eadem* [always the same], — is the *name* of it. As Aristotle remarks, what the Ionian philosophers were trying to find out as the principle of things was what they were made of. Aristotle himself, as I need not remind you, recognizes four distinct kinds of cause, which go to determining a fact, the *matter* to which it owes its existence, the *form* to which it owes its nature, the *efficient cause* which acts upon it from past time, and the *final cause* which acts upon it from future time. Oh, but it is commonly said, these are merely verbal distinctions. This to my apprehension is one of those superficial explanations, which pass current till men examine them, and serve, like the elegant banker's memorandum, *pour donner le change* to the unwary [to sidetrack the unwary]. They seem to me to mark different types of retroductively inferred facts, — facts which it was supposed furnished the universal process of Nature[,] the occasions from which different features of the [facts] were brought about. The conception is that Nature syllogizes from one grand major premise; and the causes are the different minor premises of nature's syllogistic development. It is generally held that the word cause has simply been narrowed to that one of the four Aristotelian causes which was named from the circumstance that it alone produces an *effect*. But this notion that our conception of cause is that of the Aristotelian efficient cause will hardly bear examination. The efficient cause was in the first place generally a thing not an event, then something which need not do anything; its mere existence might be sufficient. Neither did the effect always necessarily follow. True when it did follow it was said to be compelled. But it was not necessary in our modern sense. That is, it was not invariable. Even in ancient literature we occasionally meet with the idea that a cause is an event of such a kind as to be necessarily followed by another event which is the effect. This is the current idea, now. But it is only in the last two centuries that it has become the dominant conception. It is not so with the most accurate thinkers of the time of Descartes. Those whose admiration for John Stuart Mill knows no bounds consider it one of his most admirable *aperçus* that he regards the cause as the aggregate of all the circumstances under which an event occurs. Whether it be admirable or not, it was certainly a commonplace remark before John Mill ever set pen to paper. But the truth is that the remark is founded upon a misconception. So far as the conception of cause has any validity, — that is to say, as I shall show you, — in a limited domain, the cause and its effect are two *facts*. Now, Mill seems to have thoughtlessly or nominalistically assumed that a fact, is the very objective history of the universe for a short time, in its objective state of existence in itself. But that is not what a fact is. A fact is an abstracted element of that. A fact is so much of the reality as is represented in a single *proposition*. If a proposition is true, that which it represents is a *fact*. If according to a true law of nature as major premise it syllogistically follows from the truth of one proposition that another is true, then that abstracted part of the reality which the former proposition represents is the *cause* of the corresponding element of reality represented by the latter proposition. Thus, the fact that a body is moving over a rough surface is the cause of its coming to rest. It is absurd to say that its color is any part of the cause or of the effect. The color is a part of the reality; but it does not belong to those parts of the reality which constitute the two *facts* in question.

But the grand principle of causation which is generally held to be the most certain of all truths and literally beyond the possibility of doubt, so much so that if a scientific man seeks to limit its truth it is thought pertinent to attack his sincerity and moral character generally, this prin-

ciple involves three propositions to which I beg [your] particular attention. The first is, that the state of things at any one instant is completely
and exactly determined by the state of things at *one* other instant. The
second is that the cause, or determining state of things, precedes the
effect or determined state of things in time. The third is that no fact
determines a fact *preceding* it in time in the same sense in which it determines a fact *following* it in time. These propositions are generally held
to be self-evident truths; but it is further urged that whether they be so
or not, they are indubitably proved by modern science. In truth however
all three of them are in flat contradiction to the principles of mechanics.
According to the dominant mechanical philosophy, nothing is real in
the physical universe except particles of matter with their *masses*, their
relative *positions* in space at different instants of *time*, and the immutable
laws of the relations of those three elements of space, time, and matter.
Accordingly, at any one *instant* all that is real is the masses and their
positions, together with the laws of their motion. But according to Newton's second law of motion the positions of the masses at any one instant
is not determined by their positions at any other single instant even with
the aid of the laws. On the contrary, that which is determined is an
acceleration. Now an acceleration is the relation of the position at one
instant *not* to the position at another instant, but to the positions at a
second and a third instant. Let *a, b, c* be the positions of a particle at
three instants very near to one another, and at equal intervals of time,
say, for convenience one second. Then we may make a table thus: [see
Table 1 on following page].

Or if the intervals are not equal [see Table 2 on following page].

It will be perceived that there is an essential *thirdness*, which the
principle of causality fails to recognize, so that its first proposition is
false. The second proposition, that the cause precedes the effect in time
is equally false. The effect is the acceleration. The cause which produces
this effect under the law of force is, according to the doctrine of the
conservation of energy, the relative positions of the particles. Now
the acceleration which the position requires does not come *later* than
the assumption of that position. It is, on the contrary, absolutely simultaneous with it. Thus, the second proposition of the principle of causation
is false. The third is equally so. This proposition is that no event determines a previous event in the same sense in which it determines a subsequent one. But, according to the law of the conservation of energy, the
position of the particle relative to the centre of force, expressed by *b*
determines [what] the acceleration shall be at the moment the particle

[Table 1]

Dates	Positions	Velocities	Acceleration
0^s	a		
		$(b - a)/(1^s - 0^s)$	$[(c - b)/(2^s - 1^s) - (b - a)\,(1^s - 0^s)]/(1\tfrac{1}{2}^s - 0\tfrac{1}{2}^s)$
1^s	b		$= (c - 2b + a)/(1\tfrac{1}{2}^s - 0\tfrac{1}{2}^s)^2$
		$(c - b)/(2^s - 1^s)$	
2^s	c		

[Table 2]

Dates	Positions	Velocities	Acceleration
t_0	a		
		$(b - a)/(t_1 - t_0)$	$[(c - b)/(t_2 - t_1) - (b - a)/(t_1 - t_0)]/[1/2(t_2 + t_1) - 1/2(t_1 + t_0)]$
t_1	b		$= [c(t_1 - t_0) - b(t_2 - t_0) + a(t_2 - t_1)]/(t_2 - t_1)(t_1 - t_0)] \times 1/2(t_2 - 2t_1 + t_0)$*
		$(c - b)/(t_2 - t_1)$	
t_2	c		

*[Peirce made an error in this algebraic transformation; "$1/2(t_2 - 2t_1 + t_0)$" should read "$1/2(t_2 - t_0)$."]

is in that position. That is to say, taking the number b whose value expresses the position of the particle, we can calculate from this number alone, by the application of a rule supplied by the law of the force, a number which I may denote by $\mathbf{F}b$, which is the numerical value of the acceleration.

$$\frac{c - 2b + a}{(1\tfrac{1}{2}^{s} - 0\tfrac{1}{2}^{s})^{2}}$$

So that we have the equation

$$\frac{c - 2b + a}{(1\tfrac{1}{2}^{s} - 0\tfrac{1}{2}^{s})^{2}} = \mathbf{F}b.$$

Now, if we know the positions, a and b, of the particle at the two earlier dates, this equation, does enable us to calculate the position, c, of the particle at the last date. But since a and c enter into this equation in the same way, and since the difference of dates in the denominator is squared, so that if they are interchanged it makes no difference, because the square of the negative of a number is the number itself, it follows that the very same rule by which we could calculate the value of c, that is, the position at the latest of the three dates, from a and b those at the two earlier dates, may equally be applied, and in precisely the same form to calculating the position, a, of the particle at the earliest date from, c and b, its positions at the two later dates. Thus, we see, that according to the law of energy, the positions at the two later instants determine the position at the earliest instant, in precisely the same way and no other in which the positions at the two earlier instants determine the position at the latest instant. In short, so far as phenomena governed by the law of the conservation of energy are concerned, the future determines the past in precisely the same way in which the past determines the future; and for those cases, at least, it is a mere human and subjective fashion of looking at things which makes us prefer one of those modes of statement to the other. Thus, all three of the propositions involved in the principle of causation are in flat contradiction to the science of mechanics.

But when from the world of physical force we turn to the psychical world all is entirely different. Here we find no evident trace of any state of mind depending in opposite ways upon *two* previous states of mind. Every state of mind acting under an overruling association produces another state of mind. Or if different states of mind contribute to producing another, they simply act concurrently, and not in opposite ways, as the two earlier positions of a particle of matter do, in determining a third position. I come down in the morning; and the sight of the newspaper makes me think of the Maine, the breakfast is brought in, and the sight of something I like puts me into a state of cheerful appetite; and so it goes all day long. Moreover, the effect is not simultaneous with the cause. I do not think of the explosion of the Maine simultaneously with seeing the newspaper, but after seeing it, though the interval be but a thirtieth of a second. Furthermore, the relations of the present to the past and to the future, instead of being the same, as in the domain of the Law of Energy, are utterly unlike. I *remember* the past, but I have absolutely no slightest approach to such knowledge of the future. On the other hand I have considerable *power* over the future, but nobody except the Parisian mob imagines that they can change the past by much or by little. Thus all three propositions of the law of causation are here fully borne out.

Even supposing the physical and the psychical laws not to be precisely as they seem to be, yet, though the gulph between the two worlds would not be of so absolute a nature, still in regard to the general features we cannot be mistaken.

But further than that, we can assert that not only is the psychical world within us governed by the law of causation, but even phenomena of psychical interest without us, even those of inanimate matter so far as they attract everyday notice, either are, or have the *semblance of being,* under the same governance. In order to bring this highly significant fact into evidence, it will be necessary for me to explain two characteristics of phenomena that are determined by forces obeying the law of the conservation of energy. I am sorry that I shall once more be obliged to employ some very simple algebra. The first of the two characteristics I speak of is this, that if any force obeying the law of the conservation of energy, or as we usually say, any *conservative force,* that is any force whose value depends exclusively on the situation of the body acted on relatively to the bodies that act on it, if any such force, I say, can produce any *given motion,* then the very same force can equally produce the reverse motion. That is to say, if at any one instant all the particles were to strike fixed plastic plane surfaces, and were to strike them square, so as to rebound in the directions from which they came and with unchanged velocities, each would move backward through precisely the same path that it had moved forward, and with the same velocities no matter for how long a time the motion might have been going on. This really follows from what I have shown that conservative force determines the past in the same way that it determines the future. An extremely elementary demonstration would be easy; but I omit it to save time. The other characteristic of conservative force, is as its name implies that the Energy is conserved, that is, that the *living force* or square of the velocity of a particle, is simply a function of the position relative to the interacting particles, the exact function depending on the nature of the force *plus* a quantity constant throughout the motion, which has a value depending on the accidents of the particular case. You are so familiar with this that I will not waste time in proving it. But I will mention that it readily follows from the fact, that a second difference multiplied by the sum of the two adjacent first differences is equal to the difference of the squares of those differences, which is obvious

$$\Delta_1$$
$$\Delta^2$$
$$\Delta_2.$$

For since $\Delta^2 = \Delta_2 - \Delta_1$ obviously $(\Delta_1 + \Delta_2) \Delta^2 = (\Delta_2)^2 - (\Delta_1)^2$. Now employing these two characteristics, and especially the former, as criteria, we at once recognize that almost all the phenomena of bodies here on earth which attract our familiar notice are non-conservative, that is, are inexplicable by means of the Law of the Conservation of Energy. For they are actions which cannot be reversed. In the language of physics they are irreversible. Such for instance is birth, growth, life. Such is all motion resisted by friction or by the viscosity of fluids, as all terrestrial motion is. Such is the conduction of heat, combustion, capillarity, diffusion of fluids. Such is the thunder bolt, the production of high colors by a prism, the flow of rivers, the formations of bars at their mouths, the wearing of their channels, in short substantially everything that ordinary experience reveals except the motions of the stars. And even those we do not see to be reversed, though we may well believe them reversible. About the only familiar actions which appear to sense reversible are the motion of a projectile, the bending of a bow or other spring, a freely swinging pendulum, a telephone, a microphone, a galvanic battery, and a dynamo. And all but two of these are unfamiliar to man in his early development. No wonder the doctrine of the conservation of energy was a late discovery.

It is certainly a desideratum in philosophy to unify the phenomena of mind and matter. The logic of retroduction directs us to adopt Monism as a provisional hypothesis of philosophy, whether we think it likely or not; and not to abandon it till the position is stormed and we are forced out of it. In view of this, it becomes exceedingly interesting to inquire how the physicist explains those actions which seem to violate the law of energy. Now such of them as physicists have deeply studied, are all explained by the action of *chance*. For example, if one horizontal layer of air moves northerly, passing over another layer at rest, the reason why the northerly current will be retarded is that the molecules are flying about in all directions and hence chance will carry a good many of them from one layer to the other. And these chance molecules so carried from either layer to the other will be so numerous, that it is practically certain that on the average they will have as much northerly motion as the average of all the molecules in the layer from which they have emerged. Thus, after a while the average northerly motion of the molecules in each layer approximates toward that of the other layer. And to say that the average northerly motion of the molecules of the upper layer becomes less is the same as to say that the northerly motion of that layer as a whole becomes less for the motion of the layer as a whole is nothing but the average motion of its molecules.

Now in order that we may make any application of this method of explaining non-conservative quasi-forces to psychical phenomena, it is necessary to make an exact analysis and description of its essential elements, omitting all circumstances that do not contribute to the effect. To this end, the first requisite is a definition of *Chance*, not as to the causes that produce it, but as to the phenomenon itself. Surely, I need not waste breath in refuting that feeblest of attempts at analysis which make chance to consist in our ignorance. For that has already been sufficiently done in the *Logic of Chance* of John Venn, a logician some of whose opinions may be untenable but whose thought is apt to penetrate beneath the form to the matter he discusses, and after examining a hundred or two logical treatises one begins to think that a high distinction. It is the operation of chance which produces the retardation of the upper layer of air we were just considering; but surely it is no ignorance of ours that has that effect. Chance, then, as an objective phenomenon, is a property of a *distribution*. That is to say, there is a large collection consisting say, of colored things and of white things. Chance is a particular manner of distribution of color among all the things. But in order that this phrase should have any meaning, it must refer to some definite arrangement of all the things.

Let us begin by supposing that the multitude of colored things is *denumeral,* and that that of the white things is likewise *denumeral.* The denumeral multitude, as I explained in a former lecture, is that of all the whole numbers. Every denumeral collection may be numbered. That is, the number 1 may be affixed to one of its objects, 2 to another, and so on in such a way that every object of the collection receives a number. When that is done I call the relation of an object receiving any number but 1 to the object receiving the next lower number a *generating relation* of the collection. It is by no means indispensable to introduce any mention of numbers in defining a generating relation. I only do so for the sake of using ideas with which you are familiar and thus save time and trouble. Now I must define the important conception of *independence,* which incessantly recurs in the doctrine of chances. A character, say blueness, is said to be independent of a character, say smoothness, in a given collection if and only if the ratio of the multitude of those objects (PQ) of the collection that are both blue and smooth *to* the multitude of those objects (P$\overline{\text{Q}}$) of the collection that are blue but not smooth equals the ratio of the multitude of objects ($\overline{\text{P}}$Q) that are not blue but are smooth *to* the multitude of objects ($\overline{\text{P}}\,\overline{\text{Q}}$) that are not blue and not smooth. Mr. Jevons makes a fuss about proving that if P is independent of Q, so is Q of P. It is because in the proportion

$$[\text{PQ}]:[\text{P}\overline{\text{Q}}] \;=\; [\overline{\text{P}}\text{Q}]:[\overline{\text{P}}\,\overline{\text{Q}}]$$

we can transpose the means, giving

$$[\text{PQ}]:[\overline{\text{P}}\text{Q}] \;=\; [\text{P}\overline{\text{Q}}]:[\overline{\text{P}}\,\overline{\text{Q}}].$$

Now in our collection of denumeral colored things and denumeral white things, let **F** signify a particular generating relation, so that when the objects are numbered according to that relation the object numbered $n + 1$ is **F** of the object numbered n. Then, I say that a fortuitous distribution of color and whiteness in the collection consists in this that any object of the collection being colored or not is independent of it being an **F** of a colored thing, and is also independent of its being an **F** of an **F** of colored things, and is also independent of its being at once an **F** of a colored thing and an **F** of an **F** of a white thing; and in short that an object's being colored or not is independent of its having or not having any character definable in terms of **F**, color, and whiteness. That satisfactorily defines a *fortuitous distribution* when the colored things and white things are both denumeral.[1]

When either or both the two subcollections of colored things and white things are *enumerable*, that is, finite in number, such independence as the definition requires becomes impossible. Nevertheless, if both are large enumerable collections, there may be an approximation to the fulfillment of the definition, and then we loosely call the distribution fortuitous. If for example there are 500,000 colored things and 500,000 white things, then of all possible modes of sequences of 20 successive objects as to their being colored or white, there will be about one example of each. Therefore we cannot say that an object's being colored or not is independent of the sequence of color and whiteness among the twenty objects that precede it, for one of the four terms of the proportion that defines independence will probably be zero. On the other hand there will be about a thousand occurrences of each possible mode of sequence of 10 objects as to being colored or white and if from 1 object up to 10 objects, the required proportionality is nearly fulfilled, there will be no harm in calling the distribution fortuitous.

In comparing two infinite collections we have to distinguish between one being *inclusive of* more or less than the other and one being more or less *multitudinous* than the other. I call a collection *inclusive of* more than another if it includes all the objects of the latter and others besides; but to say that one collection, say the simpletons, is more multitudinous than another, say the sages, means that to every sage a distinct simpleton might be assigned, and assigned to no other sage, while it would be impossible to assign to every simpleton a distinct [sage] for him alone. Two collections may neither of them be *inclusive of* all the other *includes*, as for example the Buddhists and the Japanese; but they cannot each be *inclusive of* **all** the other includes unless they are identically the same. On the other hand, of any two collections whatsoever, one must be at least as multitudinous as the other, and each *may be* so. That is, they may be equal. Of equal collections one may be *inclusive of* more than the other; but the less multitudinous of two collections cannot be the more inclusive. All these propositions except one are easily proved; and that one is proved in the *Monist*.[2]

If of the two subcollections, the colored things and the white things, one is denumeral while the other is more than denumeral, we may still speak, and sometimes do speak, of a fortuitous distribution. It is true that for a collection more than denumeral there can be no generating relation. But still, unless the total collection is a continuum of more than one dimension, with or without topical singularities, all the objects of it may be placed in a sequence, at any rate by means of a relatively insignificant multitude of ruptures and junctions. It must be understood that the fortuitousness refers to the particular way in which the objects are placed in sequence. It must furthermore be understood that by a definite mode the whole sequence is broken up into a denumeral collection of subcollections and the fortuitousness is further relative to that mode of breaking up. [And] moreover this mode of dissection must be capable of a particular mode of variation such that the subcollections may be made all at once inclusive of less and less without limit, and the fortuitousness is still further relative to that mode of shrinking. If, then, no matter how small these subcollections are taken the character of a subcollection containing a blue thing or not containing a blue thing is independent of that subcollection having any character definable in terms of the generating relation of the denumeral collection, of containing a blue thing, and of not containing a colored thing, then the distribution is fortuitous. For example, we may say that certain marked points are fortuitously distributed upon an infinitely long line, meaning that if that line is cut up into a denumeral series of lengths, no matter how small, the lengths containing marked points will be fortuitously distributed along the whole series of lengths.

We might speak of a finite number of points being fortuitous[ly] distributed upon the circumference of a circle, meaning an approximate fortuitous distribution. When we say that a finite number [of] points are distributed *at random* on the circumference, that is quite another matter. We then have in mind a fortuitous distribution, it is true, but it is a fortuitous distribution of the denumeral cases in which a man might in the course of all time, throw points down upon the circumference.

I do not say that no sense could be attached to the term *fortuitous distribution* in case both the blue things and the white things were more than denumeral. On the contrary, the difficulty is that several senses might be attached to the phrase, and having no experience in that line of thought, I am not prepared to say which one would be more appropriate. I therefore pass that case by.

We have now determined precisely what Chance, as an objective phenomenon, consists in. In works on probabilities, of which I particularly recommend that of *Laurent*[3] as being brief and clear and yet at the same time scientific, very beautiful and valuable properties of the fortuitous distribution will be found traced out, especially that which relates to the probability curve.

In the fortuitous distribution the colored things and the white things are mixed up together with an irregularity which is perfect. It is the very highest pitch of irregularity. Departures from this, or regularities, may tend in either of two directions. On the one hand they may

mix the colored [things] and white things more perfectly and uniformly,
as when colored things and white things alternate, or they may sift them
out, as when all the colored [things] come in one series and all the white
things in another. Even the alternation might be called a sifting, for it
puts all the colored things into the odd places and all the white things
into the even places, and these constitute two distinct series. Still, having
the word *regularity* for that, we may as well restrict the word *sifting*, so
as to enable us to express the less fundamental, but still not altogether
unimportant, distinction between leaving the two series mingled and
separating them.

Let us glance for a moment at the ways in which the three states of
things, — siftedness, uniform combination, and fortuitous irregularity
of mixture are in fact brought about in nature; and then in the light of
these examples we shall be able to see how they could conceivably be
brought about.

Sifting is performed by any conservative force quite inevitably. For
example, a ray of white light strikes upon a prism. The different colors
have different refrangibilities and the light is decomposed. The action
is conservative because it is reversible. For if the dispersed light were
reflected back upon its course it would be recompounded. But this does
not happen except in the laboratory and that only imperfectly, when it
is due to the elaborate contrivance of the experimenter. Conservative
force, left to itself, can produce no such result, because it depends on
the *purposeful* exact adjustment of each pencil of light. Now one of the
first things that the mechanical philosophy discovered was that there
are no final causes in pure mechanical action. In the same way, were a
great number [of] meteors to start from the same almost infinitely distant point all moving in the same direction so as to bring them within
the sun's strong attraction; but were they to move with various velocities,
the sun's attraction would separate their motions so that when they
departed again they would all be [arranged] in the order of their velocities, the one with no velocity returning just as it came, the one with
infinite velocity proceeding in a right line unchecked, and all the rest in
more or less bent paths.

So much for sifting. Let us next consider how a state of *fortuitous distribution* is brought about. How, for example, is it that the throws of a dice occur in the utterly irregular way in which they do? It is because when we turn over the dice-box there are slight differences in the motion, and also when we put the dice into the box, there are small differences in the motion; and no regularity connects the differences of one kind with those of the other. Still, these circumstances would not in themselves give the character of fortuitous distribution to the throws, were there not a fortuitous distribution either in the differences of our motion in putting the dice into the box or else fortuitous distribution in the variations of motion in throwing them out. We see then that in this case the fortuitous distribution arises from another fortuitous distribution in one or more of the conditions of the production of the phenomenon. All this has been carefully studied by various writers on the theory of errors. Suppose we put into a jar some hot nitrogen and then some cold oxygen. At first, the molecules of nitrogen will be moving with various *vires vivae* distributed according to a modification of the probability curve and therefore fortuitously, while the molecules of oxygen will likewise have *vires vivae* distributed according to the same general law, but on the average *their* motion will be much slower. [In the] first state of things, therefore, the distribution of *vires vivae* among all the molecules considered as one collection will *not* be fortuitous. But there will be continual encounters of molecules, which, in these encounters will be governed by conservative forces, generally attractions. In consequence, [the] different modes of these encounters being distributed fortuitously, which is itself due to the fortuitous distribution of the molecules in space, and the fortuitous distribution of the directions and velocities of their motions, continual interchanges of *vis viva* will take place, so that as time goes on there will be a closer and closer approximation to one fortuitous distribution of *vis viva* among all the molecules. Here we see a fortuitous distribution in process of being brought about. That which happens, happens entirely under the governance of conservative forces; but the character of fortuitous distribution toward which there is a tendency is entirely due to the various fortuitous distributions existing in the different initial conditions of the motion, with which conservative forces never have anything to do. This is the more remarkable because the peculiar distribution which characterized the initial distribution of *vires vivae* gradually dies out. True, traces of it always remain; but they become fainter and fainter and approach without limit toward complete disappearance. The fortuitous distributions, however, which equally have nothing but initial conditions to sustain them, not only hold their ground, but wherever the conservative forces act, at once mark their character in the effects. Hence, it is that we find ourselves forced to speak of the "action of chance."

Uniform distribution presents to a superficial view diverse characters. There are just so many suicides every year; of children born every year just so many develop into giants and just so many into dwarfs. An insurance company stakes almost its existence upon the expectation that just so many losses will occur each year. The relation between temperature, pressure, and volume upon which the whole cosmos of business reposes, in so far as it depends on the regular working of steam-engines, is another case of a uniformity which is simply a necessary corollary of a fortuitous distribution. But in many cases of *uniform* distribution, so far as we can see, *fortuitous* distribution plays no part. Thus, the two kinds of electricity tend to unite in a certain fixed proportion. This is simply because one kind attracts what the other repels and these two forces vary with the distance in precisely the same way. Both are conservative forces; and the uniform distribution of the two electricities is due to the very peculiarly adjusted relation between the two conservative forces. In chemical combinations we have a very marked example of uniform distribution. We do not know by what sort of forces chemical compounds are held together. Even apart from the circumstance that some of the most readily formed bodies, such as acetylene, are endothermic, there are other considerations which show that those forces are not altogether conservative. But the bonds of atoms and their atomicities are sufficient warrant for the assertion that the forces must be exceedingly complicated and specially related to one another. I might say much more both about chemical forces and about the conditions of uniform distribution in general; but in the limits of one lecture I think it best to confine myself to the two clearer cases.

I have said that a uniformity, or regular law, may be a mere consequence of a fortuitous distribution. But if you examine any such case critically, you will find that after all, this only results, because of some regularity in the conditions. Take, for example, Boyle's law that if the density of a gas is doubled its pressure will be exactly doubled. This is because if there are twice as many molecules in the space, twice as many in a given time will pound upon the wall of the receptacle. But this results not from fortuitous distribution alone, but from fortuitous distribution conjoined with the circumstance that the paths of the molecules are all very nearly rectilinear. I will not stop to prove this, which you will find set forth both in Watson's little treatise and in the more generally interesting volume of Oscar Emile Meyer.[4] Suffice it to say that it *is* an essential condition. Now this is something which, being true of *all* the molecules, is a regularity. The simplicity of the law is due to the simplicity of this regularity. You will find, if you analyze the problem, that it must always be the case when a regularity results from a fortuitous distribution that some uniformity of the objects of the collection must come into play, and further that any simplicity the resulting law may exhibit must be due to the simplicity of that uniformity.

On the other hand, in regard to fortuitous distribution, while you may undoubtedly suppose that it arises simply from the absence of any sufficient reason to the contrary, — not that I accept the principle of sufficient reason as a general one by any means, but in this case, it amounts merely to supposing the fortuitous distribution is a pure First, without any cause or reason whatsoever, while this you may of course suppose, yet if you suppose it to have been in any case a necessary result, this necessity certainly implies that some law or uniformity is at work, but for all that it will be quite evident that the uniformity has not *per se* of its own nature produced the irregularity, but that this irregularity is due to some other irregularity, some other fortuitous distribution, in the initial conditions.

Thus it is that uniformity, or necessary law, can only spring from another law; while fortuitous distribution can only spring from another fortuitous distribution. Law begets law; and chance begets chance; and these elements in the phenomena of nature must of their very nature be primordial and radically distinct stocks. Or if we are to escape this duality at all, urged to do so by the principle of retroduction, according to which we ought to begin by pressing the hypothesis of unity as far as we can, the only possible way of doing so is to suppose that the first germ of law was an *entity,* which itself arose by chance, that is as a First. For it is of the nature of Chance to be First, and that which is First is Chance; and fortuitous distribution, that is, utter irregularity, is the only thing which it is legitimate to explain by the absence of any reason to the contrary.

These things having become clear to us, let us now, remembering that the whole aim of this discussion is to find some clue by which physical and psychical action may be unified, examine, a little, certain other features of the two classes of phenomena governed respectively by conservative forces and by the principle of causality, and see how bright or how darkling a light is shed upon them by what we have thus far made out.

Looking first at conservative forces, we remark that they govern nothing but the space relations of particles. They are the law of the mutual reactions of particles in space. And the first fact that demands our attention is that, other things being equal, particles react upon one another more strongly the nearer they are to one another. How shall we explain this fact? We shall get the right hint if we ask ourselves what would happen in case all this were suddenly reversed and particles were to act most and most directly on those particles which were most distant from them.

Would not the human race, supposing that it could survive the shock at all, be pretty sure to develop a new form of intuition[5] in which the things that now appear near would appear far? For what is the real truth of nearness? Who is my neighbor? Is it not he with whom I intimately react[?] In short, the suggested explanation is that space is that form of intuition in which is presented the law of the mutual reaction of those objects whose mode of existence consists in mutually reacting. Let us see how much this hypothesis will explain. What are its necessary consequences? I must abridge the reasoning to a mere sketch. In the first place space, as a presentation of law, must be *continuous* and without singularities. In the second place, since reaction is essentially *hic et nunc,* anti-general, it follows that the reacting objects must be entirely independent of one another in their purely spatial determinations. That is, one object being in one particular place in no way requires another object to be in any particular place. From this again it necessarily follows that each object occupies a single point of space, so that matter must consist of Boscovichian atomicules, whatever their multitude may be. On the same principle it furthermore follows that any law among the reactions must involve some other continuum than merely Space alone. Why Time should be that other continuum I shall hope to make clear when we come to consider Time. In the third place, since Space has the mode of being of a law not that of a reacting existent, it follows that it cannot be the law that in the absence of reaction a particle shall adhere to its place; for that would be attributing to it an attraction for that place. Whence it follows that in so far as a particle is not acted upon by another, that which it retains is a relation between space and time. Now it is not logically accurate to say that the law of motion prescribes that a particle so far as it is not acted upon by forces continues to move in a straight line describing equal intervals in equal times. On the contrary the true statement is that straight lines are that family of lines which particles so far as they are unacted upon describe, and that equal spaces are such spaces as such a particle describes in equal times. There are some further consequences of this principle the statement of which it will be convenient to postpone for a few minutes. In the fourth place, since Space presents a law whose prescriptions are nothing but conditions of reactions, and since reaction is Duality, it follows that the conditions of the prescriptions of space are necessarily Dual. Hence immediately follow five corollaries. The first is that all forces are between pairs of particles. The second is that when two places of the path of an isolated particle are determined the law determines all the other places; so that two different straight lines cannot have two different points in common. The third corollary is that when the places of an isolated body at two instants are given the law prescribes its places at all other instants. That is, the first differential coefficient, or mere difference between the places at two instants determine[s] its places at all other instants. That is, the velocity remains constant. From these corollaries again, together with the general principle from which they are derived, it follows that when a body is acted upon by another body, that which is directly affected is the uniform velocity in a straight line, and that in such a way that in so far as the action of the active body remains the same, two velocities, or what comes to the same thing, three positions with their dates, determine all the velocities the particle will take. This explains, therefore, why the force should produce acceleration rather than any other differential coefficient of the space relatively to the time. Hence, it further follows that a force at each moment of time acts to impart to the body a new rectilinear motion; whence it follows that forces will necessarily be compounded according to a parallelogram of forces. In the non-Euclidean geometry this is only so far modified that the parallelograms must be drawn infinitely small. And it further follows that the line of the force is the straight line through the two particles. There is still another apparent consequence; but I am not satisfied with the reasoning, since it rests upon a principle I am unable abstractly to define. I will, however, state it for what it is worth. Namely, since the force acts to impart an acceleration and since the law presented in space is perfectly general and comprehensive, it follows that the acceleration imparted may be different in kind and not merely in amount from the acceleration the particle already possesses. That is the point I consider doubtful. If it be admitted, it certainly follows that space must have at least three dimensions. Moreover, it again follows as a fourth corollary from space being a law of reactive conditions that except for the quality of the particles themselves it is the pure spatial determination which prescribes what the reaction of one particular particle upon another shall be, that is, the force between two particles depends only upon their qualities and their places at the instant. Moreover, as a fifth corollary, it follows that the mechanical law only prescribes how a *pair* of particles will act. It does not generally prescribe any relation between the actions of different pairs of particles, nor even of the action of a particle upon particles of the same kind placed differently. Hence, not only may different kinds of pairs of particles act differently, but the law of the variation of the action with the relative positions is left to depend upon the qualities of the particles, and this so completely that there is nothing to prevent a particle exercising different forces on different sides of it. In the fifth place, from the fact that space presents a law of reciprocal reactions, several corollaries follow, particularly these two. First, when one particle, A, acts on another, B, this latter, B, will likewise act on A; and moreover this action cannot impart to both the same acceleration, because the law is such as to affect their relative places. This follows by the aid of the third principle already enunciated, as we shall see. Hence, it can only impart opposite accelerations to A and B. Secondly, those two accelerations must be equal, so that the masses of all atomicules are equal. From this, again, it follows that the masses are unchangeable; and further that if two bodies, or aggregates of atomicules, react upon one another in a certain ratio to one another, in that same ratio they will also react upon any third body. A sixth principle concerning the necessity of which some doubt may be entertained is, that the law presented by space being perfectly general, every motion must admit of receiving the same kind of changes as every other. From this if it be admitted it certainly follows, though the demonstration is far too long to give, that space has either 1, 2 or 4 dimensions. Hence, since 1 and 2 dimensionality have been already excluded, the number of dimensions ought to be just 4. I will now mention the postponed corollaries from the third principle. Since space has only the being of a law, its places cannot have distinct identities in themselves, for distinct identity[6] belongs only to existent things. Hence place is only relative. But since, at the same time, different motions must be comparable in quantity, and this comparison cannot be effected by the moving and reacting particles themselves, it follows that another object must be placed in space to which all motion is referred. And since this object compares generally and thus partakes of the nature of law, it must unlike the moving and reacting bodies be continuous. It is a corrected equivalent of that which has been called the body *alpha*. It is the firmament, or Cayley's absolute. Since this is to determine every motion, it follows that it is a locus which every straight line cuts, and because space is a law of Twoness only, and for other reasons, every straight line must cut it in two points. It is therefore a real quadratic locus, severing space into two parts, and the space of existence must be infinite and limited in every direction.

I have thus briefly stated one side of my theory of space. That is without touching upon the question of the derivation of space and its properties, or how accurately it may be supposed to *fulfil its ideal conditions*, I have given a hypothesis from which those ideal properties may be deduced. Many of the properties so deduced are known to be true, at least approximately. Others, I am happy to say, are extremely doubtful. I say I am happy because this gives them the character of predictions and renders the hypothesis capable of experiential confirmation or refutation. One of the doubtful properties, the last mentioned, I have succeeded I think in proving to be true by calculations from the proper motions of the stars. Another, that about atoms attracting differently in different directions, I have succeeded in making highly probable, from chemical facts. Still, others have some evidence in their favor. The consequence most opposed to observation is the doubtful one of 4 dimensions.

Endeavoring to generalize the results that have been obtained, we may say that the continuity of space so acts as to cause an object to be affected by modes of existence not its own, not as participating in them but as being opposite to them. For instance an isolated particle is at any instant at one point; that is its actual state. But it is so affected by the state which is not actual but belongs to it by a date differing from the actual one way, that at a date differing from the actual the other way, it takes a state differing in the opposite way from its actual state. So again, when a force acts upon a body the effect of it is that the mean of the states of the body not actual but indefinitely approximating to the actual differs from its actual state. So in the action and reaction of bodies, each body is affected by the other bodies motion, not as participating in it but as being opposite to it. But if you carefully note the nature of this generalized formula, you will see that it is but an imperfect, somewhat particularized restatement of the principle that space presents the law of the reciprocal reactions of existents. Various other such imperfect formulae might be mentioned.

Let us now consider non-conservative actions. These are all distinguished by asymptotic approach to a definite state of relative rest. Conservative force can never bring about any state of rest except for an instant. It can only produce, I believe, three permanent changes.

Namely, it can permanently change the direction [of] motion of a body and this it does because the body moves away out of the range of the force, or it can cause one body to rotate round another in an inward spiral, more and more rapidly. And third a planet like Jupiter may turn the motion of a small body and then move away and leave the small body performing permanently, or quasi-permanently, an orbit round the sun. In course of time, however, Jupiter will come round again in such a way as to throw it out. This is a very curious case. Chance is an important factor of it. But all the non-conservative quasi-forces produce states of relative rest. Such for example is the effect of viscosity. These states of relative rest are states of uniform distribution which upon minute inspection turn out to be really states of fortuitous distribution. They betray their real nature by the probability curve, or some modification of it, playing a part in the phenomenon. Such, for example, is the case in the conduction of heat.

When we ask why chance produces permanent effects, the natural answer which escapes from our lips is that it is because of the independence of different instants of time. A change having been made there is no particular reason why it should ever be unmade. If a man has won a Napoleon at a gaming table he is no more likely to lose it, [than] he was to lose a Napoleon at the outset. But we have no sooner let slip the remark about the independence of the instants of time [than] we are shocked by it. What can be less independent than the parts of the continuum *par excellence*, through the spectacles of which we envisage every other continuum? And although it may be said that continuity consists in a [binding] together of things that are different and remain different, so that they are in a measure dependent on one another and yet in a measure independent, yet this is only true of finite parts of the continuum, not of the ultimate elements nor even of the infinitesimal parts. Yet it undoubtedly is true that the permanence of chance effects is due to the independence of the instants of time. How are we to resolve this puzzle? The solution of it lies in this, that time has a point of discontinuity at the present. This discontinuity appears in one form in conservative actions where the actual instant differs from all other instants absolutely, while those others only differ in degree; and the same discontinuity appears in another form in all non-conservative action where the past is broken off from the future as it is in our consciousness. Thus although the other instants of time are not independent of one another independence does appear at the actual instant. It is not an utter, complete independence, but it is absolute independence in certain respects. Perhaps all fortuitous distribution originates from a fortuitous distribution of events in time; and this alone has no other explanation than the Law of Sufficient Reason, that is, is an absolute First. It is a truth well worthy of examination that all the intellectual development of man rests upon the circumstance that all our action is subject to error. *Errare est humanum* is of all common places the most familiar. Inanimate things do not err at all; and the lower animals very little. Instinct is all but unerring; but reason in all vitally important matters is a treacherous guide. This tendency to error when you put it under the microscope of reflection is seen to consist of fortuitous variations of our actions in time. But it is apt to escape our attention that on such fortuitous variation our intellect is nourished and grows. For without such fortuitous variation, habit-taking would be impossible; and intellect consists in a plasticity of habit.

What is time? Shall we say that it is the form under which the law of logical dependence presents itself to intuition? But what is logical dependence objectively considered? It is nothing but a necessitation which instead of being brute is governed by law. Our hypothesis therefore amounts to this, that time is the form under which logic presents itself to objective intuition; and the signification of the discontinuity at the actual instant is that here new premises not logically derived by Firsts are introduced.

SEVEN

Habit

The books on physics are replete with examples of what they call "empirical laws," that is to say, formulas which are satisfied as nearly as men have succeeded in observing the facts and under certain limited circumstances, but which nobody supposes go down to the roots of existence, or to exhibit the general forms of all phenomena. They are, on the contrary, supposed to be merely special modifications which the universal formulae assume under special conditions. Of such a pseudo-law centrifugal force affords a good example. When a railway-train moves round a curve, there is always a pressure away from the centre of curvature. It must be so; for since a body not subjected to any force naturally moves in a right line, while this railway-train does not so move, it follows that the guiding rail exerts a force upon it in a direction toward the centre of curvature; and consequently by virtue of the law of action and reaction, the train must exert an equal and opposite force upon the rail. This is a perfectly real force. Namely, it is the elastic force of the iron rail which is strained by the tendency of the train to preserve a rectilinear motion. If you examine the rail you will detect manifestations of the reality of the centrifugal pressure; or if you whirl a sling, you will actually feel the centrifugal force. But now certain natural philosophers extend the formula of centrifugal force, which is a genuine force where the motion is constrained by a rigid guide to cases where there is no such constraint. They say that a planet is held to its circular orbit by the balance between centrifugal and centripetal forces. In this case, centrifugal force is a mere formula, — a formula which is undoubtedly quite correct as far as the effect goes, while yet the centrifugal force is a merely formal affair with nothing at all corresponding to it in nature. It is very much as if between two men, A and B, there has been a single transaction consisting in A lending B, $5. Now if B were to keep his books in such a manner that the state of the account as entered on those books made A owe him $100 with $105 on the opposite side of the account, the entries would in effect be correct; but yet that hundred dollars would be a fiction of book-keeping. In like manner the centrifugal force of a planet is a fiction due to using polar coördinates in place of rectangular coördinates. It is true that were the gravitation of the sun suddenly to be annihilated there would be at the first instant, an acceleration of the planet away from the circular orbit equal to the centrifugal force; and it is certainly true that what we call *force* in dynamics is nothing more than the product of an acceleration multiplied by a mass. Only, this acceleration away from the circular motion of the natural motion of the planet were it suddenly emancipated from gravitation is nothing in the world but the entry we have to make on one side of our accounts to balance the fictitious entry which we have virtually made on the other side when we took the circular motion as the standard or origin from which to reckon accelerations.

Now the question is, whether or not there is any ratiocinative method by which we can assure ourselves that any law which we may discover by the observation of nature is not like centrifugal force a mere fiction of book-keeping but represents a real and living action in nature. Many nominalistic logicians will deny at once that any such distinction can be made; but in doing so, they will be merely adhering to preconceived metaphysical opinions. They have no real evidence to offer upon the subject. Of absolute knowledge there can be no question. But if we see that as soon as circumstances are somewhat varied, the form of the law is lost, the inference would seem to be that it is not a universal or living mode of action. If on the other hand, we find that as soon as the form is prevented from manifestation in one shape it immediately reappears in another shape, and especially if it shows a power of spreading and of reproducing itself, these phenomena may be considered as evidence of genuine vitality and fundamental reality in the form of the law.

But I confess I think it will, and ought to, be harder to convince you of the truth of this general principle than it will be to assure you of the consequence which leads me to formulate it. Namely, what I wish to show is that causation, as distinct from the action of conservative force, is a real, and fundamental, and vital element both in the outer and in the inner world.

As to those explanations which the physicists propose for irreversible phenomena by means of the doctrine of chances as applied to trillions of molecules, I accept them fully as one of the finest achievements of science. Judge Stallo[1] performed an acceptable service in his earnest assault upon them, which was conducted with as much ability as so poor a cause could possibly be expected to command. Other writers have recently attempted to reinforce the attack, one of them with some understanding of the subject. But the judgement of a really scientific logic must be altogether in favor of the accepted theory. Its explanation of the facts is altogether admirable and is fortified by a variety of new phenomena which were not known at the time the theory was first proposed, but which fit into their places like the pieces of a boy's dissected map, after he has once begun to put a few of them rightly together. This explanation demonstrates that the agency of energy is disseminated through every department of physical phenomena. But in one thing it fails; namely, it fails to show the absence of a very different kind of agency; and it not only fails to show its absence, but even supplies the means of proving its presence.

Those non-conservative actions which seem to violate the law of energy, and which physics explains away as due to chance-action among trillions of molecules, are one and all marked by two characters, the first is that they act in one determinate direction and tend asymptotically toward bringing about an ultimate state of things. If teleological is too strong a word to apply to them, we might invent the word *finious*, to express their tendency toward a final state. The other character of non-conservative actions is that they are *irreversible*. If a falling stone, which moves under the conservative force of gravity, were suddenly to strike a perfectly elastic horizontal fixed surface, its motion would be reversed and it would move upwards to the point from which it fell with precisely the velocities it had in falling, only in reverse order. So it would be if every planet in the solar system suddenly had its motions reversed. Whatever motion conservative forces can effect the very reverse of that motion they are equally capable of effecting.

There is some objection to taking either of the two characters of finiosity and irreversibility as *criteria* of the conservative or non-conservative character of an action. That which strictly constitutes an action as conservative is that the forces depend solely on the relative positions of the particles, and do not depend on the velocities. But *theoretically* that which makes an action irreversible is that the forces do not depend upon odd powers of the velocities. *Practically*, however, the irreversibility is an infallible criterion. For example, the friction of sliding motion is altogether independent of the velocity; so that according to the definition it is a conservative action. The velocity of a sliding motion is retarded by friction according to precisely the same formula as the velocity of a body shot vertically upwards. The only difference is that when the instantaneous state of rest is reached, a new kind of friction, rest-friction, suddenly begins to act and breaks the continuity of the motion. Sliding friction is a unique example of a non-conservative action that simulates conservative action. The reason that it does so undoubtedly is that conservative action enters into it in a singularly uniform manner. When one solid body is set down upon another, there will be many points at which they come into contact, and where this occurs the paths of the atoms, — for I do not half believe in the molecules of solids, — will begin to be interlaced. The result is that when one begins to slide over the other, many ruptures have to be made, and before the ruptured parts have attained their positions of equilibrium they will on the average come into new contacts with the other body and thus there is a perpetual average state of elastic strain. The elastic stress of this strain is the friction, and it really is a conservative force. The parts of the action which are non-conservative are two, first and most important the ruptures, by which the elastic potential is at once converted into heat, and second and less important the contacts. You will observe that by friction the energy of molar motion is not immediately converted into heat but into elastic potential and it is only after the action is over that this becomes converted into heat and that fact explains why friction acts like a conservative force.

The resistance of a fluid according to the analysis of Newton and his contemporaries is proportional to an even power of the velocity, namely the square. It ought therefore to be reversible; and probably it would be so in part for a moment. But the truth is the whole analysis is an example of the unskillful application of mathematics, the hypothesis being too unlike the real facts to be useful. Of course, no resistance proper can be reversible.

The other character of non-conservative action, namely, its finiosity, is, as a criterion, open on the theoretical side to still more serious objection. Namely, it is not true that only non-conservative forces can bring about enduring states of things.

In the first place, let me remark that it is not generally true that a particle moving about an attracting centre describes any fixed orbit. In order that that should be the case, it is requisite that the law of the force should be subject to peculiar numerical conditions. We know that if the attraction is inversely as the square of the distance, and the velocity is not too great, the moving particle will describe an ellipse having the attracting centre at the focus. If, however, at the smaller distances the attraction is a little greater than the law of the inverse square of the distance requires, the result will mainly be that the ellipse itself will revolve slowly about the centre in the same direction in which the moving particle revolves. If there is any commensurable ratio between the periods of the two revolutions, the motion will finally return into itself; otherwise not.

If the attraction is inversely as the cube of the distance, the revolving orbit will make infinitely many revolutions while the moving body is making one half revolution in that orbit; so that it will describe a spiral line having in general an outer and an inner boundary. The outer boundary may however be at an infinite distance, or even further away. Here then we have a case in which conservative action asymptotically moves toward a final and ultimate state of things. Suppose the inner limit be distant from the centre by an insensibly minute interval. Then, it will appear to remain fixed in one spot, although it will really be in tremendously rapid motion. The fact that tremendously rapid or even infinitely rapid motion may simulate rest is what makes the conservative action simulate the finiosity of non-conservative action.

The attraction may vary according to such a law that the moving body winds in indefinitely near to the centre without ever passing out or passing through the centre. It certainly seems as if the atoms of the chemical elements may have been formed by some such aggregation. For in that way Prout's law could be accounted for.

It is important to remark that even if the attraction varies inversely as the cube of the distance, and still more easily if it varies more rapidly, the moving particle may pass through or, at any rate, *to* the centre. And this it will generally do by performing infinitely many revolutions in an infinitesimal moment of time. What the motion will be when it does arrive at the centre it is hard to say. My father in his *Analytic Mechanics* says that after that the body will proceed in a straight line. This, of course, would violate the principle of areas. He does not mention the circumstance that the direction of that straight line would in many cases be indeterminate. It appears to me that a general law being essentially continuous, to suppose an infinite velocity, or any other discontinuity in the action is to suppose that general law to be violated. If therefore a general law is such that it essentially involves such a phenomenon, the law is, in so far, self-contradictory. Still, the contradiction only amounts to this that there is a point of discontinuity in the continuum. It is only a slight departure from generality in one particular instance. It is not that the state of facts supposed is self-contradictory; but only that it is self-contradictory to suppose such a phenomenon to be a result of a perfectly general law.

If such an event can happen then it follows as a necessary consequence that there is such a thing as an absolutely chance event. For even an infinitesimal variation in the conditions will make a finite difference in the result.

But as to whether or not there is any such law, inquiry in that direction is absolutely barricaded and brought to an eternal standstill, unless there has been some logical process in nature whereby the laws of nature have been brought about. Since, therefore, it is a corollary from the First Rule of Reasoning that we must not make hypotheses that will absolutely stop inquiry, it follows that we are bound to hope that such a logical process of the evolution of law in nature may be discovered and that it is our duty as scientific men to search for it.

But let us return to those spiral motions which reach the centre only at the end of an infinite time. It must be confessed that here the simulation of non-conservative action by a conservative action is not a false or extrinsic simulation, but is true and intrinsic. It is just one of those extreme cases which throw the most light on philosophical problems and to which a powerfully solvent method of reasoning must pay particular attention. We note in the first place that the simulation depends in part on the bringing together into one infinitesimal moment motions which undo one another, and in declining to analyze this moment because it is absolutely infinitesimal. Thus the velocities in that moment, though instantaneously infinite are in their resultant zero; and with the attractive forces the same thing is true. From this point of view, it becomes absurd to say that an attraction varies inversely as the cube or any higher power of the distance down to the very centre of attraction. Indeed, a somewhat similar difficulty arises whenever there is any attraction at all at the centre.

This leads me to remark that the finiosity of non-conservative action is also manifested in hyperbolic orbits under the attraction inversely as the square of the distance. That is to say a moving body which starts from an infinite distance in one direction reaches at the end of infinite time an infinite distance in another direction.

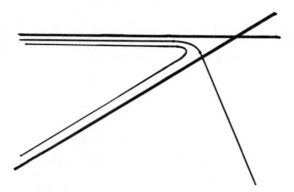

This finiosity might be regarded as due to the circumstance that time has an absolute limit. For could the motion continue beyond the infinitely distant instant of time it would continue through the infinitely distant line in the plane and complete the closed hyperbolic orbit. But I do not think that this simple way of solving the difficulty ought to be regarded as satisfactory. At any rate, if a similar solution be sought for the spiral, one is led to imaginaries, which seems to show that the mathematical hypothesis does not correspond to the facts.

It will be remarked that both these cases, that of the spiral orbit and that of the hyperbolic orbit, are connected with angular displacements. Any kind of rectilinear motion is continued by virtue of momentum, and from this circumstance arises the result that conservative forces affect not directly the velocities, but only the accelerations; and in the fact that such forces depend upon the relative positions of the particles lies their conservative character. But it is different with rotations. There is *no* momentum continuing an angular displacement as such, but only so far as that angular displacement involves rectilinear displacements. The mere rotation of an absolute particle, strictly occupying a single point, has no momentum at all. So if a rectilinear displacement is effected as in the hyperbolic orbit by means of motions which in their limits become radial, the momentum has no tendency to continue the angular motion. Thus angular motion *per se* is not a conservative action. If for example, atomicules are Boscovichian points, the attractions of those atomicules may be different on different sides of them. Many facts in elaterics, crystallography, and chemistry render it almost certain, for reasons which it would be too long here to discuss, that, as far as *atoms* are concerned, this is actually true. Suppose for the moment that it is also true of atomicules. What would be the result? As far as the mutual action of two atomicules was concerned, they would instantly turn those sides to one another which gave the minimum potential energy; and in the absence of all momentum, there would be no tendency to swing beyond that point. Those two sides would always be turned toward one another. But when there were *three* such points, the face which one atomicule turned toward another, and consequently its attraction for that other, would depend in part upon the position of the third atomicule. In this case, although the motions of translation would be conservative, the rotations of the atomicules would be regulated by the old formula of causation.[2]

Now from our modern point of view of the non-Euclidean geometry, it appears that, strictly speaking, there is no kind of motion having the properties which we associate with *translation*. That is to say there is no motion which is merely relative. It would not be convenient to attempt to explain this here, before we have examined further into the nature of Continuity.

But let me here say a word about the attempt of Ernst Mach to show that all motion, even rotation, is merely relative. Mach belongs to that school of *soi disant* [so-called] experiential philosophers whose aim is to emancipate themselves from all metaphysics and go straight to the fact. This attempt would be highly laudable, — were it possible to carry it out. But experience shows that the experientialists are just as metaphysical as any other philosophers, with this difference however, that their preconceived ideas not being recognized by them as such, are much more insidious and much more apt to fly in the face of all the facts of observation.

Newton in his *Principia* maintains that Time and Space are substances, or in the jargon of French philosophers they are *Entities*. The doctrine was a new one, well-recognized as such by Newton. Mach seems to think it was a blunder which Newton fell into inadvertently. It was nothing of the sort. We have historical testimony to show that Newton himself and his contemporaries regarded it as a peculiar, definite, and deliberate theory. Newton does not overtly argue the question in the Principia for the reason that he was a stickler for the Traditions of mathematical exposition; and that tradition compelled him to confine himself to demonstrations and comments upon demonstrations. But he contrives to make his reason plain enough. That reason is that the laws of motion make velocity of rotation to be something absolute and not merely relative. Now velocity is the ratio of the amount of a space-displacement to the amount of time in which this displacement takes place. If therefore, argued Newton, velocity is not merely *relative*, neither is a displacement in space nor a lapse of time relative; and therefore Space and Time are not mere relations but are absolute subjects or substances. Now this reasoning is founded on positive facts of observation; and it appears to me to be sound reasoning. I will not say that it draws a *necessary* conclusion; but I do say it is an excellent hypothesis to account for the facts.

Mach on the other hand lays it down as an Axiom that Space and time are merely relative. No facts lend any support whatever to such an assertion. The most that could be said, — more than is really true, — is that facts concerning the composition of motions of translation go to show that space-position has an element that is merely relative. Mach is by no means above blundering in mathematics, though his mistakes have been quietly corrected so far as possible in the American translation of his *Science of Mechanics,* which is an admirable book considered as a history of the science.[3] Mach's struggles to define angular motion as motion relative to the mean position of all the bodies in the universe are not only struggling against all observation, and not only involve the absurdity that the centrifugal force of sling would be influenced by the angular motion of stars very far away, and more influenced by the more remote than by the nearer stars, contrary to his own conception of space as an image of dynamical relations, but, what is still worse, this gratuitous theory is in mathematical contradiction to the point he most insists upon namely that rectilinear motion is purely relative.

It is true that Space, in so far as it is a continuum, is a mere law, — a mere Thirdness. But that does not stand in the way of its being a *thing* too. If besides its continuity it presents arbitrary *thisness*, we must admit that it is something more than a mere law. The question of the relativity of motion is a question of the measurement of space, not of the nature of space itself; and therefore, although motion be not relative, it would not necessarily follow that space *itself* is non-relative, however good the inference may be, considered as a retroduction. But there are characters belonging to space *per se* which seem to involve *thisness*, such as its having three dimensions, — which is an arbitrary limitation of its *cyclosis* and *periphraxis*,[4] whether these be supposed equal to 0 or to 1 are apparently arbitrary facts. You cannot reduce them to mere formalities without supposing that space has some kind of topical singularity, — which is still more manifestly an arbitrary fact of existence. As to the fourth

Listing number, all must admit that its value is 1. That is to say, a body filling all space could not by gradual degrees shrink to a point without being ruptured, while the slightest explosion which should separate the body entirely from a single place however small, — the smallest vacuous cist in it, — would suffice to enable the collapse to take place. This I believe nobody who has carefully considered the matter has doubted or is likely to doubt, — at least unless it be supposed that space has modes of connection of which observation affords not the slightest trace. Here again, then, is an arbitrary existential fact about space, which is simply the way it insists upon being, without any logical necessity. Now insistence upon being in some quite arbitrary way is Secondness, which is the characteristic of the actually existing thing. It is its self willedness.

Now if you examine the matter more closely than I have time to do in this lecture, you will find that it is precisely in those respects in which Space shows such indications of Secondness that motions act as though governed by the law of causality, while in those respects in which Space preserves all its Thirdness the motions preserve their dynamical character.

Let us next consider actions of which the space-element is not an intrinsic part. For example, I slip a nickel into the hand of a mendicant. One might say that this was a space motion. But the non-conservative friction is so great that neither the beggar nor the giver remarks any effects of *momentum*. The coin is not thrown but pushed along, and the dynamical part of the action is altogether insignificant. The fact that there is any space motion at all is accidental as far as the determination of the events goes. The money is caused to become the beggar's and remains his. Take the purest kind of temporal action. The very flow of time itself. The event passes out of the problematical state of [futurity] into the state of a *fait accompli*. All psychical action has this character. A question is answered, and answered it remains. A mere duality, a passage from a first state into a second state, here takes the place of that determination of a relation between three states which characterizes physical dynamics.

My father, Benjamin Peirce, drew my attention to the psychological peculiarity of an experiment which I am going to show you. I do not now remember how he formulated the matter. It is that a mathematical analysis of the conditions of motions often gives an expression of what happens conceived under one aspect; while anybody looking at the experiment would instinctively express what he saw under quite another aspect. [The experiment Peirce displayed to his audience was that of two equal coupled pendulums beating. One can imagine the apparatus in this way: between two rigid stands a flexible line is run horizontally; near the middle of the line, two balls are suspended, each with a supporting line, about 6 inches apart. The phenomenon Peirce is discussing here can be seen if one ball is left stationary and the other is swung. The first ball will lose oscillations as the previously stationary ball will begin to oscillate, and so on.] The dictum of the eye is that one of the pendulums is ahead of the other in its oscillations by half an oscillation, i.e. by a quarter of a vibration, and that the oscillations [of] this pendulum are continually losing their amplitude and transferring [them] to the other. This is quite true, too. But analytic mechanics looks upon the fact from quite a different point of view. According to it each pendulum oscillates in two different ways at once. One of the components of its oscillation has the period of the two pendulums when they are swinging together and both pendulums partake equally of this component, while the other component has the period of the two pendulums swinging opposite ways and the two pendulums are opposite one another in the phases of this component. I remember distinctly that my father remarked that while the view of analytic mechanics corresponds to the formula

$$\theta_1 = \Theta \cos [(a-b)t] + \Theta \cos [(a+b)t]$$

$$\theta_2 = \Theta \cos [(a-b)t] - \Theta \cos [(a+b)t]$$

the instinctive, or intuitional, view corresponds to the formula

$$\theta_1 = 2\,\Theta \cos at \,.\, \sin (bt + 90°)$$

$$\theta_2 = 2\,\Theta \sin at \,.\, \sin (bt).$$

And I further remember his remarking that the decided choice of this last view showed a peculiarity of our mental constitution. But I cannot remember that he attempted to formulate this peculiarity. It is, however, clear to me that it is nothing but our natural tendency to prefer the formula of causation. We regard the pendulum which is ahead as the agent and the one which lags behind as the patient.

To the reason of the mathematician the intuitional mode of conception is singularly crooked and unphilosophical. It happens to be pretty simple because the two pendulums are of equal weight and equal length. Were they not so, the phenomenon would appear very complicated from that point of view, though almost as simple as before from the point of view of analytical mechanics.[5]

It is now time to inquire whether psychical action be of the conservative or the causational type. You know I make no pretension to competing with the profound psychologists under whom you sit here in Harvard; and I do not promise to bring the question to a satisfactory conclusion. But I shall hope in the few minutes that I can devote to it to make you all understand what the question is, and I hope the provisional reply I make to it may recommend itself as provisional good sense.

I read out to you the rules of philosophical terminology that seem to me to recommend themselves at once to the logic of science and to the ethics of science.[6]

*   *   *

ALL THINKERS OF the least account agree that it will not do to drive one's reasoning through the jungle of philosophy with a loose rein, and that if there is to be any check *at all* upon its accuracy, it must be harnessed with a precise philosophical terminology. Now in the matter of scientific terminology, philosophers cannot do better than to trust to the experience of those scientific men who have had to deal with greater difficulties of terminology than any others, I mean the systematic zoölogists and botanists, and who have successfully *conquered* those difficulties by means of a code of rules that is easily adaptable to the terminology of philosophy. Here they are.

Rule I. Assign to every scientific conception a scientific name of its own, preferably a new word rather than one already appropriated to an unscientific and dubious conception.

That was the practice adopted by the scholastic doctors, how advantageously every student will testify. The *renaissance,* on the other hand, condemned the scholastic terms as not being Ciceronian, with the result of making *renaissance* philosophy as soft and savorless as a sage pudding. There is a rule of good writing higher than Ciceronian purity, that of expressing your thought, both accurately and *concisely.* More than a rule of good writing, this is a fundamental condition of scientific thinking; for man cannot think *at all* without formulas, nor think *powerfully* without concise formulas. This rule applies to the word *realism* which is the customary formation from a cognate word used from the time when the medieval controversy first became a great issue, to express a broad but perfectly unambiguous philosophical conception; that of a sect of metaphysical logic; so that that conception has a *right* to the exclusive use of the term; and according to the biologist code, it is almost a theft to apply the word to any other conception.

Rule II. The author of a scientific conception has the first right to name it; and his name ought to be accepted, unless there are grave substantial objections to it. But if *he* fails to give it a scientific name, some body else must do so; and in that case the earliest good scientific name shall be employed.

It is a substantial objection to a term that it is preoccupied or that cognate words are so, or that it implies a misconception. But unless the misconception is a grave one, it should not cause us to reject a name bestowed by the author of the conception. That a word is barbarous or fanciful is not a substantial objection. Yet a slight modification either of the word or of its signification, when the advantages are very decided, may be permitted.

Rule III. After a scientific conception has once received a suitable name, let it not be called by any other scientific name, old or new.

For as the conception has a right to the term, so also has the term a right to serve as the designation of the conception. This rule does not forbid us to use other names, provided it be merely as ordinary unscientific words.

In addition to those three rules, applicable to every science, a fourth, special to philosophy, is dictated by the spirit of them and indeed by that of all word-formation. For this rule expresses the way in which philosophical terms *were* formed as long as philosophy remained in enjoyment of any fixed terminology, that is, down to the time of Hegel. It is as follows:

Rule IV. As far as practicable, let the terms of philosophy be modelled after those of scholasticism.

You are aware that the whole of the Kantian language was formed in this way. Nor does Hegel himself, in my judgment, violate this principle. Where he really sometimes sinned was in stretching the application of both scholastic and common words past all recognition. He ought to have invented a system of vocables by which his categories could be designated according to their places in his scheme. That would have cut the ground from under the feet of Trendelenburg, who practically exploded Hegelianism from Germany. But whether he did right or wrong, Hegel's example certainly operated to introduce great laxity of philosophical language, and consequently of thought.

However, the abuse of the word *Realism* can certainly be charged to Hegel's account; for it began about 1800 when in consequent of Bardilis introducing a system of realism distinguished from idealistic realism, which it somewhat resembled, by being dualistic, *realism* came to be applied to that sect of philosophy which had long been called by the unexceptionable name of *dualism*. As to the French artists and *litterateurs* whose poverty of language can find no better term than *realism* to express the method which pays great attention to copying details of nature in art, it need not concern the student of philosophy at all.

When writers begin to construct their language on rules like these, to shape their style on botanists' descriptions of species, and to feel themselves as a part of the scientific world, instead of allowing the methods of their thought to be bent so far that the expression of that thought may afford an indolent pleasure to the general reader, as bent it still allows itself to be, then at last we shall be able to feel that we have settled down to a serious and worthy purpose.

* * *

THOSE REASONS for adopting them were so weighty, that I would not gauge any other consideration along side of them. But now that I am no longer arguing the question, let me add that I for one entertain a deep feeling of reverence for the traditions of the English language. It has not the amazing psychical and especially emotional wealth of German. It has not half as many words for tools and manipulations as French; nor has it the delightful social *finesse* of French. But in all that concerns logic and reasoning, it has a spirit of accuracy which is due to the fact that the language spoken in State Street and other market places preserves to an extraordinary degree the sharp distinctions of the scholastic lore of the middle ages; and where those distinctions are not available, our vernacular language still preserves the spirit of them. I regret very much that those who of late years have written in English upon philosophy and psychology seem most of them to have a contempt for all English thought and English speech so great that it produces an utter insensibility to the distinctions of the language. The French language has long been cut off from medieval traditions; and moreover it is the genius of the French to rely upon skillful phraseology to express their precise thoughts rather than upon accurate terminology. But notwithstanding this, large numbers of French words which happen to be spelled like English words but which bear quite different meanings have by recent writers been used in their French meanings threatening an utter break-down of the spirit of English speech and of English thought. For example, the word *Entartung,* having been translated into French by *dégeneration,* becomes "degeneration" in English, although what is meant is degeneracy, which is an entirely different thing. So *spontanée* becomes in this new lingo *spontaneous,* which is almost the reverse of the correct English meaning of *spontaneous. Suggestion* becomes "suggestion," regardless of the fact that suggestion was already an exact term of philosophy in English in a different sense. The German *Association* is rendered by "association," although if ever there was a school of writers who by the clearness of their definitions and the accuracy of their thought deserved to have their usage of terms respected, it was the English Associationalists. I might expend the rest of the hour on this theme. When these neologists have succeeded in thus dishonoring their mother-tongue, till no vestige of her pristine virtue remains, they will by the same act have hopelessly corrupted all the old virility and health of English thought.

However, putting aside all such regrets, which are probably futile, and saying no more about vernacular speech, I am still obliged in the interest of the logic of science to employ a scientific terminology; and this must follow the only rules by which confusion can possibly be avoided. According to those rules I am bound to use scientific terms in the senses in which they first became terms of science. Accordingly, the English associationalists having first made *association* a term of science, and they having been careful never to extend it to the operation or event whereby one idea calls up another into the mind, but to restrict it primarily to a *habit* or *disposition* of mind in consequence of which an idea of one description is likely to bring into comparative vividness of consciousness an idea of another description, or, when they applied the term association to any operation or event, to designate by it only that process of habituation by which such a habit or disposition of mind acquired strength, they having been punctilious in this matter, my code of rules obliges me logically and morally, to follow them. As for that mental event which corresponds, as we suppose, to the nervous discharge of one part of the cortex upon another, — or the action of one idea to render another idea which is associated with it, vivid by another, — for that they employed the term *suggestion.* This word is now applied mostly to motor phenomena or to such manifestations of mind as can be observed from without; and therefore, although the two meanings doubtless are in real facts connected together, the meanings themselves are different. But here a compromise is possible; for I shall violate no rule of terminology by speaking of the "suggestion" of the association-alists, as *associational suggestion* and that of the hypnotists as *nervous suggestion*. The adjectives may be dropped, — especially the former, — in cases where there is no possibility of the meaning being mistaken.

I next remark that different sense-qualities have different degrees of intensity. The sound of thunder is more intense than the sound of a dozen people clapping their hands; and the light of an electric arc is more intense than that of a star. It is also true that the sound of thunder is more intense than the light of a star, and that the electric arc light is more intense than the sound of a dozen people clapping their hands. It is not at random that I say this.[7] Besides this intensity of the sense-qualities, ideas have another mode of intensity, — their *vividness*. The contrary of *vividness* we call *dimness*. Although my personal imagination and memory of colors is very dim compared with that of most persons, yet it is decidedly above the average in accuracy; and in matching a color by memory I am no more likely to select a paler or darker color than I am to select a higher or more luminous color. This *vividness* which is so much more intense in my memory of the red pencil which I saw this afternoon than it is in my memory of a certain red fan which I possessed when I was nine years old appears, as far as I have been able to experiment, to be entirely distinct from the intensity of the qualities remembered; although, no doubt, other things being equal my memory of an intense sensation is likely to be more vivid than my memory of a faint sensation. It does not belong to the *Firstness* of the quality, but to the *Secondness* or insistency of the particular apparition of that quality.

At any one time I have a great multitude of ideas in my conscious-ness of different degrees of vividness. How vivid the most vivid of them are depends upon how wide awake I am. In any given state of mental wakefulness or alertness, there is a certain maximum limit of vividness which none of my ideas surpass, but which a few of them always attain. There is only room in my consciousness for a few at this highest level of vividness. If others force themselves up, some of those that were at the surface must subside. Below these there are others less vivid, and still deeper others that are so dim that only by intense effort, perhaps by no effort that I can possibly exert, can I assure myself of their pres-ence. And yet it may be proved indirectly that they are really there.[8] For example, I have occupied myself for weeks in answering questions about the relative intensity of excitations of sense when with the most vigorous effort I could not seem to detect the slightest difference be-

tween them, so that my answers seemed quite random guesses; and yet
the decided majority of the answers would be right every day, thus
proving that sensations were capable of affecting my answers although
I could not seem to be aware of them at all. Moreover, ideas of which
we do not seem to be aware will sometimes suggest or call up others
by association, these others being vivid enough. I have endeavored to
ascertain whether there is in any ordinary state of consciousness a definite minimum degree of vividness, as there certainly is a maximum
degree. But all my experiments upon careful mathematical discussion
point to the presence of ideas so very *dim*, or wanting in *vividness*, that
I am strongly inclined to say, as a first approximation at any rate,
that the vividness ranges all the way down to *zero*, and that every cell
that ever can be sentient is in some degree sentient as long as it is
alive, at all.

Association is of two kinds. For, on the one hand, it may be a natural
disposition, which was from birth destined to develop itself whatever
the child's outward experiences might be, so long as he was not maimed
nor virtually maimed, say by being imprisoned. This sort of association
by virtue of which certain kinds of ideas become naturally allied, as
crimson and *scarlet,* is called *association by resemblance.* The name is not a
good one, since it implies that the resemblance causes the association,
while in point of fact it is the association which constitutes the resemblance. In themselves considered any two sense-qualities are what they
are to themselves alone and have no relation to one another. But could
they be compared by a mind that brought no tinge of its own nature
into the comparison, any two ideas would appear somewhat alike and
somewhat different. But the human mind attaches a peculiar value and
emphasis to some resemblances, and that consists in this, that when one
quality is brought vividly to consciousness, others will at once have their
vividness increased, some more, some less. Thus, an idea which may be
roughly compared to a composite photograph surges up into vividness,
and this composite idea may be called a *general idea.* It is not properly
a *conception;* because a conception is not an idea at all, but a *habit.* But
the repeated occurrence of a general idea and the experience of its
utility, results in the formation or strengthening of that habit which
is the conception; or if the conception is already a habit thoroughly
compacted, the general idea is the *mark* of the habit. Some psychologists
deny the existence of association by resemblance, or say that it is at
bottom merely a special case of association by contiguity. To the arguments in defence of its fundamental character which are to be found in

common books, I will add three. The first is that it is incredible that man is so constituted that no paths of nervous discharge between parts of the cortex are naturally more or less resistant than others. But those that are less resistant must correspond to natural associations, and ideas naturally associated will resemble one another. The second argument is that without association by resemblance there could be no general ideas and no resemblances. The third argument is this. Suppose I have long been puzzling over some problem, — say how to construct a really good type-writer. Now there are several ideas dimly in my mind from time [to time], none of which taken by itself has any particular analogy with my grand problem. But someday these ideas all present in consciousness together but yet all very dim deep in the depths of subconscious thought, chance to get joined together in a particular way such that the combination does present a close analogy to my difficulty. That combination almost instantly flashes out into vividness. Now it cannot be contiguity; for the combination is altogether a new idea. It never occurred to me before; and consequently cannot be subject to any *acquired habit*. It must be, as it appears to be, its *analogy*, or resemblance in form, to the nodus of my problem which brings it into vividness. Now what can that be but pure fundamental association by resemblance?

On the other hand, the association, instead of being a natural disposition of mind, may be an acquired habit of mind. That supposes that similar ideas have been conjoined in experience until they have become associated. That is termed *association by contiguity*. Of course, psychologists have not been wanting who sought to show that there is no such thing as association by contiguity, or that it is merely a special case of association by resemblance. It is a long time since I read the work of Gay who first gave the idea of associationalism to Hartley. But I seem dimly to remember that he had a notion of that kind. A number of other principles of association have been proposed, such as contrast and causation. Association by contrast ought to be regarded as a case of association by resemblance, not in the narrow sense in which the reduction is often made but by generalizing the conception of resemblance in accordance with the logic of relatives until it embraces [a] high degree of logical relation between ideas. Contrast is a particular form, an especially prominent and familiar form, of what may be called *relational resemblance* by which I do not mean a resemblance of relations, but a connection of the kind which in the logic of relatives is shown to belong to the same class of relations to which the relation of resemblance belongs. Association by causation is an ill-defined conception embracing associations of different natures. But besides that reiterated coöccurrence which helps to consolidate an association by contiguity, another factor which plays a great part in accomplishing the association, is the experience that the combination of the ideas has important consequences. When we learn that white cats with blue eyes are deaf and have peculiar habits, such as that of following their masters like dogs, we no sooner see a white cat than we want to know what colored eyes she has. This may be called association by *relational contiguity.* That is to say not only have the two ideas frequently been experienced together, but their union has often been accompanied in experience with a third idea of an interesting kind. Another kind of association which is very important is that which makes an idea *interesting.* I purpose to term it *association by interest.* An idea occurs to us in such a way that it would, other things being equal be very dim. For example, it may result from a fortuitous putting together of two other ideas both of which are sunk deep in the subconscious mind. But if the new idea happens to be *interesting,* it will promptly become vivid. Why is this? Clearly it is because the objective selfconsciousness, or the idea which a man has of himself, consists in large measure of what may be roughly described as a composite of ideas of his aims and purposes, including all problems which exercise him. Now the separate components of this composite may for the most part be dim; but the total idea is perhaps the most vivid in consciousness at all times. Now an interesting idea is one which has an analogy, or resemblance in form, to this composite of the man's aims. It is, therefore, drawn into vividness by the vividness of that composite.

Let us now make an attempt to formulate the law of action of ideas. In the first place, an idea left to itself does not retain its vividness but sinks more and more into dimness. In the second place associated ideas in consciousness together soon undergo alterations of vividness, the dimmer ones becoming more vivid, and the more vivid ones dimmer, according to the strength of the associations. The dimmer idea never becomes more vivid than the more vivid idea had been before the change; but it may become more vivid than the idea originally the more vivid [it] is after the change; for otherwise it would hardly be possible to explain idea chasing after idea. But in the third place the action of associative suggestion does not take place instantly as soon as the two ideas are in consciousness together. There are continual changes going on in the *connections* of ideas in consciousness; and the action of associative suggestion does not take place until chance has brought the two ideas into suitable connection for acting upon one another. Thus, I stand before an emblem wondering what it means. It is vividly in my mind. Perhaps the meaning is dimly in my consciousness; but it is not until by the movements in consciousness, chance has thrown the idea of the emblem and the idea of its meaning into the right sort of connection, that they suddenly change in vividness, the idea of the emblem becoming much dimmer and that of its meaning much more vivid.

In the fourth place, this interchange of vividness is accompanied by another event which takes place altogether outside my consciousness, though there is a sign of it in consciousness. Namely, the association between the two ideas becomes strengthened, in such a way that the more vivid idea becomes more likely to call up the less vivid one on another occasion. At the same time, in the fifth place certain other associations become weakened.

Now that the mental action, as so described, is upon the surface, at least, causational and not conservative is quite obvious. There is no reversibility in it, and the traces of anything like momentum are slight and doubtful. At the same time, it would be possible to suppose that it was a conservative action affected to such a degree by resistances, that the momentum had no sensible effect.

The established cerebral theory will easily account for all the five features of mental action which I have mentioned; and that theory is favorable to the view that while the action is of a mixed nature, the non-conservative elements are the predominant ones. For there can hardly be a doubt that the peculiar properties of protoplasm depend upon the enormous complexity of its molecules, and upon those molecules being frequently broken up and reunited in new connections, and upon the circumstance that in the quiescent state the molecules are in stationary motion, while in the active state they are partly broken up and the fragments are wandering. Now all this may be summarized by saying that its properties depend upon Bernoulli's law of high numbers, and every action depending upon that law is, so far as it is so dependent, purely causational and not conservative.

Although the cerebral theory is established and although it is of priceless value to psychology in its present stage of development, it by no means follows that it will never be superseded. That method may perhaps lead to a purely psychical way of investigating the mind. We must wait and see whether it will or not; but meantime for various reasons which I cannot now enter upon that is what I am inclined to expect.

We have, then, these two modes of action, the conservative and the causational, the former rather the dominant one in pure physics, the [latter] dominant in psychics. Our logical impulse, which prompts us to try to understand the universe, and as an essential condition of doing so to bring all its action under a single principle, this impulse, I say, compels us to *hope* that it may in some way be shown either that all causational action is conservative at bottom or that all conservative action is causational at bottom.

But I am quite sure that, as far as I personally am concerned, if I had not been moved by any consideration which touched me more nearly than such a vast and shadowy hope can do, I never should have been moved to do all the hard work I have done for the last fifteen years in trying to reason this matter out. I must confess that for me a living motive must have smaller dimensions than that very general hope. But I am a physicist and a chemist, and as such eager to push investigation in the direction of a better acquaintance with the minute anatomy and physiology of matter. What led me into these metaphysical speculations, to which I had not before been inclined, I being up to that time mainly a student of the methods of science, was my asking myself, how are we ever going to find out anything more than we now do [know] about molecules and atoms? How shall we lay out a broad plan for any further grand advance?

As a first step toward the solution of that question, I began by asking myself what were the means by which we had attained so much knowledge of molecules and ether as we already had attained. I cannot here go through the analysis, although it is very interesting. But that knowledge has been based on the assumption that the molecules and ether are like large masses of ordinary matter. Evidently, however, that similarity has its limits. We already have positive proof that there are also wide dissimilarities; and furthermore it seems clear that nearly all that method could teach has been already learned.

We now seem launched upon a boundless ocean of possibilities. We have speculations put forth by the greatest masters of physical theorizing of which we can only say that the mere testing of any one of them would occupy a large company of able mathematicians for their whole lives; and that no one such theory seems to have an antecedent probability of being true that exceeds say one chance in a million. When we theorized about molar dynamics we were guided by our instincts. Those instincts had some tendency to be true; because they had been formed under the influence of the very laws that we were investigating. But as we penetrate further and further from the surface of nature, instinct ceases to give any decided answers; and if it did there would no longer be any reason to suppose its answers approximated to the truth. We thus seem to be reduced to this alternative. Either we must make some very broad generalization as to the character of Nature's ways, which may at least tell us that one theory about molecules and ether is better worth trying than another theory, or else we had better abandon altogether a line of inquiry, — I mean into the inmost constitution of matter, — which is likely to prove a mere waste of time.

But meantime our scientific curiosity is stimulated to the highest degree by the very remarkable relations which we discover between the different laws of nature, — relations which cry out for rational explanation. That the intensity of light should vary inversely as the square of the distance, is easily understood, although not in that superficial way in which the elementary books explain it, as if it were a mere question of the same thing being spread over a larger and larger surface. I cannot stop to give the true explanation, but I will just give you two hints. The first is that the basis of the measurement of light is the convention that we will call the light of two candles double the light of one. The other hint is that according to the superficial explanation of the school-books, you would expect the brightness of the image of a star made by a perfect lens to be proportional to the area of the lens, while in point of fact it is proportional to the square of that area. But given that the law of variation of light with the distance is known, what an extraordinary fact it is that the force of gravitation should vary according to the same law! When both have a law which appeals to our reason as so extraordinarily simple, it would seem that there must be some *reason* for it. Gravitation is certainly not spread out on thinner and thinner surfaces. If anything is so spread it is the potential energy of gravitation. Now *that* varies not as the inverse square but simply [as] the distance. Then electricity repels itself according to the very same formula. Here is a fluid; for electricity is really something like a fluid. It is not a mode of motion. Here is a fluid repelling itself but not at all as a gas seems to repel itself, but following that same law of the inverse square. I have not time to instance other extraordinary relations between laws of nature. But I cannot refrain from alluding to that most extraordinary law of Mendeléef.

According to the strictest principles of logic these relations call for explanation. In order to find such explanation, you must deduce the fundamental laws of the physical universe as necessary consequences of something. That is you must explain those laws altogether.

Now were it merely a question of the *form* of the law, you might hope for a purely *rational* explanation, — something in Hegel's line, for example. But it is *not* merely that. Those laws involve *constants*. Light for example moves over 300,000,000 centimetres *per* second. A mass at a distance of one centimetre from a gramme of matter receives in consequence of gravitation an increment of velocity toward that mass every second of [980.1037] centimetre per second. The explanation of the laws of nature must be of such a nature that it shall explain why these quantities should have the particular values they have. But these particular values have nothing rational about them. They are mere arbitrary *Secondnesses.* The explanation cannot then be a purely rational one. And there are numberless other facts about nature which if my logic is not quite at fault absolutely and decisively refute the notion that there can be any purely rational explanation.

What kind of an explanation can there be then? I answer, we may still hope for an evolutionary explanation. We may suppose that the laws of nature are results of an evolutionary process. In the course of this process of evolution[,] light[,] let us suppose[,] age by age[,] moves faster and faster, and we have now arrived at the stage of the process in which it moves just so fast. Now logic does not demand any further explanation than that. The same applies to gravitation. You might ask me whether the relation between the velocity of light and the modulus of gravitation does not require explanation. I answer that it does not because the dimensions of the quantities are different. One involves the unit of mass and the other does not. But two universal constants are as many as can be allowed without explanation of their relations, except that there may be besides a constant of space.

By a process of reasoning, then, of the nature of which I thus give you some hint, though given in full it would be seen to be drawn from a great variety of different evidences, I reached the conclusion that a theory of the evolution of the laws of nature must be sought.

But if the laws of nature are the result of evolution, this evolutionary process must be supposed to be still in progress. For it cannot be complete as long as the constants of the laws have reached no ultimate possible limit. Besides, there are other reasons for this conclusion. But if the laws of nature are still in process of evolution from a state of things in the infinitely distant past in which there were no laws, it must be that events are not even now absolutely regulated by law. It must be that just as when we attempt to verify any law of nature our observations show irregular departures from law owing to our errors, so there are in the very facts themselves absolutely fortuitous departures from law trillions of trillions of times smaller no doubt, but which nevertheless must manifest themselves in some indirect way on account of their continual recurrence. I do not mean to say that it is a strictly necessary consequence that there should be this element of absolute chance in nature, and my first theory attempted to avoid it. But as I went on, I found other reasons to support this view of which I will endeavor to give you some idea in the next lecture.

But if the laws of nature are results of evolution, this evolution must proceed according to some principle; and this principle will itself be of the nature of a law. But it must be such a law that it can evolve or develop itself. Not that if absolutely absent it would create itself perhaps, but such that it would strengthen itself, and looking back into the past we should be looking back [to] times in which its strength was less than any given strength, and so that at the limit of the infinitely distant past it should vanish altogether. Then the problem was to imagine any kind of a law or tendency which would thus have a tendency to strengthen itself. Evidently it must be a tendency toward generalization, — a generalizing tendency. But any fundamental universal tendency ought to manifest itself in nature. Where shall we look for it? We could not expect to find it in such phenomena as gravitation where the evolution has so nearly approached its ultimate limit, that nothing even simulating irregularity can be found in it. But we must search for this generalizing tendency rather in such departments of nature where we find plasticity and evolution still at work. The most plastic of all things is the human mind, and next after that comes the organic world, the world of protoplasm. Now the generalizing tendency is the great law of mind, the law of association, the law of habit taking. We also find in all active protoplasm a tendency to take habits. Hence I was led to the hypothesis that the laws of the universe have been formed under a universal tendency of all things toward generalization and habit-taking.

The next problem was to find a method of reasoning by which I could deduce with mathematical certainty the exact nature and formulae of the laws which would be formed under the influence of such a tendency and having deduced them to compare them with nature and thus see whether the theory was tenable or not.

Now I have had some remarkable successes in this line; and have also been led to make some remarkable predictions which remain yet to be compared with observation.[9] Of the method of reasoning I have used I shall give you some slight idea in the next lecture.

EIGHT

The Logic of Continuity

Of all conceptions Continuity is by far the most difficult for Philosophy to handle. You naturally cannot do much with a conception until you can define it. Now every man at all competent to express an opinion must admit as it seems to me that no definition of continuity up to quite recent times was nearly right, and I maintain that the only thoroughly satisfactory definition is that which I have been gradually working out, and of which I presented a first *ébauche* when I had the honor of reading a paper here in Cambridge in 1892,[1] and the final form of which I have given you sufficient hints in these lectures. But even supposing that my definition, which as yet has not received that sanction which can only come from the critical examination of the most powerful and exact intellects, is all wrong, still no man not in leading strings as to this matter can possibly think that there was anything like a satisfactory definition before the labors of Dr. Georg Cantor, which only began to attract the attention of the whole world about [1890].

But after a satisfactory definition of continuity has been obtained the philosophical difficulties connected with this conception only begin to [be] felt in all their strength. Those difficulties are of two kinds. First there is the logical difficulty, how we are to establish a method of reasoning about continuity in philosophy? and second there is the metaphysical difficulty, what are we to say about the being, and the existence, and the genesis of continuity?

As to the proper method of reasoning about continuity, the dictate of good sense would seem to be that philosophy should in this matter follow the lead of geometry, the business of which it is to study continua.

But alas! the history of geometry forces upon us some sad lessons about the minds of men. That which had already been called the Elements of geometry long before the day of Euclid is a collection of convenient propositions concerning the relations between the lengths of lines, the areas of surfaces, the volumes of solids, and the measures of angles. It concerns itself only incidentally with the intrinsic properties of space, primarily only with the ideal properties of perfectly rigid bodies, of which we avail ourselves to construct a convenient system of measuring space. The measurement of a thing was clearly shown by Klein, twenty-five years ago, to be always extrinsic to the nature of the thing itself. Elementary geometry is nothing but the introduction to *geometrical metric,* or the mathematical part of the physics of rigid bodies. The very early Greek geometers, I mean for example [Peirce left a blank to fill in later], who is said to have written the first *Elements,* I have no doubt, considered metric as the philosophical basis and foundation, not only of geometry, but of mathematics in general. For it is to be remarked that considerably the larger part of Euclid's Elements is occupied with algebra not with geometry; and since he and all the Greeks had a much stronger impulse to get to the logical foundation of any object of study than we have, and since it is only the first book of Euclid in which the logic has been a matter of deep cogitation, it is plain that it was originally, at least, conceived that those geometrical truths in the first book of the Elements lay at the foundation even of algebra itself. But Euclid certainly, and in *my* opinion much earlier Greeks, had become acquainted with that branch of geometry which studies the conditions under which different rays of light indefinitely prolonged will intersect in common points or lie in common planes. There is no accepted name for this branch. It is sometimes called descriptive geometry; but that is in violent conflict with principles of nomenclature, since descriptive geometry is the accepted name of a branch of geometry invented by Monge and so named by him, — a branch closely allied to this other doctrine but not the same. Clifford called the branch of which we are speaking, Graphics (which conveys no implication); other writers call it synthetic geometry (though it may be treated analytically), geometry of position (which is the name of something else), modern geometry (where in fact it is ancient), intersectional geometry (though projection plays as great a *role* as section in it), projective geometry (though section is as important as projection), perspective geometry, etc. I would propose the name *geometrical optic.* Euclid, I say, and earlier Greeks were acquainted [with] this geometrical optic. Now to any person of discern-

ment in regard to intellectual qualities and who knows what the Greeks
were, and especially what the Greek geometers were, and most particularly what Euclid was, it seems to me incredible that Euclid should have
been acquainted with geometrical optic and not have perceived that it
was more fundamental, — more intimately concerned with the intrinsic
nature of space, — than metric is. And indeed *a posteriori* evidences that
he actually did so are not wanting. Why, then, did Euclid not say a single
word about this optic in his elements? Why did he altogether omit it
even in cases where he must have seen that its propositions were indispensable conditions of the cogency of his demonstrations? Two possible
explanations have occurred to me. It may be that he did not know how
to prove the propositions of *optic* otherwise than by means of *metric;* and
therefore, seeing that he could not make a thorough job, preferred
rather ostentatiously and emphatically (quite in his style in other matters), omitting all mention of optical propositions. Or it may be that,
being a university professor, he did not wish to repel students by teaching propositions that had an appearance of being useless. Remember
that even the stupendous Descartes abandoned the study of geometry.
And why? Because he said it was *useless.* And this he said *a propos* of
conic sections! That he should have thought conic sections useless, is
comparatively pardonable. But that he the Moses of modern thinkers
should have thought that a philosopher ought not to study useless things
is it not a stain of dishonor upon the human mind itself?

In modern times the Greek science of geometrical optic was utterly
forgotten, all the books written about it were lost, and mathematicians
became entirely ignorant that there was any such branch of geometry.
There was a certain contemporary of Descartes, one Desargues, who
rediscovered that optic and carried his researches into it very far indeed.
He showed clearly and in detail the great utility of the doctrine in perspective drawing and in architecture, and the great economy that it
would effect in the cutting of stones for building. On the theoretical
side he pushed discovery to an advance of a good deal more than two
centuries. He was a secular man. But he worked alone, with hardly the
slightest recognition. ⟨Without one word of encouragement, just as such
a mind would do in America today.⟩ Insignificant men treated him with
vitriolic scorn. His works, though printed, were utterly lost and forgotten. The most voluminous historians of mathematics though compatri-
ots did not know that such a man had ever lived, until one day Michel
Chasles walking along the *Quai des Grands Augustins* probably after a
meeting of the *Institut,* came across and bought for a franc a MS copy

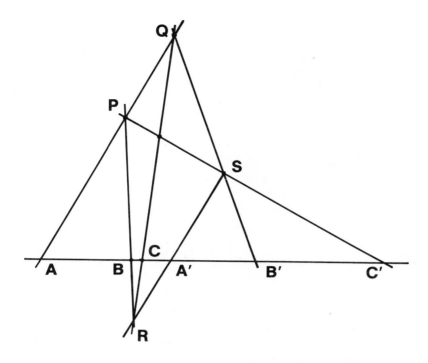

of one of those printed books. He took it home and studied it. He learned from it the important theory of the Involution of Six Points; and from him the mathematical world learned it; and it has been a great factor in the development of modern geometry. There can be no possible doubt that this knowledge actually came from the book of Desargues, because the relation has always borne the strange name Involution which Desargues had bestowed upon it, — and the whole theory is in his book although it had been totally unmentioned in any known treatise, memoir, or programme previous to the lucky find of Chasles. When will mankind learn the lessons such facts teach? That had that doctrine not been lost to all those generations of geometers, philosophy would have been further advanced today, and that the nations would have attained a higher intellectual level, is undoubtedly true, — but that may be passed by as a bagatelle. But why will men not reflect that but for the stupidity with which Desargues was met, — many a man might have eaten a better dinner and have had a better bottle of wine with it? It needs not much computation of causes and effects to see that that must be *so*. Six collinear points are said to be *in involution*, provided that four points can be found such that every pair of them is

in one straight line with *one* of the six, but not with *all* the six. Thus
AA′BB′CC′ are in involution because of the four points PQRS.

In 1859, Arthur Cayley showed that the whole of geometrical metric is but a special problem in geometrical optic. Namely, Cayley showed
that there is a locus in space, — not a kind of a locus, but an individual
place, — whose optical properties and relations to rigid bodies constitute
those facts that are expressed by space-measurement.

That was in [1859.] It attracted the admiration and assent of the
whole mathematical world, which has never since ceased to comment
upon it, and develop the doctrine. Yet a few years ago I was talking
with a man who had written two elementary geometries and who perhaps was, for aught I know still is, more influential than any other
individual in determining how Geometry shall be taught in American
schools at large, and this gentleman never heard of Projective Geometry
neither the name nor the thing and his politeness never shone more
than in his not treating what I said about Cayley with silent contempt.

But many years before Cayley made that discovery, a geometer in
Göttingen, Listing by name, — a name which I will venture to say that
Cayley, learned as he was in all departments of mathematics heard for
the first time many years later, probably from Tait, who knew of him
because he and Listing were both physicists, — this Listing had in 1847
four years before Riemann's first paper discovered the existence of quite
another branch of geometry, and had written two very long and rich
memoirs about it. But the mathematical world paid no heed to them till
half a century had passed. This branch, which he called Topology, but
which I shall call Topic, to rhyme with *metric* and *optic*, bears substantially
the same relation to optic that optic bears to metric. Namely, *topic* shows
that the entire collection of all possible *rays*, or unlimited straight lines, in
space, has no general geometrical characters whatever that distinguish it
at all from countless other families of lines. Its only distinction lies in its
physical relations. Light moves along rays; so do particles unacted on
by any forces; and maximum-minimum measurements are along rays.
But the whole doctrine of geometrical optic is merely a special case of
a topical doctrine.

That which *topic* treats of is the modes of connection of the parts
of continua. *Geometrical topic* is what the philosopher must study who
seeks to learn anything about continuity from geometry.

I will give you a slight sketch of the doctrine. We have seen in a
previous lecture what continuity consists in. There is an endless series
of abnumeral multitudes, each related to the next following as M is

related to 2^M, where we might put any other quantity in place of 2. The least of these abnumeral multitudes is 2^N [that is, 2 to the power $\aleph_0$] where N is the multitude of all whole numbers. It is impossible that there should be a collection of distinct individuals of greater multitude than all these abnumeral multitudes. Yet every one of these multitudes is possible and the existence of a collection of any one of these multitudes will not in the least militate against the existence of a collection of any other of these multitudes. Why then, may we not suppose a collection of distinct individuals which is an aggregate of one collection of each [of] those multitudes? The answer is, that to suppose an aggregate of *all* is to suppose the process of aggregation *completed*, and that is supposing the series of abnumeral multitudes brought to *an end*, while it can be proved that there is no last nor limit to the series. Let me remind you that by the *limit* of an endless series of successive objects we mean an object which comes after all the objects of that series, but so that every *other* object which comes after all those objects comes after the limit also. When I say that the series of abnumeral multitudes has no limit, I mean that it has no limit among multitudes of distinct individuals. It will have a limit if there is properly speaking any meaning in saying that something that is *not* a multitude of distinct individuals is *more* than every multitude of distinct individuals. But, you will ask, can there be any sense in that? I answer, yes, there can, in this way. That which is possible is in so far *general,* and as general, it ceases to be individual. Hence, remembering that the word "potential" means *indeterminate yet capable of determination in any special case,* there may be a *potential* aggregate of all the possibilities that are consistent with certain general conditions; and this may be such that given any collection of distinct individuals whatsoever, out of that potential aggregate there may be actualized a more multitudinous collection than the given collection. Thus the potential aggregate is with the strictest exactitude greater in multitude than any possible multitude of individuals. But being a potential aggregate only, it does not contain any individuals at all. It only contains general conditions which *permit* the determination of individuals.

The logic of this may be illustrated by considering an analogous case. You know very well that ⅔ is not a whole number. It is not any whole number whatever. In the whole collection of whole numbers you will not find ⅔. That you know. Therefore, you know something about the entire collection of whole numbers. But what is the nature of your conception of this collection? It is general. It is potential. It is vague, but yet with such a vagueness as permits of its accurate determination in regard to any particular object proposed for examination. Very well, that being granted, I proceed to the analogy with what we have been saying. Every whole number considered as a multitude is capable of being completely counted. Nor does its being aggregated with or added to any other whole number in the least degree interfere with the completion of the count. Yet the aggregate of *all* whole numbers cannot be completely counted. For the completion would suppose the *last* whole number was included, whereas there is no last whole number. But though the aggregate of all whole numbers cannot be completely counted, that does not prevent our having a distinct idea of the multitude of all whole numbers. We have a conception of the entire collection of whole numbers. It is a *potential* collection indeterminate yet determinable. And we see that the entire collection of whole numbers is more multitudinous than any whole number.

In like manner the potential aggregate of all the abnumeral multitudes is more multitudinous than any multitude. This potential aggregate cannot be a multitude of distinct individuals any more than the aggregate of all the whole numbers can be completely counted. But it is a distinct general conception for all that, — a conception of a potentiality.

A potential collection more multitudinous than any collection of distinct individuals can be[,] cannot be entirely vague. For the potentiality supposes that the individuals are determinable in every multitude. That is, they are determinable as distinct. But there cannot be a distinctive quality for each individual; for these qualities would form a collection too multitudinous for them to remain distinct. It must therefore be by means of relations that the individuals are distinguishable from one another.

Suppose, in the first place, that there is but one such distinguishing relation, r. Then since one individual is to be distinguished from another simply by this that one is r of the other, it is plain that nothing is r to itself. Let us first try making this r a simple dyadic relation. If, then, of three individuals A,B,C, A is r to B and B is r to C, it must be that A is r to C or else that C is r to A. We do not see, at first, that there it matters which. Only there must be a general rule about it, because the whole idea of the system is the potential determination of individuals by means of entirely general characters. Suppose, first, that if A is r to B and B is r to C then in every case C is r to A, and consequently A is not r to C. Taken then any fourth individual, D, Either [see table on next page.]

A is r to D

If A is r to D, since C is r to A
    D is r to C
    D is r to B
    Since B is r to C
    C is r to D
    absurd

Then either B is r to D   or
    C is r to B
    absurd

        D is r to A
Either C is r to D   or
    A is r to C
    absurd

        D is r to C
Either B is r to D   or
    C is r to B
    absurd

    D is r to B
Since B is r to C
    C is r to D
    absurd

That rule, then, when you come to look into it will not work. The other rule that if A is r to B and B is r to C then A is r to C leads to no contradiction, but it does lead to this, that there are two possible exceptional individuals[,] one that is r to everything else and another to which everything else is r. This is like a limited line, where every point is r that is, is to the *right* of every other or else that other is to the right of it. The generality of the case is destroyed by those two points of discontinuity, — the extremities. Thus, we see that no perfect continuum can be defined by a dyadic relation. But if we take instead a triadic relation, and say A is r to B for C, say to fix our ideas that proceeding from A in a particular way, say to the right, you reach B before C, it is quite evident, that a continuum will result like a self-returning line

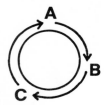

with no discontinuity whatever. All lines are simple rings and are topically precisely alike except that a line may have *topical singularities*. A *topical singularity* of a place is a place within that place from which the modes of departure are fewer or more than from the main collection of such places within the place. The topical singularities of *lines* are singular points. From an *ordinary* point on a line a particle can move two ways. Singular points are points from which a particle can move either no way, or in *one* way, or else in *three* ways or more. That is they are either, first, *isolated points* from which a particle cannot move in the line at all, or secondly, *extremities*, from which a particle can move but one way, or thirdly, *furcations*,

from which a particle can move in three or more ways. Those are the only topical distinctions there are among lines. Surfaces, or two dimensional continua, can also have singularities. These are either *singular points* or *singular lines*. The singular lines are either isolated lines, which may have singular points at which they are not isolated, or they are *bounding edges*, or they are lines of which the surface splits into different sheets. These singular lines may themselves have singular points, which are subject [to] interesting laws. A student would find the singular lines of surfaces a good subject for a thesis. Isolated singular points of surfaces are either entirely detached from the surface or they are points at which different sheets or parts of the same sheet are tacked together. But aside from their singularities surfaces are of different kinds. In the first place, they are either *perissid* or *artiad*. A perissid surface is one which, although unbounded, does not enclose any space, that is, does not necessarily cut space into two regions, or what comes to the same thing, it has only one side. Such is the plane surface of geometrical optics, and in fact, such is every surface of odd order. The perissid surfaces are mathematically the simpler; but the artiad surfaces are the more familiar. A half twisted ribbon pasted together so that one side becomes continuous with the other side is an example of a bounded perissid surface. If you pass along a plane in geometrical optic, you finally come back to

the same point, only you are on the other side of the plane. An artiad surface, on the other hand, is for example the bounding surface between air and the stone of any finite stone, however, curiously it may be cut. Moreover, a surface may have a *fornix* or any number of *fornices*. A fornix is a part of the surface like a railway-tunnel which at once bridges over the interval between two parts of the surface, and so connects them, and at the same time, tunnels under that bridge so that a particle may move on the surface from one side of the bridge to the other without touching the bridge. A flat-iron handle, or any handle with two attachments has a surface which is a *fornix* of the whole surface of which it forms a part. Both perissid and artiad surfaces can equally have any number of fornices, without disturbing their artiad or perissid character.

If I were to attempt to tell you much about the different shapes which unbounded three dimensional spaces could take, I fear I might seem to talk gibberish to you, so different is your state of mental training and mine. Yet I must endeavor to make some things plain, or at least not leave them quite dark. Suppose that you were acquainted with no surface except the surface of the earth, and I were to endeavor to make the shape of the surface of a double ring clear to you. I should say, you can imagine in the first place a disk with an outer boundary.

Then you can imagine that this has a hole or holes cut through it.

Then you can imagine a second disk just like this and imagine the two to be pasted together at all their edges, so that there are no longer any edges. Thus I should give you some glimmer of an idea of a double ring. Now I am going in a similar way to describe an unbounded three-dimensional space, having a different shape from the space we know. Begin if you please by imagining a closed cave bounded on all sides. In order not to complicate the subject with optical ideas which are not necessary, I will suppose that this cave is pitch dark. I will also suppose that you can swim about in the air regardless of gravity. I will suppose that you have learned this cave thoroughly; that you know it is pretty cool, but warmer in some places, you know just where, than others, and that the different parts have different odors by which they are known. I will suppose that these odors are those of neroli, portugal, limette, lemon, bergamot, and lemongrass, — all of them generically alike. I will further suppose that you feel floating in this cave two great balloons entirely separated from the walls and from each other, yet perfectly stationary. With the feeling of each of them and with its precise locality I suppose you to be familiarly acquainted. I will further suppose that you formerly inhabited a cave exactly like this one, except it was rather warm, that the distribution of temperature was entirely different, and that [the] odors in different localities in it with which you are equally familiar, were those of frankincense, benzoin, camphor, sandal-wood, cinnamon, and coffee, thus contrasting strongly with those of the other cave. I will further suppose the texture-feeling of the walls and of the two balloons to be widely different in the two caves. Now, let us suppose that you, being as familiar with both caves as with your pocket, learn that works are in progress to open them into one another. At length, you are informed that the wall of one of the balloons has been reduced to a mere film which you can feel with your hand but through which you can pass. You being all this time in the cool cave swim up to that balloon and try it. You pass through it readily; only in doing so you feel a strange twist, such as you never have felt, and you find by feeling with your hand that you are just passing out through one of the corresponding balloons of the warm cave. You recognize the warmth of that cave[,] its perfume, and the texture of the walls. After you have passed backward and forward often enough to become familiar with the fact that the passage may be made through every part of the surface of the balloon, you are told that the other balloon is now in the same state. You try it and find it to be so, passing round and round in every way. Finally, you are told that the outer walls have been removed. You swim to where they were. You feel the queer twist and you find yourself in the other cave. You ascertain by trial that it is so with every part of the walls, the floor, and the roof. They do not exist any longer. There is no outer boundary at all.

Now all this is quite contrary to the geometry of our actual space. Yet it is not altogether inconceivable even sensuously. A man would accustom himself to it. On the mathematical side, the conception presents no particular difficulty. In fact mathematically our own shaped space is by no means the easiest to comprehend. That will give you an idea of what is meant by a space shaped differently from our space. The shape may be further complicated by supposing the two balloons to have the shape of anchor-rings and to be interlinked with one another.

After what I have said, you cannot have much difficulty in imagining that in passing through one of the balloons you have a choice of twisting yourself in either of two opposite ways, one way carrying you into the second cave and the other way into a third cave. That balloon surface is then a *singular surface*.

I will not attempt to carry you further into geometrical topic. You can readily understand that nothing but a rigidly exact logic of relations can be your guide in such a field. I will only mention that the real complications of the subject only begin to appear when continua of higher dimensionality than 3 are considered. For then first we begin to have systems of relations between the different dimensions.

A continuum may have any discrete multitude of dimensions whatsoever. If the multitude of dimensions surpasses all discrete multitudes there cease to be any distinct dimensions. I have not as yet obtained a logically distinct conception of such a continuum. Provisionally, I identify it with the *uralt* vague generality of the most abstract potentiality.

Listing, that somewhat obscure Göttingen professor of physics, whose name must forever be illustrious as that of the father of geometrical topic, — the only intrinsic science of Space, [—] invented a highly artificial method of thinking about continua which the great Riemann independently fell into in considering the connectivity of surfaces. But Riemann never studied it sufficiently to master it thoroughly. This method is not all that could be desired for continua of more than 3 dimensions, which Listing never studied. Even for our space, the method fails to throw much light on the theory of Knots; but it is highly useful in all cases, and is almost all that could be desired for tridimensional space. This method consists in the employment of a series of numbers which I proceed to define. By a *figure*, modern geometers do not mean what *Euclid* meant at all. We simply mean any place or places considered together. An indivisible place is a *point*. A movable thing which at any one instant occupied a point is a *particle*. The place which a particle can occupy during a lapse of time, one point at one instant and another at another instant, is a *line*. A movable thing which at any one instant occupies a line is a *filament*. The place which a filament can occupy in a lapse of time is a *surface*. A movable thing which at any one instant occupies a surface is a *film*. The place which a film can occupy in a lapse of time is a *space*, or as I would call it a *tripon*. A movable body which at any one instant occupied a *tripon* is a *solid*, or as I would call it a *trion*. Thus for higher dimensional places we have the *tetrapon*, the *pentapon*, etc. And for the movable things in them the *tetron*, *penton*, etc.

Now then for Listing's numbers.

I call the first of them the *Chorisis*. He calls it simply the number of separate pieces. I give it a name to rhyme with his Cyclosis and Periphraxis; and with the analogous name I give it an analogous definition. Namely, the *chorisis* of a D-dimensional figure, is the number of simplest possible D-dimensional places that must be removed from it, in order to leave room for no particle at all. That is but a roundabout way of expressing the number of separate pieces. At first, I wished to define it as the number of simple D-dimensional places that must be removed in order to leave no room for a pair of particles which cannot move within the figure so as to coalesce. This would be one less than the number of pieces. But I subsequently surrendered to Listing's own view.

The second Listing number he calls the *Cyclosis*. The cyclosis of a D-dimensional figure is the number of simplest possible places of D − 1 dimensions which have to be cut away from the figure, to preclude the existence in the remaining place of a filament without topical singularities which cannot gradually move within that place so as to collapse to a particle. For example, this line

has a cyclosis equal to 1. For you must cut it through to preclude a ring shaped filament which is incapable of collapsing by any gradual motion within the figure. On the other hand the surface of the blackboard has its cyclosis equal to *zero*, because any ringshaped filament in it has room gradually to shrink to a particle. It is true that when the ringshaped filament shrinks to a particle there is a breach of continuity at the last instant; but when we define cyclosis we *except* that final breach of continuity. A similar remark applies to all the other numbers. An annular surface bounded by two rings has a cyclosis equal to 1. For it has to be cut through on one line to prevent the existence of a ringshaped filament which cannot gradually shrink within the annular surface to a particle. The surface of an anchor-ring has a cyclosis equal to 2. For to preclude the existence of the noncollapsible filament it is necessary first to cut round the bar of the ring and after that to slit the bar along all its length. The space which the solid iron of the anchor-ring fills has a cyclosis equal to 1. For simply sawing it through in any plane is sufficient to preclude a noncollapsible filament. [A] spiral line having one end and winding in toward the centre at such a rate as to be infinitely long, has a cyclosis *zero*. For although it be infinitely long in measure, measure does not concern topical geometry. The line has an end at the centre, and its infinite windings will not prevent any filament in it from shrinking in it to a particle. The plane of imaginary quantity which the theory of functions studies has a cyclosis equal to zero. For take a straight line extending through the zero point and the point at infinity

though the modulus of its point of greatest modulus is infinity, yet measure does not concern topical geometry and it may continuously contract to a circle and finally to the origin. But the plane of perspective geometry is of an entirely different shape. Its cyclosis is 1. For consider a ray or unlimited straight line. That ray cuts the ray at infinity. In the plane of imaginary quantity there *is* no line at infinity, but only a point. Here, there is a ray at infinity. Here it is

Here is the movable filament cutting it

That filament cuts that ray *once* and once only. But the ray at infinity returns into itself as anybody would see who stood upon a boundless desert plane and viewed his horizon round and round. That horizon would be that ray. Now, disturb and move it as you will, the filament will always cut that fixed ray in an odd number of points. Thus it can never cease to cut it. For if it did it would cut it in *zero* points and zero is an even number. Thus we see that any ray, or any curve of odd order, is the place of an unshrinkable filament. But every such line cuts every other. Hence if the surface were separated along a single line of that kind, no unshrinkable filament could any longer exist in it. Those of you who are acquainted with non-Euclidean geometry might ask me how it would be in hyperbolic space. I reply it is the same thing precisely. Perspective geometry no more concerns itself with measure than does Topical, or Intrinsic, geometry. It is true that according to the mode of measurement used in hyperbolic geometry, all the parts of the plane at finite distance are enclosed within one circle. The parts of the plane outside the circle have then *no existence,* that is to say we are utterly cut off from volitional reactions with them. But they are none the less real on that account. You must recognize them, or fill your mind with senseless exceptions to all the laws of optics. Two rays continue to intersect in one point, although that point may be outside our universe. Only it now becomes a matter of indifference to us what the shape of the plane may be, since whether it have a cyclosis zero or a cyclosis 1, the part of the plane in our universe is a simple disk.

Listing's third number he calls the Periphraxis. The periphraxis of a figure of D dimensions is the number of simple places of D − 2 dimensions which must be taken away to prevent a non-singular film from gradually collapsing to a filament within the figure. Thus a cave with 2 balloons in it has a periphraxis equal to zero. For it is necessary to build out two barriers to preclude a sac from containing one balloon or the other, so that sac cannot collapse. The periphraxis of the space of perspective geometry is 1. But that of the geometry of quaternions is *zero*.

Listing's fourth number he calls the *Immensity*. It might be called the "fourth Listing." It is the number of simple places of D − 3 dimensions which must be taken away to preclude a non-singular noncollapsible solid, or trion. As Listing remarks, for all figures in our space this number is equal to *zero* excepting only for the entirety of space itself, for which it is 1.

For anybody who wishes to study this subject I will say that one of Listing's two papers[2] is in the *Göttinger Studien* page 771, and my impression is that it is in the excellent library of Columbia University. The other memoir which relates to Listing's Census Theorem, which is mainly if not wholly an artificial theorem, — true indeed but yet a mere formality, or affair of book-keeping (although this memoir is most important and it is in it that the author develops his numbers), is in the *Göttinger Abhandlungen*. I think vol. VII. Both memoirs are full of interest and excessively easy to read. Listing himself makes the Cyclosis and Periphraxis of space equal to zero, showing how little he knew of mathematics.

I have occupied far too large a part of my hour with this matter and must now leave entirely untouched two methods of my own invention for treating problems upon which Listing's numbers fail to throw much light.

Every attempt to understand anything, — every research, — supposes, or at least *hopes,* that the very objects of study themselves are subject to a logic more or less identical with that which we employ.

That the logic of the universe is more rudimentary than our subjective logic is a hypothesis which may be worth examination in some stage of culture, but it is too violently at war with all the lessons which this age has learned for any man nowadays to embrace it with that ardor with which a man must embrace the theory which he is to devote his best powers to developing and bringing to the test of experience. Whatever else may be said for or against that hypothesis, that which we of these times ought to try is rather the hypothesis that the logic of the universe is one to which our own aspires rather than attains.

Now continuity is shown by the logic of relatives to be nothing but a higher type of that which we know as generality. It is relational generality.

How then can a continuum have been derived? Has it for example been put together? Have the separated points become welded, or what?

Looking upon the course of logic as a whole we see that it proceeds from the question to the answer, — from the vague to the definite. And so likewise all the evolution we know of proceeds from the vague to the definite. The indeterminate future becomes the irrevocable past. In Spencer's phrase the undifferentiated differentiates itself. The homogeneous puts on heterogeneity. However it may be in special cases, then, we must suppose that as a rule the continuum has been derived from a more general continuum, a continuum of higher generality.

From this point of view we must suppose that the existing universe with all its arbitrary secondness is an offshoot from, or an arbitrary determination of, a world of ideas, a Platonic world; not that our superior logic has enabled us to reach up to a world of forms to which the real universe with its feebler logic was inadequate.

If this be correct, we cannot suppose the process of derivation, a process which extends from before time and from before logic, we cannot suppose that it began elsewhere than in the utter vagueness of completely undetermined and dimensionless potentiality.

The evolutionary process is, therefore, not a mere evolution of the *existing universe,* but rather a process by which the very Platonic forms themselves have become or are becoming developed.

We shall naturally suppose, of course, that existence is a stage of evolution. *This existence* is presumably but a *special* existence. We need not suppose that every form needs for its evolution to emerge into this world, but only that it needs to enter into *some* theatre of reactions, of which this is one.

The evolution of forms begins, or at any rate, has for an early stage of it, a vague potentiality; and that either is or is followed by a continuum of forms having a multitude of dimensions too great for the individual dimensions to be distinct. It must be by a contraction of the vagueness of that potentiality of everything in general but of nothing in particular that the world of forms comes about.

We can hardly but suppose that those sense-qualities that we now experience, colors, odors, sounds, feelings of every description, loves, griefs, surprise, are but the relics of an ancient ruined continuum of qualities, like a few columns standing here and there in testimony that here some old-world forum with its basilica and temples had once made a magnificent *ensemble*. And just as that forum, before it was actually built, had had a vague under-existence in the mind of him who planned its construction, so too the cosmos of sense qualities which I would have you to suppose in some early stage of being was [as] real as your personal life is this minute, had in an antecedent stage of development a vaguer being, before the relations of its dimensions became definite and contracted.

The sense-quality is a feeling. Even if you say it is a *slumbering* feeling, that does not make it less intense; perhaps the reverse. For it is the absence of *reaction*, — of feeling *another*, — that constitutes slumber, not the absence of the immediate feeling that is all that it is in its immediacy. Imagine a magenta color. Now imagine that all the rest of your consciousness, memory, thought, everything except this feeling of magenta is utterly wiped out, and with that is erased all possibility of comparing the magenta with anything else or of estimating it as more or less bright. That is what you must think the pure sense quality to be. Such a definite potentiality can emerge from the indefinite potentiality only by its own vital Firstness, and spontaneity. Here is this magenta color. What originally made such a quality of feeling possible? Evidently nothing but itself. It is a First.

Yet we must not assume that the qualities arose separate and came into relation afterward. It was just the reverse. The general indefinite potentiality became limited and heterogeneous. Those who express the idea to themselves by saying that the Divine Creator determined so and so, may be incautiously clothing the idea in a *garb* that is open to criticism, but it is, after all, substantially the only philosophical answer to the problem. Namely, they represent the ideas as springing into a preliminary stage of being by their own inherent firstness. But so springing up, they do not spring up isolated; for if they did, nothing could unite them. They spring up in reaction upon one another, and thus into a kind of existence. This reaction and this existence these persons call the mind of God. I really think there is no objection to this except that it is wrapped up in figures of speech, instead of having the explicitness that we desire in science. For all you know of "minds" is from the actions of animals with brains or ganglia like yourselves or at furthest like a cockroach. To apply such a word to *God* is precisely like the old pictures which show him like an aged man leaning over to look out from above a cloud. Considering the *vague intention* of it, as conceived by the *non-theological artist*, it cannot be called false, but rather ludicrously figurative.

In short, if we are going to regard the universe as a result of evolution at all, we must think that, not merely the existing universe, that locus in the cosmos to which our reactions are limited, but the whole Platonic world which in itself is equally real, is evolutionary in its origin, too. And among the things so resulting are time and logic. The very first and most fundamental element that we have to assume is a Freedom, or Chance, or Spontaneity, by virtue of which the general vague nothing-in-particular-ness that preceded the chaos took a thousand definite qualities. The *second* element we have to assume is that there could be accidental reactions between those qualities. The qualities themselves are mere eternal possibilities. But these reactions we must think of as *events*. Not that *Time* was. But still, they had all the here-and-nowness of events. I really do not see how the metaphysician can explain either of those elements as results, further than this, that it may be said that the accidental reaction was, at first, one of the special determinations that came about by pure spontaneity or chance.

Let me here say one word about Tychism, or the doctrine that absolute chance is a factor of the universe. There is one class of objectors to it who are so impressed with what they have read in popular books about the triumphs of science, that they really imagine that science has *proved* that the universe is regulated by law down to every detail. Such men are theologians, perhaps, or perhaps they have been brought up in surroundings where everything was so minutely regulated that they have come to believe that every tendency that exists at all in Nature must be carried to its furthest limit. Or, there is I know not what other explanation of their state of mind; but I do know one thing; they cannot be real students of physical science, — they cannot be *chemists*, for example. They are wrong in their logic. But there is *another* class of objectors for whom I have more respect. They are shocked at the atheism of Lucretius and his great master. They do not perceive that that which offends them is not the Firstness in the swerving atoms, because they themselves are just as much advocates of Firstness as the ancient Atomists were. But what they cannot accept is the attribution of this firstness to things perfectly dead and material. Now I am quite with them there. I think too that whatever is First is *ipso facto* sentient. If I make atoms swerve, — as I do, — I make them swerve but very very little, because

I conceive they are not absolutely dead. And by that I do not mean exactly that I hold them to be physically such as the materialists hold them to be[,] only with a small dose of sentiency superadded. For that, I grant, would be feeble enough. But what I mean is, that all that there is is First, Feelings; Second, Efforts; Third, Habits; — all of which are more familiar to us on their psychical side than on their physical side; and that dead matter would be merely the final result of the complete induration of habit reducing the free play of feeling and the brute irrationality of effort to complete death. Now I would suppose that that result of evolution is not quite complete even in our beakers and crucibles. Thus, when I speak of chance, I only employ a mathematical term to express with accuracy the characteristics of freedom or spontaneity.

Permit me further to say that I object to having my metaphysical system as a whole called Tychism. For although tychism does enter into it, it only enters as subsidiary to that which is really, as I regard it, the characteristic of my doctrine, namely, that I chiefly insist upon continuity, or Thirdness, and in order to secure to thirdness its really commanding function, I [find it indispensable] that it is a third, and that Firstness, or chance, and Secondness, or Brute reaction, are other elements without the independence of which Thirdness would not have anything upon which to operate. Accordingly, I like to call my theory Synechism, because it rests on the study of continuity. I would not object to Tritism. And if anybody can prove that it is *trite*, that would delight me the chiefest degree.

All that I have been saying about the beginnings of creation seems mildly confused enough. Now let me give you such slight indication as brevity permits of the clue to which I trust to guide us through the maze.

Let the clean blackboard be a sort of Diagram of the original vague potentiality, or at any rate of some early stage of its determination. This is something more than a figure of speech; for after all continuity is generality. This blackboard is a continuum of two dimensions, while that which it stands for is a continuum of some indefinite multitude of dimensions. This blackboard is a continuum of possible points; while that is a continuum of possible dimensions of quality, or is a continuum of possible dimensions of a continuum of possible dimensions of quality or something of that sort. There are no points on this blackboard. There are no dimensions in that continuum. I draw a chalk line on the board. This discontinuity is one of those brute acts by which alone the original vagueness could have made a step toward definiteness. There is a certain element of continuity in this line. Where did this continuity come from? It is nothing but the original continuity of the black board which makes everything upon it continuous. What I have really drawn there is an oval line. For this white chalk-mark is not a *line,* it is a plane figure in Euclid sense, — a *surface,* and the only line [that] is there is the line which forms the *limit* between the black surface and the white surface. Thus discontinuity can only be produced upon that blackboard by the reaction between two continuous surfaces into which it is separated, the white surface and the black surface. The whiteness is a Firstness, — a springing up of something new. But the boundary between the black and white is neither black, nor white, nor neither, nor both. It is the pairedness of the two. It is for the white the active Secondness of the black; for the black the active Secondness of the white.

Now the clue that I mentioned consists in making our thought diagrammatic and mathematical, by treating generality from the point of view of geometrical continuity, and by experimenting upon the diagram.

We see the original generality like the ovum of the universe segmentated by this mark. However, the mark is a mere accident, and as such may be erased. It will not interfere with another mark drawn in quite another way. There need be no consistency between the two. But no further progress beyond this can be made, until a mark will *stay* for a little while; that is, until some beginning of a *habit* has been established by virtue of which the accident acquires some incipient staying quality, some tendency toward consistency.

This habit is a generalizing tendency, and as such a generalization, and as such a general, and as such a continuum or continuity. It must have its origin in the original continuity which is inherent in potentiality. Continuity, as generality, is inherent in potentiality, which is essentially general.

The whiteness or blackness, the Firstness, is essentially indifferent as to continuity. It lends itself readily to generalization but is not in itself general. The limit between the whiteness and blackness is essentially discontinuous, or antigeneral. It is insistently *this here.* The original potentiality is essentially continuous, or general.

Once the line will stay a little after it is marked, another line may be drawn beside it. Very soon our eye persuades us there is a *new* line, the envelope of those others.

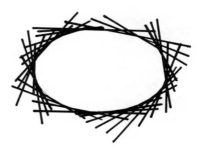

This rather prettily illustrates the logical process which we may suppose takes place in things, in which the generalizing tendency builds up new habits from chance occurrences. The new curve, although it is new in its distinctive character, yet derives its continuity from the continuity of the black board itself. The original potentiality is the Aristotelian matter or indeterminacy from which the universe is formed. The straight lines as they multiply themselves under the habit of being tangent to the envelope, gradually tend to lose their individuality. They become in a measure more and more obliterated and sink into mere adjuncts to the new cosmos in which they are individuals.

Many such reacting systems may spring up in the original continuum; and each of *these* may itself act as first line from which a larger system may be built in which it in turn will merge its individuality.

At the same time all this, be it remembered, is not of the order of the existing universe, but is merely a Platonic world, of which we are, therefore, to conceive that there are many, both coördinated and subordinated to one another; until finally out of one of these Platonic worlds is differentiated the particular actual universe of existence in which we happen to be.

There is, therefore, every reason in logic why this here universe should be replete with accidental characters, for each of which in its particularity there is no other reason than that it is one of the ways in which the original vague potentiality has happened to get differentiated.

But, for all that, it will be found that if we suppose the laws of nature to have been formed under the influence of a universal tendency of things to take habits, there are certain characters that those laws will necessarily possess.

As for attempting to set forth the series of deductions I have made upon this subject, that would be out of the question. All that I have any thought of doing is to illustrate, by a specimen or two, chosen among those which need the least explanation, some of the methods by which such reasoning may be conducted.

Various continua to which the inquirer's attention will be directed in the course of this investigation must be assumed to be devoid of all topical singularities. For any such singularity is a locus of discontinuity; and from the nature of the continuum there may be no room to suppose any such secondness. But now, a continuum which is without singularities must, in the first place, return into itself. Here is a remarkable consequence.

Take, for example, Time. It makes no difference what singularities you may see reason to impose upon this continuum. You may, for example, say that all evolution began at this instant, which you may call the infinite past, and comes to a close at that other instant, which you may call the infinite future. But all this is quite extrinsic to time itself. Let it be, if you please, that evolutionary time, our section of time, *is* contained between those limits. Nevertheless, it cannot be denied that time itself, unless it be discontinuous, as we have every reason to suppose it is not, stretches on beyond those limits, infinite though they be, returns into itself, and begins again. Your metaphysics must be shaped to accord with that.

Again, the lowest Listing number, the number of separate pieces, cannot be *zero;* for such a hypothesis would annul the whole continuum. Nor can the highest Listing number be *zero,* unless the continuum has singularities. But the intermediate Listing numbers may be *zero* or almost any numbers. If metaphysics is really to be made a definite science, and not child's play, the first inquiry concerning any general must be, first, what its dimensionality is, and secondly, what those intermediate Listing numbers are; and whatever your answer is, it will generally be found to lead you into those difficult but definite questions, out of which we are accustomed in inductive science to think that the true theory is pretty sure to grow. It is one of the great merits of the method of thought that the logic of relatives inculcates that it leads to such definite questions.

For example, take the continuum of all possible sense qualities after this has been so far restricted that the dimensions are distinct. This is a continuum in which firstness is the prevailing character. It is also highly primitive; and therefore we ought to suppose, till the contrary is proved, that the intermediate Listing numbers are all *unity.* For *zero* is distinctly a dualistic idea. It is mathematically A − A, i.e. the result of the inverse process of subtraction. Now an inverse process is a *Second* process. It is true that there is another sort of zero which is a *limit*. Such is the vague zero of indeterminacy. But a limit involves Secondness prominently, and besides that, Thirdness. In fact, the *generality* of indeterminacy *marks* its Thirdness. Accordingly, *zero* being an idea of Secondness, we find, as we should expect, that any continuum whose intermediate Listing numbers are zero is equivalent to a pair of continua whose Listing numbers are 1. For instance, a perspective plane has a cyclosis equal to 1, while a ball has a cyclosis equal to 0. Now a ball is, topically speaking, of the same shape as two planes after the singularity of the pair has been removed. I will show you that this is true. Let the one plane be that of the blackboard, and let the other be oblique to it. Let this mark represent their ray of intersection. This ray is a singular line upon the two planes considered as one surface. In order to remove this singularity, we must split it down, so as to leave the right hand side of the blackboard plane, joined along the right hand parts of the split line to that part of the oblique plane that is in front, while the left hand part of the black board plane is joined along the left hand parts of the split line to the part of the oblique plane behind the black board. Thus this ray becomes two rays. But two rays *intersect*. So that a singular point still remains. We must, then, cut through that singular point, making two points of it; and leaving the right side of the black board plane joined to the forward part of the oblique plane and the left side joined to the other part. We now move apart those two hyperbolic branches that the two rays have made until they have made nearly a completed circuit of the plane. They no longer cut the ray at infinity, and we have an eggshaped solid which is topically just like a ball. Thus I have shown how *secondness* enters into the *zero* cyclosis.

It is the same with the other intermediate Listing numbers; and we must assume that all the Listing numbers of the continuum of sense-qualities are equal to 1. This is confirmed by carrying the evolution of the continuum and its definiteness a step further. Namely, we will now suppose that each quality has acquired a settled identity in all its different degrees, so that the continuum is ready for the application of measurement. This measurement is a network figure imposed upon the blank continuum. It is true that it is in large measure arbitrary. It is *our* creation. Nevertheless, we shall adapt our creation as far as possible to the real properties of the continuum itself. Besides, there are certain modes of measurement which are impossible without breach of continuity in certain shapes of continua. For example, anybody can see that the same system of coördinates which could be applied to defining positions of points on a sphere, say latitude and longitude, would have to be modified in order to apply it to the definition of positions on an anchor-ring. On the sphere, longitude returns into itself after every 360°, and there are two points, the poles, whose longitudes are indeterminate; while latitude extends through 180° and then stops. But on the ring there will be one series of lines which will go round the bar of the ring without ever cutting one another and another series going round the hole of the ring without cutting one another. This is a much simpler system of measurement than any that is possible on the sphere. Now in the network figure of coördinates which conforms best to the properties of the continuum of pure quality, there is a line for each quality, along which line that quality only varies in intensity. All these lines come together at the absolute zero of quality. For in the *zero* of intensity quality is indistinguishable in its inmost nature. But those lines meet nowhere else. In the infinite degree qualities may dazzle our senses; but in themselves they are different. Hence, the continuum of quality is such that unlimited lines may cut one another an odd number of times, namely, *once* only. Now this would be impossible were the intermediate Listing numbers *even*, say zero. Our hypothesis that they are odd is therefore confirmed. I must add that the measurement of quality is evidently hyperbolic which weakens considerably the force of the last argument.

As another example consider the continuum of Space. In my lecture on the subject I pointed out to you how though it is a continuum, and therefore a Thirdness, the whole nature and function of space refers to Secondness. It is the theatre of the reactions of particles, and reaction is Secondness in its purity. For this and other reasons, which I omit for the sake of brevity, we must as our first retroduction assume that the intermediate Listing numbers for space are all *zero*. When we come to consider the principles of hydrodynamics we find that view confirmed. I cannot enter into details; but the motions of a frictionless incompressible fluid is as though it were composed of interpenetrating parts shot out in straight lines from sources and disappearing into sinks. But that implies that all the straight lines radiating from a single point will meet again in another single point which supposes the Cyclosis and Periphraxis of Space to be *zero*. There will be some difficulties connected with this view, but I do not think them serious; and at any rate this will serve as another illustration of the manner in which reasoning about continuity can be applied to give real vitality to metaphysical reasoning, and to cure it of its deathly impotency.

I should have been glad if I could have set forth all this in greater detail; but that would have required mathematics. I should have liked to interest you in a number of my ??scientifically?? important and philo-sophically significant results which I have been obliged to leave alto-gether unmentioned. I wish I could also have expounded some theories of other thinkers which, although I cannot accept them, seem to me to be well worthy of the most careful consideration. But to treat a theory like this, the whole life of which lies in minute diagrammatic reasoning, in eight lectures was inevitably to make it seem excessively abstruse and, at the same time, to do no more than exhibit a fragment here and there selected as being comparatively easy of presentation. The subject of mathematical metaphysics, or Cosmology, is not so very difficult, pro-vided it be properly expanded and displayed. It deeply concerns both physicist and psychist. The physicist ought to direct his attention to it, in order that he may be led to contemplate the intellectual side of his own science. Especially, the chemist, whose attention is forced to theory, needs above all to study the theory of theorizing. Psychologists have not yet dropped their excellent habit of studying philosophy; but I venture to think that they are not fully alive to all the value for their science of certain higher mathematics and to the virtues of mathematical thinking. The failure of Herbart[3] whose attempt was made before either Mathe-matics or Psychology was ripe for it, does not argue that no success can be attained in that line. I have presented, — or no, I have not presented anything in these lectures, but I have talked about the most abstract parts of Cosmology; but this subject embraces many topics which have not that character, such as the question of the present state of the evi-dences of the Conservation of Energy and the question of the nature of the influences which hold together the constituent elements of chemical compounds. In short there is a great variety of different ways in which Cosmology is both curious and useful for widely different classes of minds. We all know the kind of man who is warranted never to be interested in it, the man who lays out a system of ideas in his youth and stands on his platform with stalwart constancy like Casablanca on the burning deck. But if a mind is not absolutely argon and helium, but is capable of being drawn by any means within an alien sphere of attraction, no study is more calculated to bring about that event than this. It is decidedly a difficult subject on which to break ground for oneself. Economy of time, avoidance of a terrible waste, requires the student to take counsel of the experience here of a mathematician, there of a logician, again of a physicist or chemist, and continually of a psychologist. It is, by the way, precisely in psychology, where you are the strongest that I have to confess myself the weakest. For that reason, in these lectures I have touched as little as possible upon psychology, preferring to deal with topics of Cosmology where I should be more at home, although you were less so. Crabbed and confused as all these circumstances have caused these conferences to become, you have been kind enough to listen to them, and really I dare not acknowledge, as it is in my heart to do the whole warmth of my thanks, for fear you might think it out of measure. But should it happen to any of you to select for his life's explorations a region very little trodden, he will, as a matter of course, have the pleasure of making a good many discoveries of more fundamental importance than at all remain to be made in any ground that has long been highly cultivated. But on the other hand, he will find that he has condemned himself to an isolation like that of Alexander Selkirk. He must be prepared for almost a lifetime of work with scarce one greeting, and I can assure him that if, as his day is sinking, a rare good fortune should bring a dozen men of real intellect, some men of great promise others of great achievement, together to listen to so much of what he has learned as his long habit of silence shall have left him the power of expressing in the compass of eight lectures, he will know then an almost untasted joy and will comprehend then what gratitude I feel at this moment.

NOTES

INDEX

Notes

Introduction: The Consequences of Mathematics

1. Letter to Francis Russell, 23 September 1894, quoted in Carolyn Eisele, *Studies in the Scientific and Mathematical Philosophy of Charles S. Peirce*, ed. R. M. Martin (The Hague: Mouton, 1979), p. 156.

2. For examples, see "What Pragmatism Is" (*P* 1078), *The Monist*, 15(1905): 161–181 (republished in *CP* 5), *MSS* 320, 322, and L427 (from about the same period).

3. On mathematics as an observational, experimental science of diagrammatic thought, see Don D. Roberts, *The Existential Graphs of Charles S. Peirce* (The Hague: Mouton, 1973), as well as Kenneth Laine Ketner, "Peirce on Diagrammatic Thought," in *Zeichen und Realität*, ed. K. Oehler (Tübingen: Stauffenburg Verlag, 1984); "Semeiotic Is an Observational Science," in *Iconicity: Essays on the Nature of Culture*, ed. P. Bouissac and R. Posner (Tübingen: Stauffenburg Verlag, 1986); "Peirce's 'Most Lucid and Interesting Paper': An Introduction to Cenopythagoreanism," *International Philosophical Quarterly* 26(1986): 375–392; "Charles Sanders Peirce," in *Classical American Philosophy*, ed. J. Stuhr (New York: Oxford University Press, 1987), 13–92. See also the comments on Lecture Four in the present volume.

4. Walker Percy, "The Divided Creature," *Wilson Quarterly* 13(1989): 80. See also Percy's *The Message in the Bottle* (New York: Farrar, Straus and Giroux, 1975).

5. For a brief autobiography, see Stuhr (ed.), *Classical American Philosophy*. For a discussion of Arisbe, see Max H. Fisch, *Peirce, Semeiotic, and Pragmatism: Essays by Max H. Fisch*, ed. K. L. Ketner and C. J. W. Kloesel (Bloomington: Indiana University Press, 1986), chapter 12.

6. The first two paragraphs of this letter were printed at *CP* 8.249–250; however, the major portion, transcribed here, was omitted.

7. In 1887 Peirce produced a thoroughgoing critical review of this book,

which was considered by many to have made a good case for psychic phenomena (for the review, see *P* 352, "Criticisms on 'Phantasms of the Living.' An Examination of the Argument of Messrs. Gurney, Myers, and Podmore," *Proceedings of the American Society for Psychical Research*, o.s. 1[1887]: 157–179). A considerable controversy in print arose between Peirce and the authors of the book (see *O* 353, *P* 354). James had been scientifically interested in the American Society for Psychical Research, in whose journal Peirce's review appeared.

8. Peirce favored the hypothesis that Christianity was a development of earlier Asian traditions, especially Buddhism. Among his contemporaries, he was not alone in this notion. Similar views were advocated by Arthur Lillie, *The Influence of Buddhism on Primitive Christianity* (London: Swan Sonnenschein and Company, 1893), and William Benjamin Smith, *Der Vorchristliche Jesus* (Gieszen: Verlag von Alfred Töpelman, 1906). Peirce knew Smith's work quite well and mentioned it often. No mention of Lillie has been found in Peirce's writings, but there are many similarities with Peirce's hypotheses. Another possible line of influence in this matter is through the Booles: see *N* 3:197–199. For a quick comparison of Peirce and Buddha on religion, see Donald H. Bishop, "Peirce and Eastern Thought," in *Proceedings of the C. S. Peirce Bicentennial International Congress*, ed. K. L. Ketner et al. (Lubbock: Texas Tech University Press, 1981).

9. Although Peirce cared little for the synoptic gospels, he deeply admired the Gospel of John. For instance, see "Evolutionary Love," *The Monist* 3(1893): 176–200 (*P* 521, republished in *CP* 6), and "The Marriage of Religion and Science," *The Open Court* 7(1893): 3559–3560 (*P* 545, republished in *CP* 6). The skeptical tone here about religion is not at all typical of Peirce in general. For studies of Peirce's considerable contributions to our understanding of religion, see Donna M. Orange, *Peirce's Conception of God* (Bloomington: Indiana University Press, 1984), and Michael L. Raposa, *Peirce's Philosophy of Religion* (Bloomington: Indiana University Press, 1989). See also Kenneth Laine Ketner, "The Importance of Religion for Peirce," in *Gedankenzeichen*, ed. by R. Claussen and R. Daube-Schackat (Tübingen: Stauffenburg Verlag, 1988).

10. A partial transcript of the prospectus is also given at *CP* 8, pages 282–286; see also *N* 2: 18.

11. The complete text may be seen at *NEM* 3: 788–800.

12. Prior to 1898, these were *P* 439 (1891), "The Architecture of Theories"; *P* 474 (1892), "The Doctrine of Necessity Examined"; *P* 477 (1892), "The Law of Mind"; *P* 480 (1892), "Man's Glassy Essence"; *P* 521 (1893), "Evolutionary Love"; *P* 525 (1892), "Reply to the Necessitarians"; *P* 620 (1896), "The Regenerated Logic"; and *P* 637 (1897), "The Logic of Relatives."

13. Sara Bull, "The Cambridge Conferences," *The Outlook*, August 1897.

14. Mortimer Smith, *The Life of Ole Bull* (Princeton: Princeton University Press, 1943), p. 168.

15. *Lewis G. Janes* (Boston: James H. West Company, 1902). This is a memorial volume by a number of friends of Janes. In his description of the role of Janes as director of the Cambridge Conferences, Thomas Wentworth Higginson mentioned (page 53) a number of "special courses or speakers," including "Mr. Charles Sanders Peirce, the eminent mathematician, a course of eight lectures on 'Reasoning and the Logic of Things'."

16. Peirce had just developed a new graphical system of logic in a paper

he described shortly before his death as the "most lucid and interesting" he had written. *MS* 482 is a surviving draft of this paper.

17. It would be easy to dismiss such remarks as these, as some scholars have tended to do, as the bitterness of a hermit. But Peirce was not a recluse, and he was well-informed, through such sources as his kinsman, Senator Henry Cabot Lodge, and his brother Herbert, who as an American diplomat to the Russian court later materially aided the negotiations that ended the Russo-Japanese war. James Mills Peirce, also a brother (the J. M. P. mentioned below), was professor of mathematics and dean of the graduate school at Harvard.

18. George S. Morison, *The New Epoch as Developed by the Manufacture of Power* (Boston: Houghton Mifflin and Company, 1903; Arno reprint 1972), in which the oration, entitled "The New Epoch and the University," is chapter 6. Peirce's ideas appear most strongly in paragraphs 2–4 of the version of the address in the book.

19. William James, *Philosophical Conceptions and Practical Results* (Berkeley: The University Press, 1898).

20. Max H. Fisch, "American Pragmatism before and after 1898," in *American Philosophy from Edwards to Quine*, ed. R. W. Shahan and K. R. Merrill (Norman: Oklahoma University Press, 1977).

21. In a short unpublished note shown to Putnam a number of years ago.

22. See *NEM* and *HP*, plus Joseph W. Dauben, "Peirce's Place in Mathematics," *Historia Mathematica* 9(1982): 311–325.

23. Abraham Robinson, *Non-Standard Analysis* (Amsterdam: North Holland, 1966).

24. Peirce in fact believed in points at infinity, but in the sense of projective geometry, not in the sense of contemporary nonstandard analysis. See Lecture Eight.

25. "Seems" is appropriate because Peirce's presentation is so brief. Peirce described the series of cardinals aleph-null, the cardinal of the power set of aleph-null, the cardinal of the power set of the power set of aleph-null, and so on. These Peirce took to be all the infinite cardinals there are, apart from the cardinal called Ω in this essay, which is the cardinal of what we would call a proper class but not a set. The fact that he didn't believe there are sets of cardinals other than these strongly suggests that his universe of sets is the one described here. It also indicates that he assumed the Generalized Continuum Hypothesis, almost certainly without recognizing that it is an independent assumption.

26. Hilary Putnam, "Mathematics without Foundations," in *Mathematics, Matter and Method*, volume 1 of *Philosophical Papers* (Cambridge: Cambridge University Press, 1975). See also Charles Parsons, *Mathematics in Philosophy* (Ithaca: Cornell University Press, 1983), and Geoffrey Hellman, *Mathematics without Numbers* (Oxford: Clarendon Press, 1989).

Comments on the Lectures

1. For further information about this side of Peirce's thought, see Peter Skagestad's excellent study, *The Road of Inquiry: Charles Peirce's Pragmatic Realism* (New York: Columbia University Press, 1981).

2. Although, again like Peirce, James hoped that there might eventually be found a set of religious and ethical views on which all could converge, a "final opinion," and he held that, whether this happens or not, the notion of a "final opinion" is an indispensable regulative idea.

3. "The cries of the wounded" is from James's "The Moral Philosopher and the Moral Life," published in 1891. Reprinted in *The Will to Believe and Other Essays in Popular Philosophy* (Cambridge: Harvard University Press, 1979).

4. We mean, of course, that Peirce had such a position in the present lectures. Peirce often changed his position in the course of his long and productive life, and to what extent any given approach characterized his philosophy in any other period of that life is a question that we cannot address here.

5. See, in this connection, Stanley Cavell's *Themes out of School: Effects and Causes* (San Francisco: North Point Press, 1984) as well as the novels and essays of Walker Percy; most of Percy's essays have been collected in *The Message in the Bottle* (New York: Farrar, Straus and Giroux, 1975), and in *Signposts in a Strange Land*, ed. P. Samway (New York: Farrar, Straus and Giroux, 1991).

6. Alisdair MacIntyre, *Three Rival Versions of Moral Enquiry; Encyclopaedia, Genealogy and Tradition* (Notre Dame, Indiana: University of Notre Dame Press, 1990), chap. 1.

7. For Peirce's central role in inventing modern symbolic logic, see Hilary Putnam, "Peirce the Logician," in *Realism with a Human Face* (Cambridge: Harvard University Press, 1990). See also the papers by Quine and Dipert forthcoming in *Peirce and Contemporary Thought,* the plenary lectures of the Charles S. Peirce Sesquicentennial International Congress (Lubbock: Texas Tech University Press).

8. The opposing "Diodoran" view is that "All A are B" implies that there is at least one A, and that "If p, then q" is not automatically true whenever p is false. The stumbling block for the "Diodorans" has always been their inability to state a criterion for when "If p, then q" *is* true. Peirce's standpoint, that we should adopt the convention that "If p, then q" *is true whenever p is false* (and true whenever q is true) and not worry about whether this does or does not agree with "ordinary usage," has become the standpoint of virtually all logicians today.

9. It may be written with the aid of symbolic logic as $(x)(x$ is in *this here range* $\supset (x$ bankers $\supset x$ timids)). This contemporary notation is a direct descendant of the notion introduced by Peirce. (See the paper by Putnam cited in note 7.)

10. In his other writings Peirce often used the term "abduction" for what he here called "retroduction."

11. Von Mises's idea was that a characteristic π occurs "randomly" in a series M just in case the frequency of π is the same in *every* infinite subsequence of M. This is easily seen to be impossible unless all but a finite number of M are π or all but a finite number of M are non-π; for, in an infinite series in which there are infinitely many elements that are π and infinitely many that are not π, one can always find two infinite subsets, in one of which the characteristic π occurs with limit relative frequency one and one of which π occurs with limit relative frequency zero. Peirce himself gave a definition of "fortuitous distribution" in Lecture Six (using the notion of "definable relations") which is close to the

modern definition of randomness (if we assume that the imprecise notion of "definability" involved can be made precise by identifying it with *recursive* definability); but it appears that Peirce regarded "fortuitous distribution" and "randomness" as two distinct concepts, for some reason. Certainly the definition of randomness in the present lecture is much inferior to the definition of "fortuitous distribution" in the later lecture.

12. In an infinite population, as Peirce himself noted, "the probability that an M is π is 1" is compatible with there being Ms that are not π; this shows that his claim that *Barbara* is the limiting case of his probability inference in the first figure fails when infinite classes are concerned.

13. Even this would not help in the case of an infinite population, because for an infinite population the single case probability that one particular S is drawn on particular occasion is zero. Peirce himself (like other frequentists, e.g., Reichenbach in the present century) rejected the idea of single case probability. On this, see Peirce's "The Doctrine of Chances" (P 120, *The Popular Science Monthly* of 1878 12: 604–615, republished in W 3 and CP 2), and Putnam's discussion in the closing pages of *The Many Faces of Realism* (LaSalle, Ill.: Open Court Publishing Co., 1987).

14. But note the definition of "fortuitous distribution" in Lecture Six (referred to in note 11 above).

15. It should be mentioned that in his argument Peirce exploited the fact that in his notation r need not be a single real number but may be a set of real numbers. (Strictly speaking, he needs r to be either a single real number or a *measurable* set of real numbers, but the concept of Lebesgue measure was not available when Peirce was writing!)

16. This view has, of course, been vigorously defended by Karl Popper in the present century. For Peirce, however, retroduction is not the *only* strategy by which science proceeds, although it is certainly the most important. Moreover, falsifiability is not the only factor to be considered in Peirce's Economy of Research, as it is in Popper's.

17. For some background on Peirce's doctrine of the Economy of Research, see note 10 in Lecture Four.

18. In *The Taming of Chance* (New York: Cambridge University Press, 1990), Ian Hacking has recently noticed that this Peircean anticipation of Neymann-Pearson statistical theory occurred as early as the 1860s.

19. Schröder, Whitehead, Zermelo, Löwenheim, all learned of quantification theory from Peirce in the last two decades of the nineteenth century; before 1900, Frege's independent—and slightly earlier—invention of a version of second-order logic was virtually unknown and ignored. See Putnam, "Peirce the Logician," in *Realism with a Human Face* for details.

20. See Don Roberts, *The Existential Graphs of Charles S. Peirce* (The Hague: Mouton, 1973); see also the works of Ketner and Burch cited in notes 4 and 5 to Lecture Three.

21. These three rules are stated at CP 4, paragraphs 505, 506, and 508. It is not widely known that during his lifetime Peirce did publish a good account of his graphical approach to logic. It is found within the entry for "Symbolic Logic," in the *Dictionary of Philosophy and Psychology*, ed. James Mark Baldwin

(New York: The Macmillan Company, 1902), vol. 2, pp. 645–649, beginning at "If symbolic logic be defined as . . ." Peirce wrote many of the entries on logical subjects (along with Christine Ladd-Franklin and others) for Baldwin's *Dictionary;* another topic particularly relevant to these lectures is "Relatives, logic of," beginning on page 447 in the same volume. For a complete listing of Peirce's contributions to Baldwin, see Kenneth Laine Ketner, *A Comprehensive Bibliography of the Published Works of Charles Sanders Peirce,* 2d ed. (Bowling Green, Ohio: Philosophy Documentation Center, 1986).

22. We discover from Frege's *Nachlass* that he retracted this view late in his life, however.

23. For mathematically sophisticated readers: one way in which a present-day Peircean might argue that "logic is mathematics" (rather than mathematics being logic) is to point out that it is part of the notion of a *proof* in logic that the whole deduction—whether it be a diagram or a series of lines or a proof tree or whatever—be *finite.* But "finite" is an essentially mathematical notion, and our access to its "interpretation" is a murky business. There is a dream which the famous logician Jeff Paris (who works in nonstandard analysis) is supposed to have had, in which God asks "How do you know *two* is finite?" Paris replied, "I can prove it is." God retorts, "How many lines does your proof have?"

24. Peirce's powerful and classic critique of Descartes by way of his attack on Cartesian "paper doubt" and by arguing that in philosophy "we must begin where we are"—as opposed to some ideal starting point—is found most prominently in "Questions Concerning Certain Faculties Claimed for Man," *Journal of Speculative Philosophy* 2(1868): 103–114 (*P* 26), republished in *CP* 5 and in *W* 2.

25. Again, this theme is prominent throughout Peirce's career, but for examples see his review of *The Works of George Berkeley* in *The North American Review* 113(1871): 449–472 (*P* 60), republished in *CP* 8 and *W* 2.

26. See Bernard Williams, *Ethics and the Limits of Philosophy* (Cambridge: Harvard University Press, 1985).

27. See David Wiggins, *Needs, Values, Truth* (London: Basil Blackwell, 1987).

28. For an account of Dewey's views, see H. Putnam and R. A. Putnam, "Epistemology as Hypothesis," in *Transactions of the Charles S. Peirce Society* 26 (1990): 407–434.

29. Note that it is Mill's account of *deduction* that is favorably mentioned; Peirce regarded Mill's account of *induction* as much inferior to Whewell's (and he was surely right).

30. See the Comments for Lecture Three, above.

31. Philip Kitcher, *The Nature of Mathematical Knowledge* (Oxford: Oxford University Press, 1984).

32. See Kripke's *Naming and Necessity* (Cambridge: Harvard University Press, 1972).

33. For the use of Ω here see the discussion of Peirce's view of the continuum in the general introduction.

34. This is normally concealed in physics by defining the "state" of a system so that giving the "state" at any one time includes giving the *velocities* at that

time, and not just the positions and the masses, charges, and other constants of the bodies. But this makes the "state" at one time a *limit* of conditions at different times, and not a description of what is actual at the time in question.

35. This is no longer true in today's relativity physics, however! (Yet, some interpretations of quantum mechanics do require instantaneous action at a distance.)

36. Some authors have suggested that the causality of *quantum physics* is, however, not time-reversible.

37. At least this is what Peirce claimed. That our introspectively observed mental life *really* has the property that "the state of things at one instant is completely and exactly determined by the state of things at *one* other instant" will no doubt strike some of us as an implausible claim!

38. For a latter-day discussion of the problem Peirce raised here, see Hans Reichenbach, *The Direction of Time* (Berkeley: University of California Press, 1956), edited by Maria Reichenbach. Reichenbach ascribes the irreversibility of the sorts of processes Peirce called "non-conservative" to the Second Law of Thermodynamics, according to which entropy (in a closed system) always increases. This explanation goes back to Boltzmann; Peirce referred approvingly to Boltzmann (although not by name) in Lecture Seven, but presumably he did not think the Boltzmannian explanation, although correct as far as it goes, to be sufficient. The reason for Peirce's dissatisfaction is implicit in the passage we have taken as the epigraph to our comments on this lecture: Boltzmann had simply to *assume* the existence of an appropriate statistical distribution at some time in the past.

39. Other terms are "Gaussian distribution" and (in popular writing) "bell-shaped curve."

40. Peirce's remark that "utter irregularity, is the only thing which it is reasonable to explain by the absence of any reason to the contrary" may not go as far as he thought to explain the existence of fortuitous distributions, however, for such a distribution is not *utterly* irregular; it requires the existence of *infinitely many limits of the relative frequency,* since the limit of the relative frequency of the attribute "colored" is required to exist both in the whole sequence and in all its "definable" (i.e., recursive) subsequences, if the distribution is to be fortuitous, and all these limits must be the same. Peirce here traded on the intuitive connotations of "chance." Some people would argue that in an *utterly irregular* world there would be no limits of the relative frequency at all, and hence no "probabilities" in Peirce's sense.

41. That the mode of existence of physical objects, so far as it can be an object of knowledge, consists in mutually reacting (mutually affecting one another's motions) was argued by Kant in his *Metaphysical Foundations of Natural Science.*

42. Roger Joseph Boscovich (1711–1787) was "the first scientist to develop a general physical theory using point particles." See the article on Boscovich (from which this quotation is taken) in *The Encyclopedia of Philosophy,* vol. 1, General Editor Paul Edwards (New York: Macmillan, 1967).

43. But note that this argument was rejected by Kant in the Second Antinomy as an attempt to use reason beyond the limits of experience.

44. In projective geometry, the properties of figures studied are those which are invariant under point projection (Peirce used the terms "perspective geometry" and "geometric optic" for projective geometry in Lectures Seven and Eight). Projective geometry is characterized by a very elegant property called "duality": if the words "point" and "straight line" can be interchanged in any theorem the result is also a theorem. (E.g., two points determine a straight line; two straight lines determine a point—to make this last statement hold, we imagine that parallel lines meet at a "point at infinity" and that any two points at infinity lie on a "line at infinity.") Although Cayley's method of subsuming metric geometry under projective geometry is still much admired by projective geometers, it should be remarked that it has some drawbacks: for example, the "distance" between any two gauge points turns out to be zero! (Distance can also be an imaginary number in some cases.) It is not clear whether Peirce was aware of these drawbacks.

45. C. W. O'Hara and D. R. Ward, *An Introduction to Projective Geometry* (Oxford: The Clarendon Press, 1937), p. 226.

46. There is an empirical assumption here—one which we believe Peirce made consciously—that whether mass points at given locations tend, other things being equal, to interact more or less strongly is independent of the *kind* of interaction involved (gravitational or electromagnetic, etc.).

47. Peirce apparently considered the metric of time to be intrinsic.

48. Peirce meant that if the accelerations were the same, not only in magnitude but also in direction, there would be no change in the relative positions, and hence no reaction at all.

49. Here Peirce seems to have employed the isotropy of space (which is built into the conception of space as a mere form of representation). If the acceleration of either one of two interacting bodies were not in the direction of the line connecting them (attraction or repulsion), there would have to be something singling out the direction of acceleration from all the other directions which make an identical angle with the line connecting the two bodies; but this cannot be anything about space itself. One might object that what singles out a preferred direction could be some *asymmetry* in one of the bodies; since Peirce himself allowed such a possibility when he wrote that "there is nothing to prevent a particle exercising different forces on different sides of it." But in Lecture Seven Peirce stated that, "As far as the mutual action of two atomicules was concerned, they would instantly turn those sides to one another which gave the minimum potential energy; and in the absence of all momentum there would be no tendency to swing beyond that point." Perhaps this bears on this difficulty.

50. See the work cited in note 41.

51. John Dewey, *Experience and Nature* (LaSalle: Open Court, 1926), pp. 407–408.

52. The kind of spontaneous creation of particles that was postulated by Fred Hoyle's (unsuccessful) "Steady State Cosmology" is a good example of the sort of event Peirce had in mind. Incidentally, rare chance events (spontaneous "collapses of the wave packet," rather than particle creations) play a role in a recent quantum-mechanical theory by three Italian physicists, Rimini, Ghirardi, and Weber. These are also a good example of the sort of rare spontaneous event Peirce was led to postulate on metaphysical grounds.

53. We write "allegedly" because it is controversial to the present day whether such explanations do account for all the apparently irreversible phenomena that we observe. Cf. Reichenbach's *The Direction of Time*, cited in our comments to Lecture Six, for a defense of the view that they do.

54. Reichenbach, *The Rise of Scientific Philosophy* (Berkeley: University of California Press, 1951), pp. 160–161.

55. For details, see the work cited in note 53.

56. Cf. our comments on Lecture Six.

57. Cf. our discussion of Peirce's theory of the continuum in the introduction to this volume.

58. See note 44 to our comments on Lecture Six.

59. For a detailed explanation, see chapter 9 in C. W. O'Hara and D. R. Ward, *An Introduction to Projective Geometry*.

60. Cf. "Mathematosis," in W. V. Quine, *Quiddities* (Cambridge: Harvard University Press, 1987), pp. 127–129.

61. As we have explained above, the Boltzmannian method—statistical mechanics—still assumes the existence of "fortuitous distributions" as an *unexplained* fact.

62. Cf. Reichenbach, *The Philosophy of Space and Time* (New York: Dover, 1958).

63. Peirce had an easier time than Reichenbach, however, because in Peirce's physics there are actual point particles whose inertial motions can define straight lines.

64. The idea of founding mathematics upon modal logic was rediscovered (in ignorance, at that time, of Peirce's ideas) by H. Putnam. Cf. "Logic Without Foundations," in *Philosophical Papers*, vol. 1, *Mathematics, Matter and Method* (Cambridge: Cambridge University Press, 1975), extended and modified by Charles Parsons, *Mathematics in Philosophy, Selected Essays* (Ithaca: Cornell University Press, 1983), especially chapters VII and XI, and very much further worked out by Geoffrey Hellman, *Mathematics Without Numbers* (Oxford: The Clarendon Press, 1989).

65. *CP* 6: 86–87.

66. *CP* 6: 415.

67. See David Lewis, *Counterfactuals* (Cambridge: Harvard University Press, 1973), especially pp. 84–91, for a defense of the reality of possible worlds.

68. For discussions of Peirce's way of dealing with the conception of God and other religious matters, see Donna Orange, *Peirce's Conception of God* (Bloomington: Indiana University Press, 1984); Michael Raposa, *Peirce's Philosophy of Religion* (Bloomington: Indiana University Press, 1989); K. L. Ketner, "The Importance of Religion for Peirce," in *Gedankenzeichen*, ed. R. Claussen and R. Daube-Schackat (Tübingen: Stauffenburg Verlag, 1988).

69. "Line" was used by Peirce in the sense of "curve," not in the restricted notion of straight line, throughout these Lectures.

70. He is, however, treated as one of the precursors of topology in H. Seifert and W. Threfall, *Lehrbuch der Topologie* (Teubner, 1934). Today it is Riemann who is generally considered the founder of modern topology. Peirce's judgment that Riemann "never studied [topology] sufficiently to master it thoroughly" is eccentric. The fact is that while Listing did define a few topological

invariants (which Peirce called the Listing numbers), Riemann was the first mathematician to define a set of invariants which provide a *complete* classification of two-dimensional manifolds (the analogous problem for three-dimensional manifolds is still unsolved). (Today these invariants are, paradoxically, not called "Riemann numbers" but "Betti numbers"!) By the time Peirce was writing, Poincaré, his contemporary, had defined the fundamental group. We do not know whether Peirce was familiar with either the Betti numbers or the introduction of group-theoretic methods into topology (although we suspect that he was not). Incidentally, Peirce said in the present lecture that Listing was wrong to think the fourth Listing number of space is zero, and that it is actually one; Peirce was thinking of projective space and Listing of ordinary Euclidean space, but in addition Peirce was making a mathematical error. (Removing *any finite number* of points from projective space still leaves the entire space noncollapsible, which means the fourth Listing number is infinite.)

71. To see that the entire space can be collapsed onto a point P, consider the following continuous mapping: if each point Q in the space "moves" by a distance of rL in the direction of P in time r, where L is the length of the line segment PQ, then in one unit of time every Q will "reach" P. Note that this fails if there are points at infinity!

72. The same error occurs in *NEM* 3: 505 ("since space has apeiry [fourth Listing number] 1"; Peirce was talking about "space as linear perspective pictures it," i.e., projective 3-space).

73. If D is the number of dimensions of the manifold in question, the second Listing number is the number of "simplest possible places" (i.e., connected manifolds) of $D - 1$ dimensions which have to be removed to preclude the existence in the space that is left of a curve which *cannot* be continuously shrunk to a point by a mapping which stays within the space that is left. The third Listing number is the number of "simple places" (connected manifolds) of $D - 2$ dimensions which have to be removed to preclude the existence in the space that is left of a surface which *cannot* be shrunk to a curve by a mapping which stays within the space that is left.

74. Peirce's mistake about the fourth Listing number of projective space obviously plays a role here.

75. In the sense of what today would be called generalized Riemannian coordinates. Such coordinates are not required to be perpendicular, and coordinate lines may intersect more than once.

One: Philosophy and the Conduct of Life

This lecture is *MS* 437.

1. Peirce held that our ability to hypothesize successfully rested upon our instincts. This approach is ably presented in Maryann Ayim, *Peirce's View of the Roles of Reason and Instinct in Scientific Inquiry* (Meerut, India: Anu Prakashan, 1982).

2. A few years later Peirce revised this position on Ethics to make it a normative science, still considerably different from the topic he discussed here

under that term. For a complete account of Peirce's ideas about normative science, see Vincent Potter, *Charles S. Peirce on Norms and Ideals* (Worcester, Mass.: University of Massachusetts Press, 1967).

Two: Types of Reasoning

This lecture is *MS* 441.

1. In this passage, Peirce had first written "conjunctive" but later replaced it throughout with "copulative."
2. This essay is *P* 31, published in *Proceedings of the American Academy of Arts and Sciences* 7(1868): 261–287, read before the Academy 9 April 1867; republished in *W* 2: 23–48 and *CP* 2: 461–516.
3. Peirce discussed these concepts in *P* 637, "The Logic of Relatives," *The Monist*, 7(1897): 161–217; republished in *CP* 3: 456–552, compare *MS* 798.
4. *P* 268, *Studies in Logic, By Members of the Johns Hopkins University*, edited by C. S. Peirce, (Boston: Little, Brown and Company, 1883). A reprint edition has been published by John Benjamins Company (Amsterdam, 1982); Peirce's articles from this volume are also published in *W* 4.
5. Peirce had first written "the Kantian logician Fries," but later struck the reference to Kant. Peirce discussed his notion of the leading principle of an argument in "On the Natural Classification of Arguments."
6. "On the Natural Classification of Arguments" was read before the American Academy of Arts and Sciences in 1867 and published in 1868 (see note 2 above). In 1878, as the sixth and last in the "Illustrations of the Logic of Science" series Peirce published "Deduction, Induction, and Hypothesis," *P* 123, *Popular Science Monthly* 13(1878): 470–482; republished in *W* 3: 323–338 and *CP* 2: 619–644. The first two papers of this series—"The Fixation of Belief" and "How to Make Our Ideas Clear"—introduced pragmatism as a maxim of scientific methodology.

Three: The Logic of Relatives

The "Exordium for Lecture Three" is *MS* 751. Its content seems to dictate insertion between Lectures Two and Three. The title has been supplied by us.

While it is not a certainty that the text for Lecture Three is *MS* 439, it is quite probable that it was, given the following evidence. First, *MS* 439 exhibits many of the features this lecture must have, including a preliminary account of Existential Graphs. It seems to fit descriptions of Lecture Three given at paragraph six of Lecture Four. The seventeenth paragraph of this MS—"Although I am debarred . . ."—seems to link this text to the Cambridge Conferences lectures. The topic at the end of the previous lecture flows nicely into the topic that introduces this MS. See also the seventh note for this lecture, which records a comment by William James (written by James in the margin of a page of this MS) urging Peirce to link up with the "common mind." Finally, the last fifteen paragraphs of this MS seem to be especially tailored for this lecture series.

The reader should consider it to be possible that by the phrase "Logic of Relatives," Peirce seems to have meant something much broader than some formal logical system the subject matter of which is relations, as evidenced below by his inclusion of a discussion of his categoriology under that topic. Often it seems to have been an alternative name for his entire effort to provide what might be called an overall epistemology for science. Of course, in a narrow sense, the phrase could be approximately translated into contemporary terms as "the formal logic of propositional functions." But note that "approximately" carries a heavy burden in that remark.

1. The mention of 1866 is probably a reference to "On the Natural Classification of Arguments" once again. The "Kantian step" can be followed in *P* 32, "On a New List of Categories," *Proceedings of the American Academy of Arts and Sciences* 7(1868): 261–287, republished in *CP* 1 and in *W* 2.

2. At this point in the text Peirce deleted the following sentence: ⟨The word Mediation would have been better.⟩

3. This is a reference to "On a New List of Categories"; see note 1 above.

4. Some bibliographic background for this paragraph may be useful for readers. Robert Leslie Ellis is identified in *W* 2: xxxiii. George Bruce Halsted was Peirce's friend and correspondent, and professor of mathematics at the University of Texas. DeMorgan's memoir is "On the Syllogism, No. IV, and on the Logic of Relations," *Transactions of the Cambridge Philosophical Society* 10(1864): 331–358 (read 1860). Peirce's own appreciation of DeMorgan may be found in his obituary for *The Nation*, republished in *N* 1: 41 and 42 (also in *W* 2: 448–450). Peirce's 1870 memoir is *P* 52, "Description of a Notation for the Logic of Relatives, resulting from an Amplification of the Conceptions of Boole's Calculus of Logic," *Memoirs of the American Academy of Arts and Sciences* n.s. 9(1870): 317–378, republished in *CP* 3 and in *W* 2. Peirce's mention of an 1883 paper of his on dyadic relatives, as well as one by Mitchell, is a reference to *Studies in Logic*, *P* 268 (Boston: Little, Brown and Company, 1883); the one by Peirce is entitled "Note B: The Logic of Relatives." Peirce's development of Entitative and Existential graphs is described by Ketner in "Peirce's 'Most Lucid and Interesting Paper': An Introduction to Cenopythagoreanism," *International Philosophical Quarterly* 25(1986): 375–392, and in "Identifying Peirce's 'Most Lucid and Interesting Paper,'" *Transactions of the Charles S. Peirce Society* 23(1987): 539–556. For a convenient introduction to Peirce's graphical logic, see Kenneth Laine Ketner, *Elements of Logic: An Introduction to Peirce's Existential Graphs* (Lubbock: Texas Tech University Press, 1990), which includes computer programs.

5. Earlier, Peirce's reduction theorem had not been thought to have been established. However, it has recently received a strong defense and proof in Robert W. Burch, *A Peircean Reduction Thesis: The Foundations of Topological Logic* (Lubbock: Texas Tech University Press, 1991). Burch also shows that Peirce's reduction thesis—contrary to received opinion—is consistent with reductions to the dyadic by Quine or Löwenheim.

6. Francis Ellingwood Abbot was Peirce's Harvard classmate (1859) and lifelong friend. Peirce admired his *Organic Scientific Philosophy: Scientific Theism* (Boston: Little, Brown and Company, 1885), which Peirce reviewed in *The Nation* (see *N* 1: 71–74).

7. A marginal note by William James appears at this point in the manuscript: "This is too abrupt along here. Should be more mediated to the common mind. W. J."

Four: The First Rule of Logic

This lecture is *MS* 442 and 825.

1. At this point Peirce struck out the following bracketed material, probably to conform to time limitations. ⟨I am happy to find this point receives valuable confirmation of an entirely independent thinker, whose care and thoroughness gives weight to all he says, Dr. Francis Ellingwood Abbot.⟩

2. Peirce struck the following bracketed material, probably to conserve time. ⟨But, then, Whewell was a most admirable reasoner, who is underestimated simply because he stands detached both from the main current of philosophy and from that of science. It is worth the journey to the Rheingau, simply for the lesson in reasoning that one learns by reading upon the spot that remarkable work modestly thrown into the form of Notes on German Churches. As for the History of the Inductive Sciences, it comes as near to standing for what Dr. Carus calls a κτῆμα εἰς ἀεί as anything in philosophy can do. Mill's Logic was written to refute this book. I certainly would not have Mill's Logic lost, false as it is to the theory of Inductive Reasoning; but the contrast between Whewell's deep acquaintance with the springs of science and Mill's exterior survey is well shown by the circumstance that whatever scientific reasonings Whewell has praised have been more and more confirmed by Time while every one of the examples which Mill picked out as choice specimens of successful inductions in his first edition have long been utterly exploded.⟩

3. Peirce struck the following bracketed material, probably to conserve time. ⟨I have been reading Alexandre Dumas's charming Impressions du Voyage. It is full of slips of the pen. He says Pisa when he means Florence, Lorenzo when he means the Old Cosimo, the 18th century when he means the 13th, 600 years when means 500. The new word comes to me and is substituted just as if I had seen it. For it makes sense; and what I see printed does not. Finally, retroduction lets slip out of attention the special characters involved in its premises, because they are virtually contained in the hypotheses which it has been led to presume. But as our study of the subject of the hypothesis grows deeper that hypothesis will be sure gradually to take another color, little by little to receive modifications, corrections, amplifications, even in case no catastrophe befalls it.⟩

4. The following bracketed material was deleted by Peirce, probably to save time.

⟨Since I myself am in no sense a teacher, but only a learner, and at the very foot of my class at that, for the reproach made against me is a just one that I am all the time modifying my doctrines, it is only to please you and not by any means myself that I have elected to address you upon topics of vital importance. To me no subject could possibly be more distasteful. For I know nothing about matters of vital importance. All I *think* I know concerns things which I

hope may prove of subsidiary importance. As to topics of vital importance I
have nothing to inculcate but sentiments. True, I am a sentimentalist in theory.
I believe sentiment is far more deeply important than science. But by my training I am nothing [but] a scientific man myself and am quite out of my element
in talking about things vitally important. My only excuse for attempting it is my
desire to conform to your wishes. But I find that struggle as I may and do, I
cannot keep dry details altogether out of my lectures. For if I did I should have
nothing to say.⟩

5. Here we have some of those ideas of Peirce that were "borrowed" in
Morison's 1896 Harvard Phi Beta Kappa oration, as noted in the introduction.

6. Peirce struck out the following bracketed material, probably to conserve
time. ⟨In favor of pure mathematics we must, indeed, make an exception. It is
true that even that does not reach certainty with mathematical exactitude. But
then the theorems of pure mathematics, take them, as Captain Cuttle would do,
"by and large," are without doubt exactly and certainly true, for all purposes
except that of logical theory. Pure mathematics, however, is no science of existing things. It is a mere science of hypotheses. It is consistent with itself; and
if there is nothing else to which it professes to conform, it perfectly fulfils its
promise and its purpose. Certainly, you will not find in any modern book of
pure mathematics any further profession than that. But mathematicians are not
in the habit of setting down statements they are not prepared to prove; and it
may very well be that they generally entertain a somewhat different idea of their
science. All the great mathematicians whom I have happened to know very well
were Platonists, and I have little doubt that if the contributors to the leading
mathematical journals were polled, it would be found that there were among
them a larger proportion of Platonists than among any other class of scientific
men. I believe the great majority of them would regard the formation of such
conceptions as that of imaginary quantity and that of Riemann surfaces as mathematical achievements, and *that,* considering those hypotheses not as mere instruments for investigating real quantity, but in themselves. They would rank
them as having a much higher value than anything in the Arabian Nights, for
example. Yet why should they do so, if those hypotheses are pure fictions?
There is certainly something to which modern mathematical conceptions strive
to conform, be it no more than an artistic ideal. And the true question is whether
they fulfil their endeavor with any greater success than other human works. If
it be only beauty that is aimed at, then mathematical hypotheses must be ranked
as something similar but inferior to the Alhambra decorations, — as pretty but
soulless. If on the other hand they are essays at the portrayal of a Platonic world,
then we can only say that they are so exceedingly slight and fragmentary as
hardly to enable us to understand their drift and not at all to find room for any
application of the conception of accuracy.

⟨So much for the certainty of deductive science. As to induction it is,
upon the face of it, merely probable and approximate, and it is only when it is
confined to finite and denumeral collections that it attains even that grade of
perfection. It only infers the value of a ratio and therefore when applied to any
natural class which is conceived to be more than denumeral, no amount of
inductive evidence can ever give us the *slightest reason,*—[nor,] would not justify

the very slightest inclination to believe, — that an inductive law was without exception. Indeed, every sane mind will readily enough admit that this is so as soon as a law is made clearly to appear as a pure induction and nothing more.⟩

7. Peirce deleted the following bracketed material.

⟨Passing to retroduction, this type of reasoning cannot logically justify any belief at all, if we understand by belief the holding of a proposition as a definitive conclusion. It is here to be remarked that the word hypothesis is often extended to cases where it has no proper application.⟩

8. The next paragraph has delete marks in the manuscript. We place the paragraph in the main text, however, because it is probable that an early editor, not Peirce, made those marks. Our hypothesis is strengthened by the fact that without this paragraph, the transition to the next paragraph is abrupt. With this paragraph, the transition is appropriate and smooth.

9. This sentence is the first from a different *MS*, number 825. Because they share the same coded markings, it is clear that *MS* 825 originally belonged with *MS* 442, the main record of this lecture. The question of the proper placement of *MS* 825 within this lecture, however, remains. It is possible Peirce may have deleted it to save time, but we think not. We place it here where it provides an eloquent closing.

10. Peirce had some interesting ideas on the Economy of Research. While any hypothesis could be tried, he thought it part of the logic of science to consider which inquiry ought to be pursued in view of economic factors. He first published on this topic early in his career in "Note on the Theory of the Economy of Research" (*P* 160), republished in *CP* 7 and in *W* 4; see also *HP* for additional texts. Carolyn Eisele has provided background on the topic in *Studies in the Scientific and Mathematical Philosophy of Charles S. Peirce*, ed. R. M. Martin (The Hague: Mouton, 1979), chap. 24. Nicholas Rescher has written on the topic in *Peirce's Philosophy of Science* (Notre Dame, Ind.: University of Notre Dame Press, 1978).

Five: Training in Reasoning

This lecture is *MS* 444 and 445.

1. This is almost certainly a self-reference, for Peirce studied oenology during one of his trips to France.

2. A shift to *MS* 445 begins with the next sentence.

3. Peirce deleted the following bracketed lines. ⟨When I did find this out, which was not until about 15 years ago, it seemed to me that it was a very useless power; for I could remember colors better than most of those whose imaginations reproduced them; and besides it seemed to me that the obtrusion of that element must interfere with attention to the essential features of the image. It was not until 5 or 6 years ago, that I met with a lady (not, by the way a particularly fine or cultured mind, but rather with a good deal of the Boston crudeness) who had the power in one of its higher degrees and who yet convinced me by various experiments that she was far more expert than I in observing other features of the mental image. This led me to collect additional instances; and⟩

4. Peirce deleted the following bracketed lines. ⟨Although I have never myself cultivated this power, yet I see it developed so generally in artists and musicians, that the evidence convinces me that it is capable of being strengthened by practice as any other power.⟩

5. Peirce deleted the following bracketed lines. ⟨[It] woke me up, and made great efforts of *all* kinds easy. In particular, it helped me away from that disposition, which is called "effeminacy,"—by a most unfounded libel upon women, — which⟩

6. Peirce deleted the following bracketed lines. ⟨Those who possess the art of fasting find that some aid. But to fret about it, or think about it at all, has just the opposite effect.⟩

7. Peirce deleted the following bracketed lines.

⟨This too will aid you in acquiring the art of expression. Thought without expression is mere sentiment, and that extreme mobility which you want to cultivate in thought, you would not wish to extend to sentiment. The foundation of a good philosophical style of writing ought to be laid in algebra. But remember that good reasoning is not an affair of words but of a diagrammatic expression, though words are necessary to state it in its generality.

⟨All this attention to system, and to records, and to words is also the true art of cultivating a retentive memory.⟩

Six: Causation and Force

This lecture is *MS* 443.

An earlier title of this lecture was "Time and Causation." Peirce deleted the following alternate opening.

⟨I confess my ingenuity fails to find a valid excuse for including Time and Causation among Topics of Vital Importance. The truth is, I undertook to name the subjects of my lectures before I had prepared them, and I did so very inconsiderately. I know not what I could have been thinking of when I gave one of them this title. I suppose this subject became associated in my mind with Topics of Vital Importance, owing to this point of resemblance, that I have very little to say about either. But perhaps you will find it a relief to hear one lecture that makes no pretence to any other importance than that of a discussion of one of the least understood of the topics of the most flimsy of the sciences, — I mean Metaphysics. If you will pardon the unimportance of the subject, you will find that I shall fulfil the other promise of the course that of making what I have to say fragmentary, as well as I possibly can. I shall try to make the treatment of it redeem my choice of the subject.⟩

1. Peirce deleted the following bracketed sentence: ⟨Repeat with [what?] follows next after for F.⟩

2. This is a reference to the latter sections of "The Logic of Relatives," *The Monist* 7(1896): 161–217 (*P* 637), republished in *CP* 3. This entire article is a good companion piece for study in conjunction with these lectures.

3. Hermann Laurent, *Traité du calcul des probabilités* (Paris: Gauthier-Villars, 1873).

4. Probably the best access to this work in English is the Baynes translation from the second revised edition, *The Kinetic Theory of Gases* (New York: Longmans, Green and Company, 1899). Peirce reviewed this edition in *The Nation*, 71(26 July 1900): 79, republished in *N* 2.

5. Peirce used two distinct meanings of 'intuition'; surely this case refers to the sense associated with perception and observation, not the sense meaning "special foundational knowledge."

6. At this point, Peirce deleted the following phrase: ⟨is an affair of Twoness and⟩.

Seven: Habit

This lecture is *MS* 951 and 440.

1. For an account of the works of Johann Bernard Stallo, see Herbert W. Schneider, *A History of American Philosophy* (New York: Columbia University Press, 1946), p. 417. Perhaps the work Peirce had in mind was Stallo's *The Concepts and Theories of Modern Physics* (New York, 1882), or a series of articles on physics in the *Popular Science Monthly* in 1873–4.

2. The following bracketed lines, which end in an uncorrected grammatical flaw, were marked through in green pencil, probably by Peirce.

⟨Now let me call your attention to the facts, first, that there is no reason whatever to believe that the sum of the angles of a triangle is precisely two right angles, and second, if it is not so, there is no motion save the properties which we familiarly associate with *translation*. For example, we conceive of translation as a purely relative motion, so that two particles unacted on by any forces and relatively at rest for a moment will, however fast or slow they may be moving relatively to other bodies, remain forever at rest relatively to one another. But this is not so in non-Euclidian geometry. The two particles moving side by side [is,] unless the sum of the angles of a triangle is precisely 180°, [an impossibility].⟩

3. Ernst Mach, *The Science of Mechanics* (Chicago: *Open Court* Publishing Company, 1893). Peirce participated in the preparation of the American edition; in the translator's preface one finds the following remarks. "The thanks of the translator are due to Mr. C. S. Peirce, well known for his studies both of analytical mechanics and of the history and logic of physics, for numerous suggestions and notes. Mr. Peirce has read all the proofs and has rewritten 8 in the chapter on Units and Measures, where the original was inapplicable to this country and slightly out of date."

Peirce also reviewed this edition of Mach's book in *The Nation* at 57 (5 October 1893): 251–252 (*P* 536); republished in *N* 1.

4. These are references to topological concepts, after J. B. Listing; see *NEM*, volume 2, and Lecture Eight.

5. The following bracketed lines were deleted by Peirce.

⟨I now propose briefly to examine the law of mental action in order to inquire whether that is dynamical in the conservational sense or whether it follows the law of causation. I shall employ the terminology of the old English associationalists, which is forced upon me by the rules of terminology I have laid down and which seems to me superior in accuracy to the modern German terminology. The English associationalists of the last century, such as Gay and Hartley, drew⟩

6. Probably at this point Peirce read to his audience his rules for terminology to be found in an earlier draft (*MS* 440) of one of these lectures. That passage is reproduced immediately below. For a discussion of the importance of the Ethics of Terminology in Peirce's system, see Ketner, "Peirce's Ethics of Terminology," *Transactions of the Charles S. Peirce Society* 17(1981): 327–347.

7. At this point Peirce deleted the following material. ⟨but on the basis of experiments showing that such comparisons can be made with some degree of constancy.⟩

8. Peirce was no doubt thinking of his article with his Johns Hopkins University student, Joseph Jastrow, "On Small Differences of Sensation," *Memoirs of the National Academy of Sciences, 1884* (Washington, D.C.: Government Printing Office, 1885), pp. 73–83 (*P* 303); republished in *CP* 7, page 13.

9. For some additional background on these ideas, see Carolyn Eisele, "The Correspondence with Simon Newcomb," in her *Studies in the Scientific and Mathematical Philosophy of C. S. Peirce* (The Hague: Mouton, 1979), pp. 52–93.

Eight: The Logic of Continuity

This lecture is *MS* 948.

1. The lecture was entitled "Synechism" or perhaps "Continuity," and was presented by invitation to the Graduate Philosophical Society of Harvard University, 21 May 1892 (*P* 470). It had been thought that notes for the lecture survived as *MS* 955, but very recent study clearly has shown instead that on this occasion Peirce read from another paper, "The Law of Mind" (see *P* 477, republished in *CP* 6), which appeared in *The Monist* (2:553–559) two months later. *MS* 955, however, in regard to Peirce's Cambridge Conferences lectures, is quite relevant and rewards a close study.

2. The articles by Johann Benedict Listing are: "Vorstudien zur Topologie," *Göttinger Studien* 2(1847): 811–875; "Der Census räumlicher Complexe, oder Verallgemeinerung des Euler'schen Satzes von den Polyëdern," *Abhandlungen der Königlichen Gesellschaft der Wissenschaften zu Göttingen* 10(1862): 97–182. Listing had considerable influence on Peirce (see *NEM*). See also Robert W. Burch, *A Peircean Reduction Thesis* (Lubbock: Texas Tech University Press, 1991).

3. Exactly which work of the prolific Johann Friedrich Herbart (1776–1841) Peirce had in mind is unclear. For an exhaustive bibliography of Herbart and works about him, see *Dictionary of Philosophy and Psychology*, ed. James Mark Baldwin (New York: The Macmillan Company, 1905), vol. 3, pp. 253 f.

Index

Names whose spelling or identification could not be verified are indicated by [?].